Powers of Being

Powers of Being

David Holbrook and His Work

Edited by
Edwin Webb

Madison • Teaneck
Fairleigh Dickinson University Press
London: Associated University Presses

© 1995 by Associated University Presses, Inc.

All rights reserved. Authorization to photocopy items for internal or personal use, or the internal or personal use of specific clients, is granted by the copyright owner, provided that a base fee of $10.00, plus eight cents per page per copy is paid directly to the Copyright Clearance Center, 222 Rosewood Drive, Danvers, Massachusetts 01923. [0-8386-3529-6/95 $10.00+8¢ pp, pc.]

Associated University Presses
440 Forsgate Drive
Cranbury, NJ 08512

Associated University Presses
25 Sicilian Avenue
London WC1A 2QH, England

Associated University Presses
P.O. Box 338, Port Credit
Mississauga, Ontario
Canada L5G 4L8

The paper used in this publication meets the requirements of the American National Standard for Permanence of Paper for Printed Library Materials Z39.48-1984.

Library of Congress Cataloging-in-Publication Data

Powers of being : David Holbrook and his work / edited by Edwin Webb.
    p.   cm.
Includes bibliographical references (p.) and index.
ISBN 0-8386-3529-6 (alk. paper)
    1. Holbrook, David—Criticism and interpretation. I. Holbrook, David. II. Webb, Edwin, 1943–
PR6058.04Z83   1995
828'.91409—dc20   94-23698
                                                                                                                         CIP

PRINTED IN THE UNITED STATES OF AMERICA

Contents

Editor's Note	7
Introduction	9

Part I. David Holbrook
David Holbrook: A Portrait	
BORIS FORD	27

Part II. Educationist
Teaching English: A View from the Classroom	
MICHAEL CHARLES	55
English for Living	
EDWIN WEBB	62
A Relish for the English Word	
ROGER KNIGHT	78
A Moral Approach to English	
GORDON PRADL	93
The Tradition of Poetic Humanism and the Teaching of the Arts	
PETER ABBS	112
Working on One's Inner World	
JOHN PAYNTER	125

Part III. Critic
Language and the Experiencing Self	
MARGARET WELDHEN	148
Psychoanalysis and the Humanities: The Toronto Experience	
ANDREW BRINK	159
Looking: Subjectivity and the True Self	
ANN ULANOV AND BARRY ULANOV	173
Cupid and Psyche: Understanding the Workings of the Female Mind	
PAM TAYLOR	191
England's Only Existentialist Philosopher	
ROGER POOLE	211

Part IV. Poet and Novelist

"The Petals of the Man": The Relationship of David
    Holbrook's Criticism to His Poetry
    JOHN FERNS   233

"The Probes that are Creation": A Criticism of David
    Holbrook's Poetry
    IAN ROBINSON   245

The Novels of David Holbrook
    GEOFFREY STRICKLAND   256

Select Bibliography of Works by David Holbrook   271
Notes on Contributors   277
Index   281

Editor's Note

In September 1991 Dr. Ved Varma, a retired educational psychologist and an experienced editor, contacted me to ask if I would help him to get together a *Festschrift* to honor David Holbrook on his seventieth birthday. Ved's own interest in Holbrook's work stemmed from his encounter, in his professional work, with Holbrook's *English for the Rejected* which had been, for him, an inspiring work. My first response was to say that though I thought such a tribute should be made, I was not the person to undertake the project with him. Though I had read various of Holbrook's books as I had intermittently come across them over the years, and had admired much of what I read, I had not made any kind of systematic study of his work. Nonetheless Ved, who is a charmingly persuasive man, persuaded me to think about the proposition.

I took several weeks to do so. During that period I made further exploratory researches into Holbrook's works, and became even more convinced that such a tribute should be made. And since it appeared that no one else had it in mind to assemble such a public recognition, I agreed to a meeting with Ved.

In the course of that long meeting it emerged (which is as precise a description of the event as the implication of a single word permits) that I had not only agreed to work with him on the project, but had agreed to be the senior editor, *and* to draft out a prospectus for the book. Shortly into the start of the new year, at the time I was beginning to make preliminary approaches to prospective contributors, Ved had to withdraw completely from the project because of serious ill health. He gave me his benison and proclaimed his utter, though (I thought) completely unwarranted conviction that I would see the project through successfully.

In the event, therefore, I have to accept responsibility for the sole editorship of this *Festschrift* to honor David Holbrook's achievements. Various delays mean that the appearance of this book will not coincide with that birthday it was intended to celebrate. But this note is to record the fact that, in whatever measure Ved's faith has been realized, to him must be accorded the title of "onlie begetter." For without his conceiving the idea, this book would not have been made.

Introduction

Edwin Webb

There is the story—I like it too much ever to have felt the urge to check its historical veracity—of the philosopher Schopenhauer, whose daily habit was to take a long walk accompanied by his poodle Atma ("world-soul"). One day, so the story goes, he took a straight path across the lawns and formal flower beds of a municipal garden. One of the gardeners, unstooping himself from his labors, called out brusquely to the philosopher, "Here! who do you think you are? and what do you think you're doing?" Recalled thus abruptly from his abstracted reverie, Schopenhauer replied, "Ah! if only I could answer that. . . ."

A story, as the best of fictions confirm, need not be true to contain truth. And here, what the story directs us to is no less than the twin questions of what it is to be human. It is not, I believe, mere fancy to suggest that the whole corpus of David Holbrook's writings, in whatever form and in their variety of particular concerns, gather the collective response he would make should Schopenhauer's outraged gardener call *him* to personal account. There can be, of course, no succinct and uniquely satisfying answer to the question what it is to be human; and sometimes the closest we can get to answers are in the pertinacity and the definition of the questions which we propose. In the case of David Holbrook's lifework, the questioning has been pursued with a singular dedication.

The sheer quantity and range of Holbrook's writings astonish. There are works addressing themselves to education, to philosophical and to social and literary criticism; works which gather into themselves huge tracts from the fields of psychology, psychoanalysis and philosophy, and the physical sciences among others. Simply to have extended oneself into these fields of knowledge and inquiry with such developed understanding is an outstanding accomplishment by any estimation. Then to apply this accumulation of knowledge to new and significant insight marks the distinctiveness of that inquiring mind which this book celebrates.

To these critical endeavors there must be added the fact of Holbrook as artist—or, perhaps more precisely, such writings should be seen as preceded by the fact of his poetry and novels. I mean this not in a chronological sense—the creative and critical writings go on simultaneously; but in the sense that the creative enterprise identifies, through its embodiment or assumption within the art form, matters which it is then possible to explore directly and rationally through inquiry, reflection, and the search for satisfactory explanation. Certainly the concerns of the novels and poems, and of what Holbrook is attempting by them, is counterpointed in much of the critical writings. In this regard Holbrook has an affinity with D. H. Lawrence who wrote of the consequence, for himself, of his own novels and poems. They represented to him "the absolute need one has for some sort of satisfactory mental attitude towards oneself and things in general," so making one "try to abstract some definite conclusions from one's experience as a writer and a man." In the same place Lawrence then dubbed his critical reflections "pollyanalytics," that is, "inferences made afterwards from the experience."[1]

In similar fashion I think it is the case that many of Holbrook's critical writings are just such a response to the intuitive graspings of his poetry and novels, and represent also his attempt to bring to reasoned consciousness those insights. The construction of his own "pollyanalytics" has led Holbrook to challenge, indeed condemn, significant parts of the Lawrentian presentation of reality. Yet I think the same drive toward a sense of meaning in one's living is what, finally, informs the whole enterprise of Holbrook's writings. The issues with which he is concerned are not presented as an academic exercise, the abstract of a detached and neutral working-over of ideas, even where he writes within a convention of the academic apparatus. For in all his writings one senses that Holbrook is himself palpably present. He is *there* in his work in a passionate engagement throughout to the matters he addresses. In this, *all* of Holbrook's writings—the novels, the poems, the critical-analytical work—are written from an inner response to experience. It is personal writing, at times, intimately confessional. In the procedures of some writers such a practice could well engender self-absorption, a merely egotistic display, or a withdrawal from the world of shared realities; thus leading to separation, and the making of a world compounded of private fantasy. Holbrook's introspection, and the search through realms of knowledge which it induces, is made, however, in order to enter more fully and engage more securely with the world of everyday event and circumstance. Holbrook's world of experience, the world he is at pains to make sense of, is neither remote nor rarefied; it is the stuff of living in which we daily share.

* * *

The continuous effort throughout Holbrook's writings is the endeavor to make sense of lived reality, to live with a sense of meaning—and thereby live life richly. Without attempting a summary of Holbrook's successive and various attempts to come to terms with significant aspects of experience, it is possible nonetheless, perhaps, to identify some of the central and recurring concerns. The matters I have selected are not intended to assemble an "evolution" or progression of thinking, a line of development viewed retrospectively. Rather they suggest some of the constellations of thought by which Holbrook has taken his own bearings. One such constellation is that of "philosophical anthropology."

It would be difficult to establish with which of his works Holbrook formally signaled his involvement with philosophical anthropology. The phrase appears, for example, in *Sylvia Plath: Poetry and Experience* (1976), but goes unexplained. In *Education, Nihilism and Survival* (1977)—which must have been put together in whole or in part contemporaneously—philosophical anthropology is formally identified and described. But because of the essential nature of what philosophical anthropology is, and what it attempts to do, there is a sense in which all of Holbrook's critical and educational texts had always been involved in some of its vital concerns. For philosophical anthropology should be understood not as a body of knowledge, but as a mode of inquiry; one which starts from the primary facts of human consciousness itself, including self-consciousness, and the subjective, inner world of being. Such evidences as human consciousness supplies may not be disregarded, as they are in other forms of inquiry which propose their objectivities as findings which are independent of the seeker; the disciplines of scientific rationalism, behaviorist psychology, and logical positivism, for example. The propositions which philosophical anthropology embraces include the recognition that the findings of objective, mathematico-scientific forms of inquiry can be at best, even when valid, partial realizations; that pure objectivity is in any case impossible, since all such findings, in whatever degree, are products of the human consciousness which conceives them; that the knower is implicated in the known, the known a product of the knower.

Susanne Langer addressed herself to the "Idol of Objectivity" governing the tenets of behavioral psychology which

> ... requires its servitors to distort the data of human psychology into an animal image in order to handle them by the methods that fit speechless mentality. It requires the omission of all activities of central origin, which are felt as such, and are normally accessible to research in human psychology through the powerful instrument of language. The result is a laboratory exhibit of behaviour that is much more artificial than any instrumentally deformed object, because its deformation is not calculated and discounted as the effect of an instrument.[2]

Langer's observations on the limitations of behavioral psychology can be extended to other applications. For facts, which are themselves established through the agency of human consciousness, do not speak for themselves. Further, if they are to achieve or be converted to meaning, they require that gloss which consciousness alone can supply. Meaning is an act of interpretation which facts cannot achieve for themselves. Thus philosophical anthropology seeks to combat the reductionism which exclusively empirical or mathematico-scientific methods induce. Similarly, it confronts abstraction. For philosophical anthropology takes, first, a phenomenological approach to attempts to establish meanings of consciousness, drawing heavily (as Holbrook's own writings do) upon the work of Edmund Husserl; and, among other significant thinkers, Michael Polanyi. Another major reference point, since philosophical anthropology is interpretation addressed to meaning and its understanding, is the hermeneutics of Marjorie Grene. But there are many sources, or influences, which go towards the syncretics of philosophical anthropology: psychology, psychoanalysis and psychotherapy, neurophysiology, physical and social anthropology, existentialist philosophy, sociology.... For philosophical anthropology, in Holbrook's words, "embraces all those disciplines which are concerned with exploring human existence as *experience*."[3] Yet it is not any one discipline. It is any discipline, or combinations of discipline, whose "sensibility" (one might say) shares in that essential requirement. For the field of philosophical anthropology includes, potentially, *all* manifestations of human consciousness.

Philosophical anthropology is consciousness exploring itself through rational discourse; and in that reflexivity of self-consciousness attempting to make sense of experience. It attends to "objectivities," but rather as the nexus of consciousness which so conceives them. Its distinctiveness, as a mode of inquiry differing from detached and objective study, derives from the degree of authenticity and veracity which it is prepared to acknowledge in the subjective. Thus the inquiries of philosophical anthropology may also include what can be known through reflection, introspection and insight; a focused concentration of consciousness for which we might recover the word "contemplation."

In an important way, philosophical anthropology is, therefore, an exploration of man as *animal symbolicum*, as symbol-bearing and symbol-making consciousness; and is founded upon the recognition of symbolization as the fundamental process of mind. Other than through direct behaviour, it is through symbolization—whether esoteric or communally-shared within a culture—that consciousness is known at all. Behaviour and symbolism are both charged with the subjective life of experience; so that, finally, the making of the meaning of experience—if it is both to have conviction and to be convincing—demands our subjective assent too. We give assent to such meaning because it confers upon us a full sense of our being; in it we both realize and recognize (in its fundamental sense of "knowing again") experience. Meaning of this order is not detached, abstract; it is charged with the beingness of living itself—it is existential. Such sense confers "lived meaning" to our lives, constructing our realities. "Human beings," Holbrook argues consistently throughout his various addresses to existential, lived reality, "cannot exist without a sense of meaning in their lives, and this sense of meaning is explored through symbolism."[4] It is a theme which recurs in Holbrook's literary and social criticisms as well as in those works which specifically deal in philosophical anthropology that, lacking such a sense of meaning, there is only despair at the pointlessness or absurdity of life:

> [The] way beyond nihilism and all the degradations and evils to which it has led is in the vindication of the dynamics of love and creativity, in the study of man as animal symbolicum and his need for meaning, in the face of death and nothingness: the *Dasein* problem.[5]

The *Dasein* problem, and its analysis, as Holbrook frequently characterizes man's search for meaning-in-living, takes its cue from Martin Heidegger's concept of "being-unto-death." From *da* (there) and *sein* (being) the compound implies, within being, the potential too of *becoming*. But that being is also, vitally and essentially, one whose lived sense of being *there* locates and identifies the individual against nothingness, against the deathward urge.

The *Dasein* problem is the matter of being-in-the-world and of "feeling real." But how does one create out of the Rorschach of impression and sensation, the otherwise meaningless flux of existence, a significant sense of being to set against nothingness? In large measure, it is a question of personal identity, of a self-realization of the self; so that one can then consciously relate to the "thereness" of that self; and so begin to "know" that self. But one may, of course, construct a "false" self to deny or conceal the "true" being—from which "false self" false solutions to the question of being-in-the-world will issue. To these false solutions Holbrook, again, has consistently addressed himself: to the nihilism which he sees in much contemporary culture, to Sartrean existentialism, to pornography, and to much else that is life-denying and, ultimately (he argues), established by and springing from hate.

It is an unvarying principle of Holbrook's writings, in whatever form, that the capacity for being is founded upon the principle of love. It is, in a way, the melody-line of all of his works:

> The very fact that we are that distinctive *animal symbolicum* is a product of love, for there is no other name for the mother's devoted capacity to be for her child. If our symbols and culture are given us through love, then love is the fundamental principle of the human world.[6]

Holbrook's first explorations of love began in large measure, I suspect, as a reaction to particular aspects of Freudian psychoanalytic theory. In this he found an important ally in the early critique of Freud's theories made by Ian D. Suttie (*The Origins of Love and Hate*, 1935). Later he was to find, in the work of Harry Guntrip in particular, an extension of that critique and a proposition of radical alternatives, which Suttie's death had left incomplete. I suspect, too, that there was a personal urgency to this search for alternatives. Holbrook had lived through, and seen active service in, the twentieth century's greatest expression of hate, the Second World War. Holbrook has written "indirectly" (but with an autobiographical closeness) of some part of that experience, through the persona of Paul Grimmer, in his novel *Flesh Wounds* (1966); a novel which itself bespeaks a long period of absorption. Otherwise, he has been curiously reticent about that experience and its effects—as Boris Ford, a close friend who first met Holbrook just two years after the war's end, notes in his *Portrait* within this book. The wounds caused by living through such an experience are not of the flesh only: they are psychic too. They are profound in the way which William Golding has recorded them:

Before the second world war I believed in the perfectibility of social man . . . but after the war I did not because I was unable to. I am not talking of one man killing another with a gun, or dropping a bomb on him or blowing him up or torpedoing him. I am thinking of the vileness beyond all words that went on, year after year, in the totalitarian states . . . [Such things] were done, skillfully, by educated men, doctors, lawyers, by men with a tradition of civilization behind them, to beings of their own kind . . . I would like to pass on; but I must say that anyone who moved through those years without understanding that man produces evil as a bee produces honey, must have been blind or wrong in the head.[7]

From such a witnessing one cannot, of course, "pass on" unmoved, unchanged; and Holbrook's writings, from the earliest books on, have all explored variously a need to identify those personal and social forces which would promote healthy living. He has searched always those positive life forces which enable us to *be* as fully as we may. His is therefore an insistence upon the fundamental need for love as the basis of personal identity and as the making of the bondings of society.

Holbrook seems not to have turned to the insights of psychoanalysis immediately following his own war experience; that precipitation was itself an outcome of love—through his wife's discovery of the healing process of psychotherapy. The matter is recorded briefly in *The Quest for Love* (1964), and much later treated novelistically in *Nothing Larger than Life* (1987). Certainly, from the earlier reference onwards, Holbrook turned increasingly and overtly to psychoanalysis as a means of furthering his inquiries both into literature and into society in order to uncover the motivations of love and hate. Andrew Brink notes in his essay that the enterprise (now sustained throughout Holbrook's writings over three decades) bespeaks "personal upheavals," commenting "There is a story to be told about this . . ." For so to use the concepts and theories of psychoanalysis itself implies, again in Brink's words, "facing and resolving conflict." Within that personal story of David Holbrook, drawing attention to itself largely through omission, the psychic consequences of the totality of the "war experience" must, one guesses, feature prominently. At the least, the absence of the full story is remarkable in an author who, in all other respects, uses the circumstances of personal living as the prime material for his own creative outputs.

What psychoanalysis most especially concerns itself with, at the risk of distortion through reduction, is the matter of human motivation; in particular, the undeclared (even unknown) intentions which make a person do and behave as one does. Through its references, Holbrook uses the theories of psychoanalysis to provide a means of "framing" cultural products and pursuits, individual and collective. So framed in the concepts of psychoanalysis, details of the composition hitherto concealed from superficial glance become perceptible to appraisal—and to judgment. In *Human Hope and the Death Instinct* (1971), among other writings, Holbrook has shown how connections between psychoanalysis and cultural products of the imagination connect with our modes of apprehending and coming to terms with reality. They offer, too, a moral view of culture based on the positive or destructive tendencies of such creativity. Such interpretations of psychoanalysis, employed alongside other existentialist disciplines, can thereby provide genuine illumination of creative works. Such psychodynamic criticism may, of course, challenge literary and cultural orthodoxies or fashions—and may even result in findings which discomfort us. They can also accrue, for the author of the exposure of such deeply hidden intentionality, a measure of social obloquy.

The especial inquiry which it has been Holbrook's endeavor to promote, through his various explorations, has been conducted, therefore, at profound "subtextual" levels of analysis. In this progress he has moved away from "practical criticism" and eschewed modish structuralist methodologies—simply because they are irrelevant to his discovered purposes. Holbrook approaches a work of literature not as a *text*, but as a symbol; and gives it a concentrated attentiveness much as a therapist might receive a patient's dream and then, in cooperation with the materials of that dream, together with other materials or "evidences" with which they appear to have organic connection, work over its substance to find what was symbolized though not articulated.

Holbrook's inquiries into the springs of human love start from a primary recognition of human nature as "predominantly altruistic and capable of love."[8] Where Golding's faith was shaken, and only partially retrieved subsequently, Holbrook's was reasserted—defiantly so, perhaps, in the face of the evidence of war, but perhaps, too, as the only possible alternative to a view of the human psyche as inherently evil, to use Golding's shorthand term. If, by nature, human beings have a predisposition to altruism and to love, then the causes of distortion and destructiveness must be either in the individual's nurturing or in the destructive agencies of collective society.

In addition to substantial references to Harry Guntrip in the search for satisfactory answers, Holbrook's exploration of love takes in extensively a range of theories on child development and nurturing, with the work, among others, of Melanie Klein, W. R. D. Fairbairn and D. W. Winnicott all providing important signposts. He takes special heed of the Object-relations school of thought which stresses both the necessity of, and the processes by which is achieved, the infant's early and essential feeling of "I am"—that recognition of separateness, of the individual. The "I am" feeling is the beginning of a sense of self as distinguished from all that is "not me." The "I am" is a "psychic weaning" from the mother, from the literal fact of having been a part of the mother, and is the beginning of the infant's discovery of all else in the world that is "not me." Against all that the child discovers to be "not me" the "I am" sense in part discovers and defines itself in the movement, supported by the mother's love, towards self-consciousness and self-realization.

One vital consequence of such psychic weaning, a process which is natural and normal for most infants, is that the individual can "stand alone":

> The *capacity to be alone* depends upon the individual having a personal culture by which he feels that his union with the mother is symbolised—while this in its turn establishes for him the capacity to be self-reliant and to be alone sustained by his inward possession of the mother and that culture which relates him to all other human beings.[9]

The infant's early experience of "being" is the foundation for "becoming," a way of experiencing existence which promotes, with the loving ego support of the mother, the development of the "true self." Given this, the *Dasein* problem can be faced, because an authentic sense of being has been established, from which the child can go on into maturity (which is not to suggest that the path will be easy or uncomplicated). But where the security of self is not established, where (in Winnicott's words)

> ... the mothering is not good enough, then the infant becomes a collection of reactions to impingement, and the true self of the infant becomes hidden behind a false self which complies with and generally wards off the world's knocks ...[10]

From the "false self" issue false solutions to the question of identity and of being-in-the-world, including those schizoid solutions which invert or reverse the values of living. From the fear of incomplete identity the individual imposes self on others, exploits them, and by that act of conflict tries to feel real—without ever feeling real within herself or himself.

Given, however, an essential nurturing through love and self-realization, through a "taking in of goodness," the individual learns to develop a "positive creativity," a means of addressing oneself to experience. Through such creative attitudes to experience, the individual acquires the ability "to triumph over difficulties and make things 'come good' ...."[11] But if given a "not-good-enough" environment in one's early days, must the individual be lost? Holbrook's answer calls upon the symbolization of culture, of its art and art-making, as a further means of enabling essential development to take place. It is so argued, for example, in his early writings on education, in which he sees the absolute need for the child to encounter the redemptive, or restorative capacity of art, of literature in particular; so to liberate the locked-in feelings which seek to love and be loved. For through those creative encounters which art makes possible, imagination discovers and works over the sum of individual experience so that it may be known and thereby connect, from the inner world of experience, across to the outer world of reality. In that process

> ... the creative arts are a chief source of nourishment for this [inner] life, being the means to establish bridges between inward and outer life. For this reason the central discipline in our education must be the creative arts, and their place in adult life needs to be as central.[12]

In Holbrook's scheme of things the subjective is not a selfish principle, nor is it to be fed in the name of self-indulgence. The subjective is the fundament from which springs the individual's need to make sense of experience and so enter the world of experience of others. For the subjective extends, intersubjectively, into the lives of others and is, by that process, enriched. Such a search for a sense of meaning is therefore, and necessarily, a moral pursuit:

> Our view of the world (even its *reality*) is always rooted in our subjective life. We cannot separate knowledge from the knower. Knowing is a form of being, and inevitably bound up with moral being.[13]

It is the precept of D. H. Lawrence that "The essential function of art is moral" which Holbrook is at pains, again and again, to reemphasise in his writings. The relationship between art and the morality of one's actual living is tenuous (reading a good book won't necessarily make one a good person), but it is there nonetheless. It is there in those awarenesses which, through art, we may more certainly see so that we may attend directly to them.

In Holbrook's criticisms, whether investigating the works of Mahler, or Chaucer, or Shakespeare, the contemporary literature of Dylan Thomas and Sylvia Plath, or the world of popular culture, Holbrook throughout searches the moral dimension of these products of the human imagination. He seeks out, through the metaphor and symbol of their own composition, their origination in love or hate—and their consequential effect upon our own power to be through discovering the true self of our being.

* * *

These, then, are some of the markers which distinguish David Holbrook's creative and critical enterprise. Many of these matters recur in various settings within the body of Holbrook's writing as a whole, just as they are taken up within different themes addressed by the contributors to this collection of original essays, all of them specially written for this volume. And because, in some essential ways, Holbrook's writings of whatever kind are "all of a piece" several contributors, in order to pursue their chosen theme, cross and recross the boundaries of formal categories and genres. The essays have been put in nominal groupings, nonetheless, in the hope that such an arrangement will enable the reader to gather a fuller, more representative perspective on the principal engagements of Holbrook's work.

Within the essays there are reservations and criticisms voiced too. For the real tribute is to address those issues which Holbrook himself addresses, to take seriously those matters which Holbrook takes seriously, and in so doing recognize the distinctiveness of his achievement in bringing those matters to our attention. If there are critics who do not like the answers which Holbrook puts forward, the questions remain, and remain to be answered. In such an abundance of production, it would be more than human if every one of Holbrook's works achieved uniformly the highest standard—and some of his works suffer certainly from a repetitiveness of sources and argument. Yet one must create as one must; or fail to create at all.

Far from diminished, Holbrook's creativity continues with accelerated fertility. There are yet more works on the way: works already written and awaiting publication, works written and still to find a publisher, and others in various stages of completion. This book can mark, therefore, only a stage in the progress which it celebrates.

If the occasion of a seventieth birthday is arbitrary, it is also opportune; a moment to attempt, through the collective efforts of the contributors to this book, a proper recognition and appraisal of David Holbrook's achievements to date. And if, in the recital of Holbrook's works which follows, there are detected some wrong notes, these should not detract from our appreciation of the performance and the achievement as a whole. Viewed within that perspective, there is a case to be made (as Roger Poole explicitly argues in his contribution) for David Holbrook to be recognized as a leading, contemporary, existentialist writer. He has, if we are prepared to attend to his writings, pushed on into "darkling plains" and there shed light. To such a claim for Holbrook's extensive analytical and expository writings, there is the fact, too, of his poems and novels in their own right as achieved art. There are the poems which illuminate moments of being, of potentiality and insight—and thereby assert a fuller sense of being in the quest for meaning-in-life. Such meaning, as the poems attest, is neither remote nor arcane, but is in the everyday of common experience which, however personal, may also be shared. There are the novels, too, which display an "extraordinary ability to convey the real"; which, as Geoffrey Strickland explains in his essay within this book, arises from the novelist's need "to know who and where he is"—an endeavor which demands "the contemplation of wholly different participants in the life they all share." Thus the novels and poems alike are concerned to explore and identify the inner realities of experience. They are also, one senses, those productions of Holbrook in which he is himself most closely realized and his philosophy made most actual—actual in that it is of the very stuff of the events and circumstances themselves which the writing presents.

What all of Holbrook's writings, collectively, assert is the living identity of a bravely independent imagination which *values* life, and whose positives are rare indeed within contemporary culture and cultural commentary. For in Holbrook's writings we find just such a profound affirmation of life and its rich potentialities, when we learn to live through love. To locate and activate our "powers of being" (to use one of Holbrook's own phrases) is a liberation possible only through the fullest of engagements with our livings.

* * *

If there can be a short expression to identify the importance of such a lifework as we find in David Holbrook's writings, I think I would locate it in his own affirmation that "the courage we require is the courage to be human."[14] For it is to the end of identifying and affirming those forces which enable us to be truly human, to live positively and rewardingly, that his work continuously aspires. And I hope that this *Festschrift* too, in celebrating the man and his works, is itself a celebration of the spirit of that living principle.

Notes

1. D. H. Lawrence, foreword to *Fantasia of the Unconscious* (London: Heinemann, 1961), p. 9.
2. Susanne K. Langer, *Mind: an Essay on Human Feeling* (Baltimore: Johns Hopkins University Press, 1967), vol. 1, p. 36.
3. David Holbrook, *Education, Nihilism and Survival* (London: Darton, Longman and Todd, 1977), p. 31.
4. Ibid., p. 51.
5. Ibid., p. 135.
6. Ibid., pp. 121–22.
7. William Golding, "Fable," in *The Hot Gates* (London: Faber and Faber, 1965), pp. 86–87.
8. David Holbrook, *The Quest for Love* (Methuen: London, 1964), p. 13. This work contains one of the fullest and most direct of Holbrook's summaries of object-relations theory; see pp. 27–90.
9. David Holbrook, *The Masks of Hate* (Oxford: Pergamon Press, 1972), p. 16.
10. D. W. Winnicott, quoted by Holbrook, ibid.
11. Holbrook, *The Quest for Love*, p. 57 and p. 61.
12. Ibid., p. 20.
13. Holbrook, *Education, Nihilism and Survival*, p. 47.
14. David Holbrook, *Sylvia Plath: Poetry and Existence* (London: Athlone Press, 1976), p. 285.

Powers of Being

Part I
David Holbrook

David Holbrook: A Portrait

BORIS FORD

It is not every day nor even, in my experience, more than once in a lifetime that one sits down to write a "portrait" of a friend whom one has known for many years. Where should one begin? Perhaps, for want of any brighter idea, with our most recent encounter or communication? That was a postcard from David Holbrook explaining with apologies why it would not, alas, be convenient for him and Margot, his wife, to put me up when I was proposing to visit Cambridge to do some work at the University Press. There was nothing very momentous about that. Except that David phoned the next day to apologize and explain they were leaving the following day for a fortnight's holiday in Normandy. And then, on that next day, another card arrived hoping that he and Margot would see me on their return from France.

A flavorsome card duly arrived from Normandy, of course: the meals in their two hotels were rich and superb beyond belief—some years ago the annual card from France explained that the only time they could bear to use the loo was when a rich and superb meal was being served and all the discriminating French flies moved in a dense cloud from the loo to the dining room. These three cards and one phone call, which is more than I receive from most friends in the course of a year, must surely offer a revealing clue or two about this person David Holbrook. He must be afflicted, someone suggested, with a fearfully bad conscience; but in relation to offering me a bed (and a rich and copious meal) that could hardly be, for David and Margot have put me up many more times than I can remember in the past two or three years alone. So maybe he is an anxious sort of person? Or was it possible that Margot had at long last put her foot down and said "Oh no, not again, surely!?"

The only clue one need extract from this fairly trivial episode, I am sure, is that David was being no more, or only a little more, than his normal hospitable self. Then, for another clue, it seems that David must live pen in hand; the cards and voluminous letters that arrive periodically are always handwritten with an ex-fountain pen dipped in an inkwell. Indeed, one might deduce from this and other evidence that David only lays down his pen in order to go and eat a good meal—but that would be a somewhat less than accurate deduction.

Lastly I noticed that the card from Normandy contained no hint of any memories of the day, fifty years ago, when David landed with his tank unit on the coast of Normandy, described so movingly in *Flesh Wounds*. I am not sure what to make of this omission. It is true, though I had not registered it before, that I do not remember David ever speaking about these ghastly experiences which left him wounded—but alive. It may be that until he wrote that first novel, which was not published until 1966, the Normandy nightmare was too raw and painful to talk about, for the "vast loneliness of the warring young of the forties fell on his soul."[1]

> Blast waves and smoke blinded his periscope, and then hammering blows rocked the thirty-ton tank which lurched and swayed under them. High up along the beach he saw a tank burning, and then, suddenly, under its dipped and useless gun, a row of dead beside it. The full dreadful sense of waste came flowing into his gorge, the first full flavour of machine warfare. There are moments, short moments, from which we never recover; this first minute's baptism of fire changed Paul's sensibility for ever, for ever to be a little deadened.[2]

The bombardment, which left animals lying slaughtered in the fields, "their stiffening legs cocked up in the air. . . their bodies going bloated, then oozy and slimy with decay," left Paul Grimmer anxiously "hoping to see a calf that moved . . . a living movement of beasts to gladden the scene." It seemed as if this smashing of the beautiful Normandy countryside broke his capacity "to identify himself with the gladness of natural creation, for ever." And yet, as he lay under the bursting mortar shells and "died many times in that three minutes," he saw that the early morning grass was full of rainbow-colored beetles. One of them, "jewelled like a brooch," made its awkward way from small clod to small clod:

> Paul felt a great wave of empathy with the beetle, and pressed his face down to it . . . if he gets to that clod six inches away, I shall survive this [he wagered]. If not, he, the green jewelled one, and I, will perish

together. A bomb-tail whirred into the air like something to scare a bird. His beetle made it. The mortaring stopped.³

This seems to me an inspired passage, like Paul's sight, in the midst of the "chaos, confusion, squalor [where] each man was lost in the impersonal hell, where metal chased flesh," of "an old man in dusty blue overalls, and a youngish woman in dull blue peasant apron, working in the field . . . pathetically among the craters."⁴ "Nothing larger than life," as David entitled one of his later novels.

Some years later David was commissioned by *The Sunday Times* to return to this scene and write an article about it. He ate a meal in a bistro now rebuilt in the salvaged and luxuriant countryside, and after their talk about the war, madame said that she would give him a bottle of Calvados if he were ever to return. So during this latest visit to Normandy, these many years later, he and Margot came back to the bistro, and madame, before a word of reintroduction was spoken, emerged to greet them with a bottle of Calvados.

The flesh and spiritual wounds suffered by Paul Grimmer in Normandy were not to be seen in the lackadaisical young man whom a friend had invited me to meet some time early in 1947. She told me that David had been a pupil of F. R. Leavis at Downing College a few years after me. Ensconced among the cushions on the divan, he had the air of one not much inclined to engage in conversation, least of all about wearisome topics like Cambridge English and *Scrutiny;* instead he uttered occasional *ex cathedra* remarks in what seemed to me the carefully groomed, sonorous voice of an aspiring actor. He was certainly handsome enough for the part, I noted enviously, with his green eyes and strong hair. When, after this singularly unsatisfactory encounter, I asked Milein who this "rather fearful young man" was, she said, to my surprise, that he was working as assistant editor to Edgell Rickword and Randall Swingler on their Marxist quarterly, *Our Time*.

However, I must have met David again a few times, though I have no memory of doing so, or I would hardly have suggested him as a likely person to fill an editorial post at the Bureau of Current Affairs, where I was working in my first post-war job after some years' experience of running courses and editing pamphlets for the Army Bureau of Current Affairs, or ABCA, during the war. And so began a long editorial relationship with

David, which before long, when we were both married, flowered into a close domestic friendship.

A 'Rich Roomful'

If this account of David Holbrook is not to read like an anonymous recital of his undertakings and achievements, as in an obituary, or a novelist's imaginative recreation of his inner life, it seems that there is no alternative but to continue in this subjective fashion. However, the subjectivity has been lessened as a result of talking with David's wife and, since this *Festschrift* is not being kept a secret, with David himself. Then it occurred to me to write to a number of people who have known David well over the years, some of them at different times and in different places from me. And of course there is the ample evidence provided by his own writings.

For many years David has distributed among his friends a printed sheet listing his publications, a missive which I'm sure we found welcome for the good news it gave of a friend, but also somewhat bewildering, because I for one saw little chance of keeping up with all his writings unless I were to give up reading more than an occasional novel by Jane Austen and Dickens and George Eliot and Henry James and a few others, let alone reluctant perusing of Booker finalists. For the most recent sheet lists seven volumes of poetry, eight novels, nine volumes on education, and nineteen volumes of criticism—a few of these books are held up because the publishers are in financial difficulty. Even so, five of these titles are dated 1992. And the list does not include David's many anthologies and his excellent hymnbook, on which he collaborated with Elizabeth Postan. (Nor does it include two somewhat unexpected titles which are listed under the name of David Holbrook in the Avon public library catalogue: one on playing games and the other on squash). Moreover, the list does not mention the titles of a large number of books in various stages of gestation and composition which reside in file boxes and in neat piles of typescript on the double bed in David's study.

So I am afraid I have not read all these forty-three volumes. It may well be that the only person in the world who has is David himself (unless there is a fearsomely diligent student somewhere or other who has worked his or her way through them in pursuit of a Ph.D.). From those many of his books that I have read, it is clear that they provide the best and most copious evidence about his experiences and preoccupations, his reflections and changing moods, as well as his professional and domestic life. For in various guises, he tends to be strongly present in nearly everything he writes. One senses that David Holbrook was lying at least alongside Paul Grimmer under the mortar barrage, watching that jewelled beetle. And it must surely be significant that the name of the boy and man at the center of so many of his novels is named Grimmer, which was the maiden name of David's mother.

In his poems, many of them about domestic felicities and crises, David is concerned to render the immediate firsthand experience, as when, for instance, in what is perhaps his best-known poem, *Fingers in the Door,* one feels with him as he feels with Kate:

> ... She
> Held her breath, contorted the whole of her being focus-wise,
>   against the
> Burning fact of the pain.

How does one, how does he, react to this accident which one cannot bear to contemplate?

> And for a moment
> I wished myself dispersed in a hundred thousand pieces
> Among the dead bright stars.

For many it would be a moment for a display of grief, horror, tears. For David it was a moment when "it crowded in to me how she and I were / Light-years from any mutual help or comfort," and when the experience could only be expressed and encompassed symbolically. "The need to symbolise," he has said, "is a primary one, and is everywhere neglected and abused." What can one meaningfully say, at the end of such an experience, except that

> Nothing can restore, She, I, mother, sister, dwell dispersed among
>   dead bright stars:
> We are there in our hundred thousand pieces![5]

The poem is the experience: and the experience was that of a father who happened, in that very moment, to be a poet. David's concern "to write about normal, quotidian life" might lend itself to sentimentality were it not matched, as here, by the veracity of his seeing and feeling eye, and by the distinctive quality of his responses. The poetry reveals on these occasions what it means to be sensitively alive. "Quotidian life" includes, for David, topics like *Living? Our Supervisors Will Do That for Us, A Week Teaching Poetry, Painting in the Snow, The Maverick, A Day in France,* or *The Essential Function of Art is Moral.* Some of these poems are ironic, some sardonic with disillusion, some lighthearted and amused. But people who used to associate the name Holbrook with polemical, hectoring letters to the press would have done well to turn to his poems about the daily round, about his children or his wife, about the fear of death or the yearly cycle of nature, for these would have revealed to them a more introspective and heartfelt part of his nature.

For to write about one's marriage and one's children is to have to ponder time passing. He sees an iron bed in a shop window,

> ... like the one we had
> In Cornwall once, when we first slept away
> Together. All that romance returns: the sea
> Might be inland: I hear the gulls: yet we
> Are many hours and miles from that today,
> And many beds have known our births, our losses, and our dead.[6]

His preoccupation with death, in his poetry, is almost never morbid: sometimes wistful (with an echo of Yeats):

> My daughter sat on my lap in green. . . .
> So here I swallow, . . .
> And learn to let her go separated.
>
> Mine but not mine! You and I, only two,
> One day shall sit here, quietly, in Time,
> And you shall ask me why I'm looking so
> As if I held a child's ghost, murmuring her name.[7]

Love and Let Live is this poem's title, and so it had to be, for Kate of the trapped finger did indeed "take fulfilment's wing" and now lives, married with children, in Canada. Occasionally a deep pessimism pervades the poems, but most often what is noticeable is how a somber reflection on decay and death is dissipated with a gentle symbolic touch, even at times with an unexpected élan. In *A Child Said, "I am Smoke,"* one of the children danced harmlessly at a bonfire of old lilac, and prompted the thought: ". . . if Death did snatch / At us he'd like as not take that enquiring one." But then,

> .... if this creature with her open eyes,
> Brown and believing with a fire in heaven,
> Were to close them, and be laid straight, and stiffen
> And carried to a place and burned, 'the Universe'
>
> Would have to move its vast indifference,
> The great rocks crack with love, the star interstices
> Fill with her angels, new gods as novices
> Follow her smoke wherever she should dance![8]

In a later essay Ian Robinson discusses and evaluates David's poetic achievement. Here I offer it as revealing some of his central preoccupations: "the scurrying flow of home"; "our twenty years of difficult marriage" with "long storm-bound months"; the swooping swifts "writing their joy in arabesques of play"; the brief innocence of the November day of sun. This "rich roomful of who we are" may eventuate in a "yawning vacuum", yet what counts is the "endearing talk, ironic eye, / The child's quick shaking of her hair." And finally, one of David's most moving, one might say quintessential poems, *March Evening:*

> ... lock doors, rake fire, one light
> Left for children—then let's go to bed:
> One more tired regular untroubled winter day.
> And that's by inches how we edge away,
> I think, and look out at the night.

He recalls a walk in Odsey Wood when, expecting March's flowers, they found December still:

> ... But for one small larch's
> Dead wood spurting green, and then one more,
> And then ten thousand, running across the floor,
> Wood violets snagged by the frost; and we're surrounded
> By blazes we had missed on every tree, astounded
> By what leaps out from every copse ...

He felt "The stars, the woods, laugh at us as they roar / To their new perihelion." Though "preoccupied with death," he now sees "night's tongue flicker life's renewing," and the poem ends with a wonderfully delicate moment of life-affirming intimacy:

> ... and as the black turned green, a wife's
> Hand turned my head, she kissed my mouth,
> And we began a new year's lease of life.[9]

Perhaps the final word here should be Christopher Hope's, writing of David's poems as "carried off with a grace and geniality which are due to a thorough-going openness before experience and a brave perception of the flickering potential for moments of true being.... This gives his verse its unusual dignity, its celebratory air."[10] Yet he has been unable to find a publisher for any volumes of verse since *Selected Poems 1961–1978.*

Plays of Passion

The impression David gave off at that first encounter, of being an incipient actor, may have had its origins in his sixth-form years in Norwich. His headmaster, Geoffrey Thorpe, allowed two or three boys to help Nugent Monck behind the scenes at the Maddermarket Theatre, "sweeping up the tickets, and helping prepare for this great illusion." For David this was an emancipating experience, which he has described at length in *A Play of Passion*. Paul Grimmer's first sexual passions may well be fictional; but Monck lives in his own name in the novel, and the environment he created in his theater and home was undoubtedly what David himself experienced and which he knew would be a major influence in his life:

> There was something in the air, even in the dust-motes floating in Moncklet's lilac and rose flood-lights, that offered to transcend the existence in which [Paul] felt now so imprisoned.[11]

It was David's first break away from home, and also an escape from the dread hand of the Gradgrind who succeeded Thorpe ("whom I loved"). Monck was totally committed to producing, with an amateur cast and very meager resources, the most inspiring performances of Shakespeare. They became famous in the thirties.

Paul Grimmer is not described as being stagestruck, and though he takes the "dull" part of Fabian in *Twelfth Night* he does not aspire to go on the stage, and nor, David says, did he; but being around during rehearsals he got to know the plays by heart. What meant most for him was to be among people for whom poetry was in their blood, and for whom "the search for meaning" in their speaking of Shakespeare's verse, especially on such an uncluttered and undistracting stage as Monck ensured, was "the major preoccupation of their lives." (I have an indelible memory of seeing, as a boy of sixteen, Monck's *Antony and Cleopatra,* and of hearing, for the rest of my life, the lament that Cleopatra, purple-robed and absolutely motionless, spoke over Antony's body).

As it happens, it is not one of Shakespeare's plays but Monck's version of the *Norwich Passion Play* which is described in some detail in the novel. For Paul, and no doubt for David himself, to be involved in this was to enter an almost unknown world of natural piety and faith. Though he found Monck's translation too archaic,

> the production caught the spirit of the direct, poetic enactment of the mystery; and the mystery of it was taken by the hundred or so people in Monck's converted baking-powder factory.[12]

The world that Monck "unfolded so feelingly to Paul" not only included "some of the pleasures of civilised middleclass life—the pleasures of bathing every morning, for example . . . . or of food prepared with a real interest, and served with its own setting and drama"—but above all it revealed to the maturing boy a life "lived with great intensity," a "life given over entirely to his art." The novel ends with Monck's funeral in the cathedral. He had been an atheist, "yet with such a deep veneration for the meaning of Christianity"; faced with "the strangely theatrical catafalque, and on top of it a little coffin," Paul feels at once

> the whole intolerable awfulness of death [bursting] over him, like the great stone waves of the cathedral's masonry. The cathedral dissolved in his burning tears, and he sobbed aloud, suddenly and uncontrollably distraught, utterly broken down. . . . Not only grief threw him as he stumbled around the Cathedral Close, but his recognition of his love for the man, for that small wizard, with his capacities to transform the world into art, into meaning.[13]

Monck must have been a seminal influence for David, but I doubt if this included his "deep veneration for the meaning of Christianity." Religious belief or disbelief are absent from his novels that I have read. In a later novel, partly set in a barely disguised King's College where David taught for a time, Paul never enters the chapel and it feels like a lost opportunity. In one of his critical books, *Lost Bearings in English Poetry,* he writes that he believes

> it is possible to allow the mystery of the world, or needing to admit man's spiritual needs, ... without moving into mysticism . . . . or needing to find or restore God or gods.[14]

And yet, sharing a degree of the "spiritual dimension with those who do have a faith," he believes that "We can restore man's moral being to our view of the world." That final sentence defines very well what became one of David's main "missions" in life.

English for the Rejected

Toward the end of the war David was released as a university student and within a fortnight he had returned to Cambridge to complete his degree in English literature, studying under F. R. Leavis at Downing College. As far as I know he has not described his relations with Leavis, though he can render his distinctive, flat Cambridgeshire accent and delivery to perfection. At the end of one of his poems there are five lives which I am sure depict Leavis:

> ... his supervisor can be seen any Friday
> Walking up Trumpington Street with an odd movement of the feet,
> Still looking like an old corm, lissom, and knowing
> Uncannily what's good, what's bad,
> And probably rather hard up into the bargain.[15]

As for the Leavises, they were by way of dismissing David as a Marxist, as if that were all there was to be said about him. It is true that at this time he got to know a number of Marxist writers and artists like Edgell Rickword, Randall Swingler, Richard Carline, Jack Lindsay, Francis Klingender, James Boswell and "a whole bunch of Hampstead intellectuals." As a result he found himself drawn in the direction, not of *Scrutiny* to which he never contributed, but of *Our Time* which he helped to edit on leaving Cambridge. David remained very close to Edgell Rickword, more so than to Leavis, though he was powerfully influenced and challenged by the latter. Thirty years later he was to write, from Downing College itself, his *Lost Bearings in English Poetry* in which he, in his turn, challenged in a radical but certainly no longer Marxist way some important assumptions and evaluations in Leavis's *New Bearings in English Poetry*.

The "Scrutineers" with whom David was closest were Wilfrid Mellers, Denys Thompson, and I suppose myself. For Mellers he wrote the libretti for two pastoral operas, one of which was performed and had much less success than it deserved. I have never been sure of the place of music in David's life. If it has not been as great as he would have liked, that may because he and Margot probably could not afford to buy records or go to operas. But they go to concerts and recitals, there is always music on the stand of the grand piano, and one of their daughters teaches music. And then, to everyone's astonishment, David suddenly wrote a book about Mahler's Ninth Symphony, a book strongly commended by Donald Mitchell, the Mahler scholar and biographer. He heard this symphony while lying in bed with flu and it made the deepest impression on him. Indeed, together with Mahler's *Das Lied von der Erde* and some of Schubert's songs, it became a cultural lodestar for him:

> menaced by loss of faith, by a Godless universe, by nihilism, and by his own empty, or most cynical, dynamics of self, [Mahler] struggled on to find a sense of meaning that could triumph over spiritual paralysis. . . . Blankness is transmuted in creative meaning, and so into gratitude for having existed.[16]

My professional relationship with David began in 1947 when he joined the Bureau of Current Affairs, where I had become chief editor. David was responsible for helping to edit our illustrated wall charts and pamphlets on political, social and cultural themes, which were written by "progressive" writers like Victor Bonham-Carter, Mark Abrams, Angus Maude, Gertrude Williams, John Madge, Jacquetta Hawkes, Donald McLachlan, Aldous Huxley, Leonard Woolf, Jacob Bronowski, Clough Williams-Ellis, and the like. The pamphlets were designed to form the basis of discussions in places of work and further education. David had no doubt met this kind of material published by the Army Bureau of Current Affairs during the war. Dealing with and often meeting authors of this caliber made the Bureau, directed by W. E. Williams, a very congenial and civilized organization in which to be working after the war, with its handsome offices overlooking Green Park and with the elegantly bohemian and even notorious Shepherd's Market to the rear. But it came to an abrupt end after five years, when our grant from the Carnegie Trust was not renewed.

So I went off with my family to New York and Geneva, to a post with the United Nations; and David and Margot moved to Suffolk, where he taught as a free-lance lecturer for the Workers Educational Association, his idea being that he would write during the day and earn his living in the evenings. This, David says, "was a terrible period of our lives: we were extremely poor, houseless and confused." But matters improved when he was appointed WEA tutor organiser in Leicestershire and wrote his first book, still unpublished, on T. F. Powys—except that there was no proper water supply, and the farm next door caught fire and all the pigs were burned. He found the experience of working in adult education invaluable, for it led, in 1954, to him being appointed tutor at one of Henry Morris's new Cambridgeshire Village Colleges, at Bassingbourne. Here he taught adults and looked after the evening classes; he was also given the bottom stream children to teach and told that he could do what he liked with them, which provided the material for his marvelous (and marvelously named) book, *English for the Rejected*.

As it happened, this book and its predecessor came my way, unexpectedly and by the skin of their teeth. For in 1958 I was appointed to be Education Secretary at the Cambridge University Press and there, on my desk, was a bundle of manuscripts which the outgoing Secretary said were "worthy of rejection." Towards the bottom of the pile was a manuscript by David Holbrook, which was the first I knew that he had written a book on education. I read its superb opening paragraphs (which I have slightly abbreviated):

> I remember once being shown round a huge new secondary modern school. The architecture was an achievement of the spirit. No-one could help being stirred by that building: the gay colours in the corridors and classrooms; the way the architect had scaled his rooms and all the furniture to the stature of the children; its convenience, and warmth, and generosity. In the great gymnasium the yellow pine bars and rails, the red glow of the sprung floor, made one feel an urge to leap and dance. And in the grounds there was a family group in bronze by a great contemporary sculptor.
> Nothing had been spared, not even the thought to plant flowering shrubs and trees.
> The headmaster took me into his large, wall-papered study. 'Of course,' he said, 'we only get the duds here'.[17]

English for Maturity was an immediate success, and made its author into a figure of major influence on the teaching of English to children of somewhat lesser attainment in secondary modern and comprehensive schools. As David argued with wit and passion, and with copious examples of practical work, what has to be combatted is not the dimness of children but the cynicism and snobbery of many teachers. The timetable subject called English, including literature, can be made meaningful to the "duds" as well as to grammar school highfliers for it is about living and the meaning of life.

After this best-seller and *English for the Rejected,* there followed a number of others, together with anthologies, which linked the resources of English and the value of original writing (however hesitant and modest initially) to the needs of the less privileged children. No one who has read it will forget the case history of Rose, described at length in *English for the Rejected.*[18] This "low-spirited, drab, and unhappy child", labelled "backward," wrote, during the two years that David worked with her, "poignantly real" story after story about the "one predominant problem in her life—her grief at the loss of her mother":

> I was often so moved that there could be no pretence at mere objectivity as a 'teacher of English': a sympathetic touch on the shoulder was all that needed to be said. And even to write 'Good' at the bottom seemed impertinence.[19]

These books proved to be the spearhead of a revolution in the English classroom, a revolution which ran in harness with the pioneering approaches mainly to grammar school teaching of English that Denys Thompson had been promoting for many years in a series of books, and in the pages of his periodical *The Use of English*. We had contrived, rather improbably, to launch this periodical from the Bureau of Current Affairs, and it was through this that David's close links with Denys were forged. David and I, together with Raymond O'Malley, a longstanding friend and colleague of Denys's and senior English master at Dartington Hall, made up the supporting editorial board of *The Use of English*. We met, in a lively and argumentative fashion, twice a year in Denys's home in Yoevil, where he was head of the grammar school. David came to know Denys (who had taught me in the sixth form at Gresham's School in Norfolk) as one of the wisest and most quizzically sane of educationists, and the best and most incorruptible of friends.

Nothing Larger Than Life

Around the time I was failing to reject David's *English for Maturity* he and Margot moved, in 1956, to a rambling house called Ducklake in the Hertfordshire village of Ashwell. David gave up his post at the Village College in 1962, having been elected the previous year to a fellowship at King's College, partly financed by Cambridge University Press to enable him to write a number of books. This was followed in 1965 by a Senior Leverhume Research Fellowship and three years later by an Arts Council writer's grant. Also he taught for a time at Jesus College in Cambridge, being made a College Lecturer under Raymond Williams. What with these various appointments and grants and the comparatively good royalties his books on education must have steadily been bringing in, one might imagine that the Holbrooks were now comfortably off. In fact, during most of their time at Ducklake they were often as poor as the Ashwell church mice—the Jesus appointment brought in £250 per annum.

Nonetheless, the combination of part-time teaching at Bassingbourne or tutoring at the Cambridge colleges, and writing at home in such an agreeable setting, must have suited David ideally. "Village life in Ashwell was most satisfying, and it was a splendid place in which to bring up children," he wrote recently in a letter. Wondering why his description of village life seemed so familiar, I came upon the answer when rereading *Nothing Larger Than Life,* the novel he wrote about this period of their lives:

It was a splendid place to bring up a family. The village offered the children a secure pattern of life in which everyone's role was evident, as simply as Happy Families. Maggie, at seven, could easily draw a map of the whole place with the church, chapels, pubs, prison, pound, police-house, garage, pigs, butchers and springs, all in their correct places, on a pretty stylized map. Even Cressy was safe at five going about the village freely . . .[20]

To visit the Holbrooks in Ashwell at this time was to share their sense that "It was a place without harm; a strangely innocent enclave, in a world going steadily brutal, in those decades." The novel is set in the village of Oakwell, and the Grimmer family is living in Ashlake, but apart from the barely disguised names, one might be in the midst of David's autobiography. I found that reading this novel for the first time was an eerie experience, for here was the pink-washed house and the family's life described in the most familiar detail. "It is silly," David has said, "not to use the material one has." So we read about the "Queen" of the village, as she was caustically called and whom I remember being so amusingly described by David and Margot at the time. She lets the "Grimmers" this lovely medieval house with a considerable garden for £175 per annum, and pays for them to buy some antique furniture, on condition that they make efforts to contribute something to the village. We read of "Paul's" fight to save the Verderers' being pulled down, cottages dating from about 1400 whose "loss would not only be a material loss: [their] disappearance would be a fatal blow to English consciousness, like the loss of Chaucer, or William Byrd."[21] Paul Grimmer, as may be guessed, teaches English in a nearby school and is writing a novel at home.

Though giving up his post at Bassingbourne and becoming a free-lance writer, with some tutoring on the side, was a hazardous decision, it was undoubtedly the right one, for David has said that he was happiest when writing. And he wrote a great deal in his study up the winding stairs in Ducklake. At the end of the day he might have written 1,000 words by hand, but not all for the same book, for he prefers to have several books going at the same time. But if David enjoyed writing about the parochial affairs in which he and his family were immersed at this period, it is hard to believe that he could have found it easy to write the searingly painful account of the Grimmers' marriage, and the antagonisms and jealousies and personal calamities that so nearly destroyed it. One remembers lines from his poems: "our long, storm-bound months," "Our twenty years of difficult marriage," "So, we're estranged again—how it goes on!," or the distressed and distressing poem *Image Problems:*

> Freezing fog drips: dead bleakness in the night.
> Here we lie, side by side, like animals
> Sleep-slumped in straw; but human in the hate
> That alienates our touch, as the mind swirls ....
> I can remember nothing of our loving selves,
> Exhausted I give up the quest for you ....[22]

David has said that a great part of his poetry and fiction is more or less autobiographical, arising out of a compulsion, so it seems, to work on his life experiences and ponder their meaning; and to do so, not within the covers of a private journal but in this exposed, and self-exposing, manner. In the case of *Nothing Larger Than Life,* the very faithfulness with which the Ashwell and Ducklake setting is described makes it almost impossible, at least for a friend who knew them then, to read of the marital agonies of these "storm-bound months" and years without a painful feeling of voyeurism. Yet on a second reading I could only wonder at the courage and perception with which the author explores the complex tensions which threaten this marriage and the responsibilities of each partner to ensure its survival. In the Holbrooks' own marriage, Margot has said that their relationship was saved by her eight years' of psychotherapy and the insights it provided them both with; and so, having "come through," they embarked on having a fourth child.

It is no doubt true, as David has remarked, that many writers of fiction hide their deepest problems; in his Grimmer novels he says he has attempted "to be realistic, to be true with the aid of insights from psychotherapy," even if being realistic must quite often have made very painful reading for Margot. He added that in writing about close friends one is "brought near the bone, and it is crucial to avoid paying off old scores, as Lawrence did so often, or falsifying one's relationship with people." But I think this has not been much of a temptation in his life. Many of us, I am sure, must share the feeling of one of his friends who wrote to me about "his absolute lack of envy and rancour"; another wrote, simply: "I love the generosity of his feeling." At any rate, David says that he found it a relief to write a nonautobiographical novel like *Jennifer.* But that novel only confirmed my belief that David's strength as a novelist lies in autobiography, for to me it reads too much like the fulfilling of some younger idyllic wish.

The account of the infant's cot death, however, and of the young parents' shock is notably restrained and affecting.

Sex, Culture, and Philosophical Anthropology

If the relationships between men and women have been one of David's central preoccupations in his poetry and fiction, they have also been at the heart of much of his critical and polemical writing. For some people David seems best known for his concern about pornography, which led to many stirring letters in the press and to his membership of "The Longford Committee Investigating Pornography." In 1972 he published both *Sex and Dehumanisation* and *The Case Against Pornography* (which he edited), books which certainly do not adopt the genial attitude of Bernard Williams and his Committee on Obscenity and Film Censorship towards the problem. For David, pornography demeans and exploits women, and a society which tolerates the kinds of gross obscenity and violence that can be purchased on the open market and witnessed behind open doors is a seriously sick one. Not only do "mechanistic and reductionist attitudes to sex tend to lower our human stature," David has written, "but they actually tend to promote psychic impotence and a loss of creative power in our dealings with reality. The prevalent cult of dissociated sex is thus a threat to the *imagination*."[23] In his analysis of the "cultural pollution" that is "likely to affect our psychic health," David draws on an impressive body of work by such writers as Rollo May, Ian Suttie, W. R. D. Fairbairn, Melanie Klein, D. W. Winnicott, Harry Guntrip, Marion Milner, Victor Frankl and others in philosophical biology like F. J. J. Buytendijk and Irwin Straus.

During these Ashwell years David joined the editorial board of *Universities Quarterly*, which I was editing and to which he was one of the most frequent contributors. It is hardly surprising that these articles and reviews, on a formidable range of topics in the humanities and education and depth psychology, and in the area he describes as philosophical anthropology, needed a good deal of editing, for when one considers how many books he was writing at the same time, they must have been spun more or less off the cuff at high speed ("I believe my writing is best in its first flush," he has said). He has been accused of launching himself superficially into too many fields. But what has surely been most striking has been the astonishing amount of new reading that has underpinned these very diverse and, in some instances, formidably difficult areas of thought and exploration about what it is to be human. "Philosophical anthropology," for example, which he has increasingly placed at the center of his thinking, embraces, he says, existentialism, post-critical philosophy, post-Kantian philosophy, psychoanalysis and its developing phenomenology and poetry. Through such interrelated studies David believes that "we may find succour in the present crisis of our culture," because

> In all these disciplines there develops a new and creative sense of living in time. We are not doomed to an inauthentic existence, inevitably trying to find meaning in futile attempts to define ourselves. Existence is not absurd. There does seem to be a need to recognise a 'formative principle' in the universe and the emergence of life, since no explanations which reject the idea can explain the original emergence of life, its evolution, or our development of consciousness.[24]

For most mundane mortals, to familiarize oneself with any one of these fields would be a sisyphean task. Yet in a single year there appeared *The Novel and Authenticity, Education and Philosophical Anthropology,* and a third book, *Evolution and the Humanities;* this includes, as a start, four critical chapters on Darwinism and evolutionary theory; and then chapters on (among others) Polanyi; on Sheldrake's "A New Science of Life"; on the "Selfish Gene"; on "Chance, and Dobzansky's view of natural selection as Engineer"; and on Monod's examination of whether mind can be the product of "blind chance." And so to final chapters on "Rescuing the Humanities from Darwinism." Having mastered those 200 and more pages of lightish reading, one discovers that the index lists 270 names and the bibliography 280 titles (one can only hope that David permitted himself not to read every one of them from the first to the last pages). As he puts it, in his matter-of-fact way, "I have spoken from time to time of the need for new thinking." One can only wonder, and be grateful for the quantity of new thinking that he, in these books, has undertaken on behalf of his readers.

Sitting in his study from 8 A.M.–5 P.M. writing books with one hand and reading with the other, as it were, David has always felt disheartened not to get through to his readers: who are they? how many of them are there? why is it that virtually none of them, even friends, write letters, "or even a postcard if only saying Fuck You!"? If a number of his books have received enthusiastic reviews, many others have appeared and eventually disappeared without so much as a single critical comment in any periodical. "It astonishes me," Angus Wilson wrote in a review, "that his imaginative work is not widely known." David admits he may have become paranoiac about this lack of reviewing, even wondering at times if it is the result of positive discrimination:

> Alas, the penalties for pointing out the falsities of contemporary culture are severe—one is ignored, or one's books are not reviewed. English culture is too much in the hands of fashionable nihilists and moral inversionists, and this new establishment shows itself bigoted and censorious.[25]

Unless he studiously goes the rounds of the parties and conferences, unless he engages in butterings-up and jollyings-along, is it true that an author is liable to be thought ideologically "incorrect" or to fall out of fashion?

'Something Rather Akin to Innocence'

After ten years the Grimmers find they must give up their house and leave Oakwell. Their marital "stranglehold had at last been broken," perhaps with the aid of Frances Grimmer's course of psychotherapy. "It had just happened . . . They did not know why. They only knew that they knew one another as never before." And after seventeen years, the Holbrooks too were ready to move. Friends from Ashwell have spoken of their "deep involvement in village life"; "they were the kind of people a village needs . . . . Those whose lives were touched by David and Margot at that time still think of Ducklake as the Holbrooks' home." They moved to Australia for five months, traveling by boat, and David visited schools and lectured for the Victoria State Teachers's organization and in a number of universities. This expedition gave rise to a book on the teaching of English in Australia and a rather disheartening novel *Worlds Apart,* which could have done, I feel, with a lighter and more ironic touch. The protagonist this time is not David alias Paul, but David more or less in the guise of Anthea, and it makes a significant difference, especially in the rendering of Anthea's fallings in, out of, and again into "love."

The other expedition, on their return, was to Dartington Hall School where, between 1971–73, David was "writer in residence." This experience is best described in his own words (in a letter):

> I was intended to provide some philosophical inspiration for the new approach to 'progressive' education. This was badly mishandled, and

the staff resented my presence—not least when I found that libertarianism had progressed to outright decadence: the children were taking drugs and their sexual lives were fallen to the level of a 'thoroughly decadent sensualism.' There was much drunkenness, and the headmaster, a homosexual, was often absent, keeping an antique shop in Plymouth. They were showing obscene films and letting the children into these: the staff seemed to me infantile, and so I retreated into my work. But this was the most miserable period of my life—the only place where I have been shouted down in a lecture by students and staff (for criticising a lyric by Mick Jagger!).[26]

One of David's friends has written that he "can at times be heavy-handed, with a tendency to hold the stage." Publishing forty–fifty books, the majority of them educational and critical books, is in itself undoubtedly a form of "holding the stage" for 200 pages at a time. Moreover, these books are understandably serious in tone: the themes are advanced with the support of much evidence and detailed argument, but seldom with irony, caricature, or zany humor. This might lead his readers to suppose that he must be rather formidable and even forbidding company, a Jeremiah weighed down, and liable to weigh others down, with *angst* and lamentations about the plight of society. Nothing could be further from the truth. Though he certainly has his anxieties and depressions, David is, for the most part, a lively and even boisterous person, with a sharp but never malicious wit and infectious humor, especially when emerging in a broad Norfolk accent. His explosions of stentorian laughter go along with a singularly generous feeling for people. One friend finds that David reminds him "in an odd way of a Shakespearean fool." But I think it would not be one of Shakespeare's mordant fools who would spend so much time painting the landscapes of the English and French countryside which cover every wall of his house, cultivating a large garden (with an unexpectedly copious familiarity with plants and wild life), or cooking *recherché* meals; though I suppose he might be heard playing away, in David's fashion, at the piano. In short, David has an unbounded capacity for remaining genial and human while filling creatively all the thirty-six hours of every day. It is, no doubt, this infinite variety that is reflected in the rather diverse comments and judgments of his friends:

> It is disconcerting at times to discover that he knows more about some areas of my own field [psychoanalysis] than I do myself.
>
> I have to admit I have mostly found his writing embarrassing. It seems

somehow that he has fallen between all the stools. But I believe him to have emerged as a gifted teacher who produces really good students.

His total output has been very considerable and varied. It has suffered from a certain slap-dash vigour but on the other hand might not have got produced at all were it not for that enthusiastic warmth.

I have found in his critical work what I can only crudely describe as a sloppiness of thought, a lack of rigorous grip, that lessens the force and value of the very many excellent points that he is often making. His honesty (extraordinary conscientiousness) and the clarity and purity of his sense of values are so evident in all his work—and in his social life.

In spite of his obvious intelligence and erudition there is something rather akin to innocence in the passion he brings to his beliefs. He knows about evil, but is not a cynic.

Return to Cambridge

To move, in 1973, from the Dartington fiasco to Cambridge was a positive step indeed. David was appointed assistant Director of English Studies at Downing for a year, mainly to support him while completing books; and Margot was appointed University Lodgings Officer, which David has described as "one of the most remarkable incidents in our lives." To embark on this new life outside the home in which she had worked as a housewife for twenty-four years meant that Margot could now help support the family financially—and it was as well she could, for this coincided with a period of three years when David had no book published. Above all, it must have given her a great psychological boost. And when, in 1981, David was appointed Director of English Studies at Downing, the Holbrooks suddenly found, in their latter years, that they had recognition and security—and could afford a bottle of wine each evening with the meal which David had prepared for Margot's return from her office. Home was a delightful house and garden standing back from Maid's Causeway, which Margot persuaded Peterhouse to do up and let to them—the Holbrooks have never been able to own the houses they have lived in.

David's appointment to Downing at the age of fifty-eight was a triumph for him and also, in many ways, for the college. The selection committee surely cannot have read his satirical treatment, in *Nothing Larger Than Life,* of high table conversation at

Prince's College.[27] At that earlier period when he was at Kings, writing books on education for school teachers, David found the intellectual snobbery of many of the senior academics hard to stomach. Downing might well have decided to keep up with the fashions and appoint a "brilliant" young deconstructionist or neo-Marxist. Instead the College sought the advice of the best person possible, Professor Derek Brewer, the then-Master of Emmanuel, and David was appointed. Derek Brewer knew David and his writings well and he is happy to let me quote from the letter he wrote in reply to my enquiries:

> He has written some excellent poems both about love and war. They have a touching openness and vulnerability which helps to make them memorable. He has written many other books, all of them with a crusading fervour. . . . In all of these he lashes out with great lustiness and disinterested excitement.
>
> I find David a very sympathetic figure but with a certain wildness. He is warm and generous. . . . He is a brave, enthusiastic man who is willing in every sense of the word to go over the top for his convictions and deserves to be honoured as such.

David's arrival in Downing with the reputation of being a Leavisite (though that is certainly not what Leavis would have called him) was not likely to please everyone, for at this time Leavis and *Scrutiny* were very much out of fashion. One morning, going to use the college photocopier, David found that a young research don using the machine before him had left behind a questionnaire addressed to students studying English, inviting them to express their views on David's teaching. David was understandably outraged:

> Typically naive and innocent, he cried out for 'fair play'. He created a fuss. Presently the younger scholar apologized. David was magnanimous, but I always thought a little steel entered into his academic administrative behaviour from then on. David's gentleness, the childlike trusting David behind his avuncular approach to the young seemed to develop a tougher side.

This perceptive account is from the then-Master of the College, Professor Sir John (now Lord) Butterfield. At any rate, David's teaching, in which he concentrated mainly on Shakespeare and the novel, proved very rewarding to him and also, before much time had elapsed, to his students. In addition he found that his senior colleagues were "very good people with wide interests, pursuing interesting research." The result was that David, who is, after all, a gregarious and stimulating companion, found himself much more involved than he had probably expected in the intellectual and social life of the college, which Sir John had such a talent for stimulating.

During these Cambridge years David had to contend with a major problem, the sheer difficulty of getting his books published. For someone with so many books printed this might seem the least of his worries. But I calculate that his books have been published by eighteen–twenty different publishers, and for very many of these acceptances there will first of all have been a string of rejections. "One gets knocked down by a rejection," he said; and then he finds it hard to work in his study for a day or two. If there was a blank period of three years in the seventies without a book published, there was a far more worrying span of six unpublished years in the eighties. "However, the only answer is to go patiently on with one's creative work in hope." And sure enough, the years since 1987 have seen an astonishing total of six novels and ten critical books published.

Among these are a number of literary studies, in which he takes up again his concern about the relations between men and women, such as the challengingly titled *Edith Wharton and the Unsatisfactory Man* and *Where D. H. Lawrence Was Wrong About Woman*. In addition there are at least another seven books written but not yet published. (If I may utter it in a whisper at this point, could it even be that at the age of seventy he might write one or two *fewer* books? I wonder if producing eight or nine autobiographical Grimmer novels is perhaps to count on too much staying power among his readers for so extended a story of his own past life? On the other hand, would that he could find a publisher for his poetry, in which he transmits and reflects so feelingly on the *living* moment.)

When David retired in 1989 he was made an emeritus fellow of the College, and he then landed a two year Leverhulme Emeritus Research Fellowship in order to .... write more books. Margot retired three years later and, with a base in New Hall, is studying an intriguing segment of Cambridge life: the culture of the society of landladies, who, since the early nineteenth century, have been linked to the colleges and who have looked after their often unruly young men.

So it has worked out, and is still working out, very well for them both. There have been plays of passion, and there have certainly been flesh wounds. But throughout these years nothing, for them, has been larger than life and the quest to find what it is to be human and loving.

Notes

1. David Holbrook, *Flesh Wounds* (London: Methuen, 1966), p. 110.
2. Ibid., pp. 128–29.
3. Ibid., p. 161.
4. Ibid., p. 164.
5. David Holbrook, "Fingers in the Door," *Selected Poems 1961–1978* (London: Anvil Press, 1980), p. 12.
6. Ibid., "Apprehensions of Maturity," pp. 28–30.
7. Ibid., "Love and Let Live," pp. 43–44.
8. Ibid., "A Child Said, 'I am Smoke'," pp. 49–50.
9. Ibid., 'March Evening,' pp. 22–23.
10. Christopher Hope, review in *The London Magazine,* June 1979, p. 77.
11. David Holbrook, *A Play of Passion* (London: W. H. Allen, 1978), p. 17.
12. Ibid., p. 122.
13. Ibid., p. 213.
14. David Holbrook, *Lost Bearings in English Poetry* (London: Vision Press, 1977), 44.
15. Holbrook, "Living? Our Supervisors Will Do That For Us," *Selected Poems,* p. 13.
16. Holbrook, *Lost Bearings,* p. 194.
17. David Holbrook, *English For Maturity* (Cambridge: Cambridge University Press, 2nd. ed. 1967), p. 3.
18. David Holbrook *English for the Rejected* (Cambridge: Cambridge University Press, 1964), pp. 117.
19. David Holbrook, *Children's Writing* (Cambridge: Cambridge University Press, 1967), pp. 203–4.
20. David Holbrook, *Nothing Larger Than Life* (London: Robert Hale, 1987), p. 70.
21. Ibid., p. 110.
22. Holbrook, "Image Problems," *Selected Poems,* p. 51.
23. David Holbrook, *Sex and Dehumanization* (London: Pitman Publishing, 1972), p. 8.
24. David Holbrook, *What is it to be Human? New Perspectives in Philosophy* (Aldershot: Avebury, 1990), p. 5.
25. David Holbrook, entry in *Contemporary Authors* (Detroit: Gale Research Co., 1963).
26. Featured also in David Holbrook's novel *Worlds Apart* (London: Robert Hale, 1989), pp. 174.
27. Holbrook, *Nothing Larger,* pp. 113.

Part II
Educationist

Introduction

The name of David Holbrook first became widely known through his writings on education, in particular on the teaching of English in secondary schools. And it remains the case that it is within this field he achieved, by far, his largest audience. *English for Maturity* (1961, but in fact written in 1956) set out a program for creative approaches to the teaching of English, with poetry and the poetic function of language at the center of its conception. *English for the Rejected* (1964) showed how the same governing principles had been applied by Holbrook, in his own practice, to the teaching of a class of less able, "backward" children. It was then, and remains, an inspiring book. There followed numerous other books on English and education, including diverse collections of literary resources to aid the teacher of English; all of them practical exemplifications of the literary-creative principle.

In the following section Michael Charles presents a personal "view from the classroom" of the effects of Holbrook's work upon his own practice as an English teacher. Though an individual acknowledgment both of Holbrook's influence and his practical guidance, it is representative too of similar accounts which could be made many times over by practicing teachers—perhaps especially among those who began their teaching careers in the sixties.

Edwin Webb traces an outline of the history of English teaching from its inception as a formal subject of study. Within this context there is a clear clash between those who saw English as serving, either exclusively or predominantly, limited, functional purposes, and those who saw the possibility of a radical alternative—the promotion of creative engagement as a means toward fuller development of the child. Within that emerging movement he considers the place of English as art and as art-making; as essential means towards the child's self-realization and individualization.

Roger Knight's contribution takes the theme of the "living principle" of English into the current setting of a statutory national curriculum dominated by a mechanistic model of English. There, governed by notions of "linguistic competence," sets of techniques are prescribed and are to be measured at different levels of attainment. To work in such programmed ways, Knight argues, is to trivialize language; to pay scant heed to the pupils' own "growing powers;" and to disregard almost wholly the implications of terms as significant as sensibility, feeling, culture.

Within such terms resides a profound and alternative justification for the teaching of English; one which necessarily confronts the purely instrumental. Another key point of reference may be called the moral dimension of literature. Gordon Pradl traces the line of argument from Arnold to Holbrook which insists that literature is, through and because of its shaping power, a moral exploration of meaning-in-life. "What connections exist, however tenuous," Pradl asks, "between the reading and writing of literature and the quality of private and public lives?"

The expository line pursued by Pradl affirms the value, for the child perhaps especially, of dwelling within those symbolic worlds created by literary forms. But, as Peter Abbs argues, there is the need to experience, and to create within, the other arts too. Though each of the arts has its own distinctive character, all the arts may be seen as containing a kind of knowing, a form of cognition qualitatively different from the knowledge of facts and data. Within that tradition of poetic humanism, as Abbs calls the inheritance of thought which began with the Romantics and may be tracked through to the work of Holbrook himself, there are to be found significant points of departure by which one may begin to appraise more fully the existential nature of the arts, the needs which they satisfy. The tradition to which Abbs addresses himself contains, he argues, limitations in conception. Holbrook's contribution to our understanding both extended the tradition and, so Abbs demonstrates, contributed a number of principles by which to extend a philosophy of art into classroom practice.

It is fitting, therefore, that the final contribution in this section is from John Paynter who shows how music education benefited from Holbrook's work. Holbrook, though addressing in the main the teaching of English in the classroom, nonetheless "spoke for all arts teachers" through his insistence upon creative principles. Paynter provides a worked example of children's creativity in music, drawn from the work of young children in a primary school in the Yorkshire dales. It reveals, dramatically, how children may become fully engaged in the making of art and, in that process, explore the reality of experience by "working on one's inner world."

Teaching English: A View from the Classroom

Michael Charles

When I began my teaching career in 1963 I was primarily a teacher of history, but owing to the usual shortage of English specialists I found myself teaching some English. After a few years I found that I preferred English to history and I gradually switched subjects, ending up as head of an English department in 1971. Those early years were spent in secondary modern schools, which was difficult enough in itself, but I had the added burden of having to teach a subject for which I had had no formal training. I was starting from scratch.

In the circumstances I thought it prudent to acquire some qualifications. To this end I obtained a year's secondment at Sussex University where I gained a B. Ed. Honors degree with English and Education as the main subjects. A few years later I achieved the M. A. degree in Language and Literature in Education at London University. This period of intense study was completed in the space of six years between 1974-80.

Before training in this way, I had already embarked on a process of self-education. Favoring an eclectic approach, I set about reading anything I could lay my hands on about the teaching of English in the hope that I would discover the state of the art, the most up-to-date methods.

At that time English teaching seemed to be constipated by a restricted diet of arid textbook exercises, although more imaginative approaches to the teaching of the subject were becoming fashionable and a new consensus was beginning to emerge. Of the books I read, Holbrook's *English for Maturity* seemed to be a seminal work, an essential aid to survival for a head of department who was a novice in every sense of the word. Personal experience convinces me that there are writings of Holbrook which remain essential texts for today, compulsory reading for all English teachers. When I drew up my first syllabus, Holbrook's fingerprints were everywhere.

One of the things that endeared me to Holbrook was the fact that he was concerned about the 75 percent of pupils who were stigmatized as failures because they went to secondary modern schools. What was even more impressive was the fact that he had actually spent time with less able children and was clearly convinced that they were capable, through their creative work, of achieving fluency and literacy. The title of one of his books, *English for the Rejected,* helped to lift a generation of teachers whose daily task was to cultivate civilized values in pupils from whom little was expected.

To some extent Holbrook himself seems to have accepted the prevailing propaganda of the day, believing, apparently, that there was a real difference in the intellectual abilities of grammar school and secondary modern pupils. This is a myth which has not been totally dispelled: as I write, my own local education authority is trying to resurrect the 11+ examination. The truth is that the distribution of intelligence in a community probably resembles the distribution of height: there are some people who are well over six feet and some who are very short, but the bulk of the population are much of a muchness.

Nevertheless, Holbrook was passionately committed to the secondary modern child, including children in the lower streams of the secondary modern school. He did not want them to be fobbed off with an inferior kind of education that left them more than before at the mercy of a popular culture that had been debased by rampant commercialism.

While it is true that some of Holbrook's more esoteric forays into literary criticism are redolent of the university, there is little of the ivory tower mentality in these writings on English in education. On the contrary, there is much here that is down-to-earth and rooted in the classroom. Here is a man who knows his stuff and has plenty of practical advice and suggestions for the teacher who has to face 4C every day of the week. He knows the territory because he has been there.

For the struggling beginner Holbrook throws out a lifejacket to enable you to keep your head above water. If you want to know how to encourage children to write stories and poems, he can furnish you with a step-by-step guide based on his own classroom experiences; if you want to know which novel to use with a particular year group, he has comprehensive lists for every year in the secondary school; if you want to know how to mark children's work, he can offer a policy that steers a sensible course between excessive correction and *laissez-faire* inaction.

Holbrook undoubtedly extended the range of what could be offered in the English classroom. For example, no secondary school should be without Holbrook's anthologies, *Iron, Honey, Gold.* Each anthology contains a fair sprinkling of folk songs and ballads, and pre-1900 English poetry is substantially represented. This is something that would have pleased those who helped to frame the Cox Report which recommended that there ought to be some pre-1900 English Literature in the National Curriculum for English. In the search for relevance in the sixties and seventies we were probably guilty of neglecting the literature of earlier periods.

There is nothing woolly about Holbrook's ideas. For example, he is quite specific about the teacher's input of literature: the pupil "should have read, or have read to him, in each year of his school life some 50 first-rate stories and poems."[1] This is not a bad aim although such targets often left me with a feeling of guilt because so little of the work Holbrook rightly advocated had been attempted by the end of each school year!

Some Aspects of English Teaching

Aside from his championing of the underdog, Holbrook made principled stands on other issues central to the educational debate. Teaching, he asserted, was an art. Certainly there are ways in which it can be made more efficient and productive, but it is still an art. As appraisal of teachers' effectiveness is now on the agenda perhaps we need to remind ourselves that teaching *is* an art and that you cannot teach by numbers. There are no crude benchmarks by which you can measure a teacher's performance, since teaching does not necessarily yield immediate results. Teaching must focus on a long-term goal: to equip a young person for life.

Presumably this is why Holbrook set his face against utilitarian education. For him, we do not educate for earning a living: we educate for living. This might serve as a timely antidote to received wisdom at the present time when there are calls from some quarters to introduce a vocational element into the curriculum. The school should have broader aims than that: in any case, how can one prepare pupils for jobs that may not even exist in a few years' time?

That is not to say that English teachers can wriggle out of their responsibility of preparing children for the mundane tasks of reading and writing. There *is* need to teach children to decipher a notice or write a letter of application. Holbrook accepts that this will probably fall to the lot of the English teacher and takes the commonsense standpoint that it should be discharged with a minimum of fuss.

He is not so accommodating when it comes to the treadmill of textbook exercises and snippets of grammar that sometimes masquerade as English. There is no shortcut to the mastery of English. Holbrook is unequivocal:

> the way to develop one's mastery of English is to live within a rich context of its lively use, by reading, listening, and talking.[2]

It follows from this that teachers must be widely read, their reading not limited to a single period or even a single genre, but ranging across the whole spectrum from the dawn of literacy to the present day. This demand is difficult to meet when teachers are pressed for more and more paperwork and when pastoral and academic meetings make great inroads into their free time. Holidays are about the only time when English teachers can catch up with their reading and recharge their batteries. Holbrook's own knowledge of literature seems awesome. What a mentor he would make for young teachers who in future will receive most of their training in schools.

He would undoubtedly draw their attention to the key role that schools can play in maintaining the verbal culture which we have inherited, the language of Shakespeare and the Authorized Version of the Bible, a literature that is second to none. However, we live in a visual age and the forces ranged against us are formidable: it will require all Holbrook's missionary zeal to maintain the existing position. If anything, the climate has become more hostile to the printed word; television has proved almost irresistible to the young and the not-so-young, so that even those who study literature at advanced level are just as likely in their spare time to take out a video as they are to settle down with a good book. There may have been a decline in literacy since the sixties: books that were regarded as an easy read may prove too difficult for all but a few. Laurie Lee's autobiography *Cider with Rosie*, for example, was popular with pupils in the early years of the secondary schools but is now rapidly acquiring the status of an elitist text mainly because the language is so rich in association and imagery, so compressed and so close to the borders of poetry. All the more reason, then, why we should be evangelists, showing the young through our wonder and excitement that we have something that is worth preserving.

Affirming the Culture

Linked to this militant attitude is Holbrook's vision of schools as a focal point for reestablishing a popular culture in its pristine form, disentangled from the ubiquitous tentacles of creeping commercialism—the kind of culture that existed before industrialization. Folk songs should be used "as a main instrument in crossing the gap from children's own poetry, as a kind of poetry which has an obvious function, to 'educated' poetry."[3]

This idea is amongst the intellectual baggage that I have carried with me since the sixties. It has become a source of amusement in my own department that I have argued so strongly for folk songs when we devised our programs of study to meet the requirements of the National Curriculum. Holbrook went a stage further than this and saw the possibility of collaboration with music and art: "a school could produce a festival of song and poetry every day, with perhaps one longer occasion, on one morning of the week, for the whole school."[4]

This is another idea that still exercises my mind and although I have never mounted such festivals, except on a very modest scale, I still think it is a goal worth pursuing. Such occasions could be extended further by including dance. In fact, I do not know why Holbrook with his interest in folk culture stops short of dance. This is an idea where we are indeed badly let down by commercial culture. One has only to see folk dancing in Eastern European countries to realize how important an influence dance can be in the cultural life of a community, bonding people together in a reaffirmation of shared values, as well as demonstrating, to use a cliché, poetry in motion. What a far cry this is from the floor of the contemporary discotheque where the only excitement is provided by the flickering lights and sporadic outbursts of mindless violence. The bureaucratic straitjacket in which schools now operate, the tyranny of bells and the tightrope of exams, would have to be overturned in order to allow these dreams the oxygen they need to turn them from inert concepts into living organisms. It may seem a high price to pay, but the rewards in terms of improved morale, aesthetic enjoyment and positive identification with the schools' aims could be enormous.

Given that tantalizing vista, it is easy to understand why Holbrook was less than enthusiastic about the introduction of examinations for the secondary modern child in the form of the Certificate of Secondary Education. The success of the C.S.E. examinations and, more recently, the General Certificate of Secondary Education examinations, has taken the wind out of the sails of those who espoused an antiexamination stance; but Holbrook's point that examinations promote factual learning because memorization and the regurgitation of facts can be easily measured, is still valid. Attempts to introduce some flexibility and creativity into the examination system by incorporating coursework have not won official approval; the recently restyled secondary examinations appear to be returning to earlier, more rigid, formats.

So conditioned are children to this overemphasis on facts that they view with grave distrust anyone who has the temerity to suggest that feelings are important. Holbrook wanted to "encourage the expression of feelings, in an atmosphere in which such expression was regarded as seriously as the expression of facts."[5] The teaching of poetry, for example, which, according to Holbrook, is at the center of English, should focus as much on feelings as on technical devices.

As one might expect, Holbrook takes children's writing seriously. It is accepted that in the art room children should paint and draw in a kind of workshop environment. The same kind of workshop atmosphere needs to be established in the English classroom, for in writing their own poems and stories, children come to terms with the zigzag course of their emotional development while at the same time they learn something about literary form, even though achieving mastery may be a long way off. To outsiders it may seem that in giving children space to write not much is accomplished, but this period of gestation has to be gone through. Thus English may be seen as a kind of subversive activity by those who like to see tangible results at the end of each lesson. An English inspector on a visit to my school spent one day with the department visiting several teachers. On the basis of seeing one lesson, some attempt was made to evaluate the effectiveness of each teacher. This is like assessing the quality of a sprinter on the first few strides as he explodes from the starting blocks. The fastest starts do not always end up winning the race. In this way the current emphasis on testing and getting value for money must surely militate against the long-term aims of the English specialist.

A Sense of Purpose

How, as a classroom teacher, can I sum up the debt I owe David Holbrook? First and foremost, I suppose, he armed me with a sense of purpose. He convinced me that English teachers have an important and worthwhile contribution to make. He would probably endorse E. M. Forster's view that

> we have in this age of unrest to ferry much old stuff across the river, and that old stuff is not merely books, pictures and music, but the power to enjoy them.[6]

This should not, however, restrict the role of children to that of being passive recipients of the literary heritage, for their own creative writing can be the starting point in a voyage of self-discovery through which they can gain understanding of themselves and of the community at large while giving them hands-on experience of literary form.

Above all, Holbrook's expertise on all matters relating to the classroom task has been a support and inspiration for over twenty years. Any young teacher who is confused and dispirited by all the chopping and changing that has taken place in education during the last few years would find in David Holbrook a guide whose vision and understanding are the embodiment of all that is best in the English tradition of school teaching.

Notes

1. David Holbrook, *English for Maturity*, 2nd ed. (Cambridge: Cambridge University Press, 1967), p. 27.
2. Ibid., p. 23.
3. Ibid., p. 77.
4. Ibid.
5. Ibid., p. 114.
6. E. M. Forster, *Two Cheers for Democracy* (Harmondsworth: Penguin, 1970), p. 110.

English for Living

Edwin Webb

In looking back across the topography of educational debate and the function of English within the curriculum, I am concerned only to identify, highly selectively, just a few features of the landscape. They are the ones, however, which I feel are charged with significance for the practice of education, and especially the teaching of English, for today. From such a rearward cast I hope to assemble a present perspective; one, at least, which will define more sharply the present context in which education, by decree, largely services ulterior motives. These prominent features of the view are identified particularly through the writings of just a few of the contributors to the field. They suggest a continuity of thought, of practice—despite differences among them—to which tradition the work of David Holbrook, as educationist, essentially belongs. I claim them as antecedents, not necessarily as direct influences upon Holbrook's work; though the "climate of opinion" which such writers both create and reflect can subsist in a generalized way even where we lack direct experience and specific knowledge of that work. The intention, finally, will be to focus upon that area of English teaching to which Holbrook gave most concentrated and sustained attention. That is, to the absolute need to provide a form of English which would serve existential, not instrumental ends. It is a conception of creativity which, fundamentally, is at the heart of all of Holbrook's critical writings—educational, social, and literary. It insists on the need to understand one's self in relation to the world and the world of others; to give meaning to existence; and to establish a sense of personal identity.

Education and "the Work of Life"

> Education is initiation, not apprenticeship. It has nothing to do with trade, business or livelihood; it has no connection with rates of wages

or increase of pay ... Education is a preparation for life, not merely for a livelihood, for living not for *a* living.

The words are George Sampson's.[1] They proclaim an ideal; embody a warning; and issue a challenge. The ideal to which Sampson directs us is implied in the very word "education"; its derivation from the Latin *educere*, meaning "to lead out, to bring out" and its essential relationship with *educare* which points to notions of nurturing or fostering. All of this, as a full reading of Sampson's classic work will confirm, is summarized in his use of the term "initiation." What the process of education initiates is induction into a culture within which and by means of which the child's own potential is nurtured so that, through this development, the child may learn to live as fully as possible. Sampson warns us not to forget that education, in the first place, is about living, not about earning a living. And the challenge which continues to issue from Sampson's assertion is to find the will and the means to construe an education for our children which will indeed serve *them*, rather than fit them to serve; for—

> We must really get out of the habit of talking as if education were the preparation of children merely for that part of their life which does not belong to them, as if they, as reasonable, living beings, had no existence at all.[2]

The challenge remains: how to enable children to come into possession of their lives so that they connect with their own growing experience; how to promote that curiosity which leads to learning; and how best to help them achieve a various, rich, and rewarding sense of being.

More than seventy years ago, when *English for the English* first appeared, Sampson was responding, of course, to the particular circumstances of his time. The Education Act of 1870 had paved the way towards free and compulsory elementary education for all, though that provision had not been fully implemented until about twenty years later. Just a few years before Sampson had started his own teaching career in elementary schools, the 1904 *Code for Elementary Schools* had appeared. In his introduction to the Code, Sir Robert Morant had declared unequivocally that:

> The purpose of the elementary school is to form and strengthen the character and to develop the intelligence of the children entrusted to it, and to make the best use of the years available, in assisting both

boys and girls, according to their different needs, to fit themselves, practically as well as intellectually, for the work of life.[3]

"The work of life": it is a telling phrase resonant with the heritage of the puritan work ethic and its associated notions of "duty" and of "service." Its effect is to dehumanize and to depersonalize the child, to reduce the complex circumstance of living and growing to a programmed training which will fit the child to the higher demands of the state. For beyond that statement lay the assumption—largely undeveloped as a philosophy for education but nonetheless powerful because unchallenged—that the "products" of education (the state's girls and boys) were intended primarily to service the great economic production machine. In the last decade or so we have witnessed within the English educational system a powerful reaffirmation of just this belief: both in doctrinaire assertions that the real "business" of education is preparation for the world of work, and in those many and diverse initiatives which have sought to reinstate "the work of life" as the first item on the agenda, certainly for those pupils approaching school-leaving age. Such a tension, between education as a preparation for work and education as the fullest development of the individual personality, has subsisted throughout the history of English state education. In the retrospect we can bring to the progress of the decades we can see quite clearly that these conceptions of the purpose of education shift in degree and dominance without ever having come to harmonious resolution.

Voices in Dissent

Beyond Morant's "work of life" lay the history of the notorious Revised Code (1862) instituting a system of "payment by results" as the means of funding schools. The system ensured that the Gradgrind method of teaching which Dickens had satirized in *Hard Times* (1854) achieved the widest possible application. Though the system introduced by that Code had ended officially by 1897 its effects continued to be felt for many years after. The philosophy of the *Code* had been roundly and persistently condemned by Matthew Arnold who saw that the purpose of such an education, and the means of achieving it, were in fact harmfully divisive to society. In his Reports, and in works such as *Culture and Anarchy* (1869) and *Literature and Dogma* (1873), he argued again and again against the brutalizing and dehumanizing consequences of the Revised Code and its politico-economic justification. For Arnold, on the contrary, saw education as a civilizing process, achieved through the induction of *all* children, rich and poor, into a common culture.

Soon after Arnold took up his post as an Inspector of Schools in 1851, John Henry Newman (later Cardinal Newman) advanced his own views on the nature of a liberal education in those Discourses of 1852 and Lectures of 1854–58 which comprise his work *The Idea of a University*. Here he advanced the argument that education is properly concerned with the training of the mind rather than with the diffusion of "useful" knowledge. He advanced also—in a way which Arnold was to transpose from the university context to that of schooling—an argument for the special place of literature in education. Importantly, by literature he referred not only to the classics, but to the heritage of literature in English (and to works within that canon to which Catholics would have specific objection). "Literature expresses," he wrote, "not objective truth, as it is called, but subjective; not things but thoughts." By "thought," he explained, was meant "ideas, feelings, views, reasonings, and other operations of the human mind." Thus literature

> ... consists in the enunciations and teachings of those who have a right to speak as representatives of their kind, and in whose words their brethren find an interpretation of their own sentiments, a record of their own experience, and a suggestion for their own judgments.[4]

Arnold, similarly, argued for the educative effects of literature, especially in the training of the moral sensibility. But his stand was not simply moral, confirming the entitlement of each child to possess and own the culture; it was political too—since such a common endowment, as he conceived culture, was essentially classless and, thereby, a powerful force with the potential to unite the whole body of society. Arnold's conception of culture, however, was almost exclusively bound to literature; but a culture embodies traditions which include authentic art forms, as well as realms of knowledge, other than the literary. So if an education is to lay claim to the development of the whole personality of the child, these forms of knowing and coming to terms with reality must also feature within the curriculum design.

It was Sampson's distinctive contribution to express trenchantly the conception of a liberal and humane education which would genuinely free the child from the tyranny of mechanical drudgery in school—especially since such mechanical drudgery was what awaited the vast majority of pupils when they left school and went into jobs:

> I am prepared to maintain, and, indeed, do maintain, without any reservations or perhapses, that it is the purpose of education, not to prepare children *for* their occupations, but to prepare children *against* their occupations.[5]

In his criticism of the *status quo,* Sampson saw clearly that the instrumental conception of education went more or less hand in hand with a deadening notion of what constituted English and the practices of its teaching. Both failures were intimately connected, each symptomatic of the other's condition. The fact was realized by the distinguished members of the Newbolt committee (of which Sampson was himself an influential member) in its Report issued just months after Sampson's book had appeared:

> The inadequate conception of the teaching of English in this country is not a separate defect which can be separately remedied. It is due to a more far-reaching failure—the failure to conceive the full meaning and possibilities of national education as a whole, and that failure again is due to a misunderstanding of the educational values to be found in the different regions of mental activity . . .[6]

Language, Meaning, and Personal Reality

The teaching of English (as the report exemplified) had not freed itself from the classical tradition of Latin and Greek; indeed, in the minds of many, English was a poor substitute for the study of the classical languages in any case. Much of English was taught, therefore, along the lines of its classical models, the grammar of the language itself made to conform to rules derived from Latin, rather than from the living tongue. Pupils spent inordinate amounts of time learning to parse and analyse specimens of the language; and then learning to correct further samples of language so that they too conformed to the same patterns of construction. Literature provided opportunities either for "learning by heart," such recitation justified as a general mental training, or as a means of improving pronunciation and developing the pupils' ability to read aloud. Additionally, passages of literature provided models for the pupils' own "composition" work, in which they would attempt to imitate the style—and the borrowed sentiments—of the originals. Dictation, as one would suppose, also featured strongly within English lessons.

Today, we can see that the failure of such English teaching was founded upon two major falsehoods—even though the elements of such a program, in some secondary schools (as I can attest personally), remained in place through to the late 1950s at least. The first falsehood belongs to the curiously contradictory conception of the child, who was seen simultaneously both as a miniature adult (who ought, therefore, to be able to do those exercises which adults could do), *and* as an empty vessel into which information and learning could be poured. The second damaging misconception resided in the belief that language was merely an *instrument* of thought and expression; by training in the use of the instrument, therefore, one would be able to produce the correct expression of a given thought.

Coleridge long previously had pointed out that language is not simply an instrument of thinking but is the source of thought. Language does not simply enable thinking to proceed; it is the origination of thinking—the language as expressed *is* the thought. Our use of language is creative. We do, of course, learn from the speech of others; both those thoughts which somehow bespeak us too and with which we can identify, and from the various manners of speaking by which we may begin to see *how* to speak. Listening to others, reading the words of others, will certainly help us to perceive, appreciate, and learn potentialities of the language. Miming or repeating such language I am not, however, in any fundamental sense thereby speaking for myself. No one else can speak my personality for me. It is imperative, therefore, that to some degree we create our own language, make our own construction of words, if we are to speak or write personal meaning.

We generate our own versions of language, through which we hear and see, and thereby learn, what it is we *do* think and feel. Such personally constructed language both defines and explores individual realities. *Self*-realization cannot be achieved either through a mimed repetition of the language of others or by "doing language exercises." At best, doing language exercises will make us good at doing language exercises; imitating the language of others will make of us impressionists dependent upon someone else's script. At worst, such repeated experience will disenfranchise us from language as a personal possession at all. We shall have no sense of language as an enablement to enter and possess our own world of reality and, by sympathetic extension, the worlds of others. Reflexivity of consciousness is made possible, predominantly among other modes of realization, through language. Where, therefore, the development of language in its state of "inner speech" is undeveloped or thwarted, the growth of self-consciousness too remains stunted.

Realizations such as these have accumulated an overwhelming authority in the varied researches, findings, and speculations of linguists, psychologists and philosophers—all of which point to the essential symbolizing function of language,[7] and to the human creature as *animal symbolicum*. At the time of Sampson's writing, however, a general transformation in the teaching of English still awaited, in most quarters, such a radical reconception and acceptance of the nature of language. Sampson recognized with a clarity of vision, nonetheless, something of the order of changed perception which was needed if English, as taught, was to be anything more than, or different from, a mechanical and disconnected matter to be learned via skills to be rehearsed. A good deal of the subsequent and radical change in the practice of English teaching is prefigured in his appreciation that

> English is not really a subject at all. It is a condition of existence rather than a subject of instruction. It is an inescapable circumstance of life, and concerns every English-speaking person from the cradle to the grave. The lesson in English is not merely one occasion for the inculcation of knowledge; it is part of the child's initiation into the life of man.[8]

The radical shift away from a wholly instrumental conception of education which persisted from Arnold's times to those of Sampson's—and well beyond—emerged from a confluence of voices and influences. Their effects, of course, were seldom immediately felt, and their influence was often, to begin with, local. Yet over time, through dispersion and absorption, their cumulative pressures reshaped education. There was, for example, the influence of practitioners such as Froebel, Pestalozzi, and Macmillan which contributed to a more liberal form of teaching based, variously, on a child-centered psychology, activity methods to replace rote learning, and a committed belief in the innate creativity of the child. Developmental studies of the psychology of the child showed the need to create alternative models for the teaching of children, and helped also to promote a sense of the individualism of each child despite generalized stages of development. In this context the work of Susan Isaacs, for example (*Intellectual Growth in Young Children,* 1930), became a key resource. The voice of Edmond Holmes (*What Is and What Might Be,* 1911) who had vigorously attacked the narrow utilitarian conception of education, asserting the absolute need to promote a humane education founded on the self-realization of the child, reechoed in the voices of later critics. These, and many more, gradually shaped a general climate of opinion on which the possibility of a more enlightened form of education could be founded.

Knowing, Feeling, Doing: H. Caldwell Cook

There were, too, seminal works which addressed themselves specifically to the teaching of English. Most notable among these early shaping influences was the work of H. Caldwell Cook, first in the *Perse Playbooks* (1912–17), anthologies of the stories, poems, plays and other writings produced by his pupils at the Perse School, Cambridge; then in *The Play Way* (1917), "An Essay in Educational Method" outlining Cook's creative approaches to the teaching of English.

Rereading *The Play Way* today, one is struck first of all by the generous, and wholly partisan, spirit of vitality which animates Cook's reflections. He is on the side of the child; he is for education as a liberation, opposing the mean puritan conscience which would mould and crimp the child to predetermined form. Where the end of education for Morant was "the work of life," for Cook it is "the play of life,"[9] a means to further and fuller living. With urbane irony Cook analyzes those forces which had made work of learning, and any enjoyment a less than innocent recreation:

> A puritan feels much self-gratification in toiling up a hill, and is rather ashamed of coasting down the other side . . . The puritan is of opinion that every race should be an obstacle race; and is convinced that he who goes the primrose way is destined for the everlasting bonfire.[10]

Cook advocated the replacing of the drudgery and mindless repetition which characterized so much of teaching method with *active* means of learning, preferably those which included in measure some self-direction from the pupil. This is the "play" of his method; not the idle diversion of time, but the purposive, directed employment of time. It is the play of the Latin *ludus,* the "serious play" we have come to associate, for example, with the playing-out of their games and fantasies by infants and children in which the game *is true for them while it lasts,* and will frequently be a necessary, albeit incipient, movement towards development and maturity. By adaptation of this natural impulse, Cook evolved methods of teaching which would unite *knowing,* with *feeling,* through *doing:*

> by Play I mean the *doing* anything one *knows* with one's heart in it. The final appreciation in life and in study is to put oneself into the thing studied and to live there *active.* And that is Playing.[11]

This is the "serious play" of the artist, and in Cook's manifesto of his own practice each child, individually and in cooperation with peers, becomes an artist: making poems, plays, and stories; acting or enacting plays, poems, stories; originating art as well as creatively engaging with the art of others.

True and False "Griffins": Marjorie Hourd

There is much to praise in Cook's pioneering teaching, and there are implications to his methods which still have contemporary pertinence, and which are still being worked out. For what Cook called the Play Way has become transformed into the guiding principle—though not formally acknowledged as such—of what are now known as "active strategies" for the teaching of English as endorsed by the Cox Report proposals for English within the National Curriculum.[12] There remained, however, a lingering deficit—exemplified in much of the actual literature produced by Cook's boys—which it took a later perspective fully to perceive. Thirty years after *The Play Way,* "especially through the findings of the psychologists [through whom] we have come to understand more about child nature and expression," Marjorie Hourd pointed to the essential "barrenness" in some of the compositions resulting from Cook's "literary approach." Her objections are coded in the difference between false and true "griffins"; that is

> the difference between imitation and creation. The imagination refuses to co-operate when a work of imitation is in hand. It leaves it to "the inferior faculties" to get on with the job, and "a false griffin" ensues. But when a piece of creative construction is in progress, then it sets to work at once with its unifying power, and "a true griffin" emerges.[13]

Hourd made an important distinction between "direct" and "indirect" imitation. Only the second of these, she argued, can result in authentic creation made by the children; and this possibility is itself engendered through the employment of "indirect teaching." Here, the teacher deploys a poem or passage of prose in such ways that the children "wander with it on their own and read it themselves," "muse and reflect upon it ... to bring home to it their own ideas," or "only to dream upon it, so that the symbolism and imagery and all the other suggestive forces awaken thoughts without any intermediary help apart from what will be given in the reading":

> Then, if upon this upturned soil it is suggested that they plant something of their own, there is likely to result a composition "tipped" by the passage, but woven nevertheless from their own inwards—an *original* composition.

The procedures which will lead to children's own art-making, in Hourd's account, are not aimed at getting them to act upon the poem as presented to them in order that they shall develop a conscious understanding of the poem; rather, that they should *react* to it, allowing unconscious association to be released. Then what is produced, at best, stands as an authentic representation of some aspect of the individual psyche. The child's personal development, "the process of individuation," will be "greatly helped through artistic expression."

The influence of Jung is here formally acknowledged as, in Hourd's thesis, is also the work of various other psychologists (analytical, developmental, and *Gestalt*). Another signal influence is that of Herbert Read, whose *Education through Art* (1943) placed the child's innate expressivity at the heart of the educational enterprise. To the view of creativity as largely the operation of what, in its psychoanalytical term, are the forces of *sublimation,* Hourd melded the Romantic perspectives of the Wordsworthian child and the Coleridgean Imagination.

Hourd's article of faith asserts that "a child needs expression for this world of inner reality," that is, "the psychic processes at work in the child." This "hidden life" has nonetheless a "haunting power," from which "the shy spirit in the heart of every child" strives "for release." Retelling phrases from lines in Wordsworth's *The Waggoner,* Hourd contends that in the various readings of literature (which have been identified and discussed), the child

> recognizes the familiar face of her own repressed conflicts, which will trouble her until the ghost be laid, and the debt be paid in some form of creative effort.

Such an explanation of art-making comes close to, if not actually assuming, a cathartic or purgative function for art; and, in the educational context, might seem to put the teacher in the role of therapist-confessor. In fact Hourd is at some pains to deny such a role, arguing against "the substitution of a psychological analysis of expression for the correcting and evaluating of it." Despite the denial, there is a questioning which remains: in correcting and evaluating the *expression,* has the teacher acknowledged and begun to deal with the *experience* which the expression embodies, or towards which it points? Can one deal with the expression, evaluating the language, and at the same time avoid the experience of which it is compounded?

The Ordering Processes of Art: David Holbrook

There are here, as elsewhere, contacts between Hourd's dissertation and *The Secret Places* (1964) of David Holbrook; that work of his which shares, as I sense it, most closely in the same community of beliefs (though I infer no direct influence). Holbrook's own influences here proceed most directly from psychoanalytical theory; but they lead in a direction at times parallel to that advanced on by Hourd. Here, in a way which takes further some parts of the argument as defined in *English for Maturity* (1961)—and contemporaneous with Holbrook's emerging application of psychoanalytical theory to literary criticism—we shall find his propositions for putting the *art* of literature at the center of the English-teaching enterprise. The firsthand making of art, in literary forms, *may* have a therapeutic effect or consequence for the child. But that is neither the first aim in teaching English as and through art, nor the prime function of art. On the first of these, Holbrook is quite clear:

> What the teacher seeks to promote is a real revelation of the self. He does not seek psychic manifestations of disorder, such as a psychiatrist might pursue, in order to cure. He is only incidentally and at times a therapist. He promotes the normal ordering processes of art, the poetic grapplings with the disturbances of the heart.[14]

"The normal ordering processes of art"; it is a proposition begging many questions. In part, Holbrook here is following an earlier assertion that "the creative process" is accepted, understood, and willingly engaged in by children. Given the opportunity children will make their poems, stories, pictures, and will *know* without telling that they are making art-forms. To put the matter reductively, a child knows when she is making a poem, and understands that the purpose of so doing is in some essential regard different from the purpose of making some other things with words. The child's acceptance of this may be cultural; the environment in which she grows evidences this for her. From the existence of art-forms within the culture the child learns, preconsciously and without need of telling, that art performs its own function. But the *urge* to make art in the first place betokens a prime, evolutionary psychobiological need; one which cannot be satisfied in any other way than by the making of art. The art is the expression of the need; the satisfaction of that need is achieved through the ordering processes which the making of that art imposes. Each completed work of art is therefore, in itself, a sign of order, an order compounded from the constituent elements of which it is made, and brought into relationship to form a coherent whole. Experience is ordered via the agency of mechanics which are inherent within the art-form and its medium *through which the experience is to be expressed.*

Experience which is formless may be *apprehended;* but it can not be *comprehended.* Only when given shape, only when brought into essential contiguity, can the otherwise dispersed possessions of consciousness assemble a sense of meaning. In this the function of art-making and the function of the psychoanalyst share important resemblances. The difference, in this context, resides in the psychoanalyst's referral to a repertoire of theories against which shards of individual experience may be "tested out." The "shape" of the theory is made from patterns of experience shared communally, patterns of living which seem to repeat—with individual variation of particular circumstance—from one person to another, however unusual or rare that pattern might be among a society as a whole. But a psychoanalytical theory is not the lived reality; it is a possible, and at best plausible, explanation for the origin and development of that pattern of experience. Nor is the theory, in lived experience, a "model" of what reality "is like"—which is to replace reality and deal with the metaphor as if that were the substantial and living truth; a process of transformation we designate in the term "reification." (I do not, for example, *experience* my consciousness as id, ego and superego). But what a theory can suggest and supply are terms of reference within which one can begin to talk about the experience, means by which we can conceptualize the reality of experience. Where psychoanalytic theory moves by explication, however, that metaphor which is a completed artwork moves largely through implication. The purpose of the art-metaphor, as is the aim of psychotherapy, is to liberate us to return to life. Nor can the art-metaphor be exhausted through a method of analysis. The danger of deconstructionism, for example, as a method of dealing with the metaphor of an art-form, in whatever medium, is that it can fail to return us to life; locking us, instead, within a potentially endless analysis only of the language of the metaphor.

The nature, and thereby the function of the metaphor, as art, is to give shape to a network of otherwise unformulated experience; one whose organization generates a tacit realm of understanding which is both more extensive and more inclusive than we could otherwise say in discursive language, or whose discursive version would necessarily change the nature and reality of the experience as it now lives in the metaphor. In and through the metaphor of art, we know more than we can say; we understand, where the voicing of understanding eludes us. Through these realizations we discover much of the excitement and satisfaction we gain from art. Where we can make our response explicit, we can say what we mean. Where the understanding is tacit, unvoiced, we still derive a sense of meaning—a distinguishing vitality made possible through the ordering processes of art.

The making of art provides us with a way of knowing, rather than knowledge in its conceptual form. Through that making we create a sense of a lived reality.

Using Words as Art to Deal with Life

What Holbrook asserted, in *The Secret Places* and elsewhere, was that in dealing with literature, children were "learning to use words as art to deal with life."[15] The ordering of experience, which the making of art both enables and induces, assists the individual to come to terms with the "inner," subjective life, including imaginative fantasy, as well as providing "a means to extending our exploration of the relationship between external reality and our inward understanding of it."[16] Art, in these terms, is to be understood as a resounding affirmative to the question posed by D. W. Winnicott:

> is it not largely through artistic creation and artistic experience that we maintain the necessary bridges between subjective and the objective?[17]

The work, preeminently among others, of Susanne Langer, Michael Polanyi, and Marjorie Grene, all confirm that "knowing" can exceed the evidences which "objectivity" exclusively will reveal; that there is a subjective element to all knowledge; and that understanding may be a tacit cognition. Within these perceptions we can see easily that the making of art *is* a making of meaning.

In the first of his works which directly drew upon philosophical anthropology, Holbrook expresses man's primary need as his "existential yearnings, his will-to-meaning, his quest for a sense of significance."[18] In artworks made by child and adult alike there inheres meaning. This meaning, to borrow a distinction made by Polanyi, is *existential* rather than "representative."[19] The work of art is a symbolization of the existential meaning which has been brought into being, by virtue of the creation of that context which is the work of art itself.

When we return these findings to the debate on the content and processes of English teaching, we can see readily enough the essential rightness of the argumentative line advanced, with individual variation and difference, by Sampson, Cook, Hourd, and Holbrook. The child, the growing youth, both require the experience of language as art—whatever else will feature within the whole English program. The experience of language as art includes the making of one's own literature and the reading of others' literary forms. In the creation of their own poems, stories, and other literary forms, pupils express their growing sense of reality, and in that recognition (the "bringing to mind") of experience engage, in degrees of tacit knowing, with the existential meaning of experience. That sense of lived reality will be further nurtured and, indeed, in a crucial way is made possible, through the reading of other literature. The imaginative life is nourished through this subjective engagement, as through the shared, intersubjective response of others, peers and teachers alike, to the experience of each text. Such enrichment is vital again; through a sympathetic extension of one's own subjectivity, one may then enter the worlds of others and the realities which confer upon them a sense of existential meaning, a definition of identity. To fulfil the ideal of education *(educere)* we must "lead out"—enabling the child to discover self in relation to the world of experience by giving expression to that world; but that education *(educare)* must also "nurture," provide new experience to enlarge and make fulfilling that world, and to give direction to the child's potentialities. Only through this reciprocity is the "true self" in each of us revealed and shaped—and, I would add, shaped through revealing:

If there is a 'true self' and a sense of potentialities how do we recognise those? How do we know the 'true self'? The answer is, somewhere between our own creative dynamics and culture as the embodiment of the pursuits of truth . . .[20]

In the making, reading, and response to literary forms, then, children actively construct a sense of reality—what is true for them, and for others. In their own writings, if we can devise means through which they will achieve this personal authenticity rather than mimed replication, they can locate a surer sense of self. For the making of the existential meaning of art is simply not available through other kinds of educational activity, activities which have their own justifications. Through such meaning, which draws subjectively upon the child's sense of self and the "outer" world-as-experienced, the *animal symbolicum* finds expression. And in so doing the ordering processes of art contribute crucially to development, to self-realization and individuation. If language is not developed creatively, through imaginative realizations of experience by which you can mean *personally* what you say, then it is possible that both the personal and the language development of the individual will remain impoverished. Language must be, first, as Holbrook reminds us, for living:

> The use of language for the purposes of life . . . is learned only by a rich and varied reading, talking and listening. Above all, literacy comes from much imaginative talking and writing, to extend the powers of the word, by metaphor, over the unploughed areas of our existence.[21]

Notes

1. George Sampson, *English for the English* (1921), ed. Denys Thompson (Cambridge: Cambridge University Press, 1970), p. 20.
2. Ibid., p. 28.
3. Quoted by Denys Thompson, introduction to *English for the English*, p. 3.
4. J. H. Newman, "Literature," in *The Idea of a University* (1873) (London: Longmans, Green and Co., 1898), p. 274, p. 291.
5. Sampson, *English for the English*, p. 27.
6. Board of Education, *The Teaching of English in England* (The Newbolt Report) (London: HMSO, 1921), pp. 4–5.
7. Some of these findings and their educational implications for the teaching of English are further explored in Edwin Webb, *Literature in Education: Encounter and Experience* (London: Falmer Press, 1992), especially chap. 4, "Language: the Agent of Discovery," pp. 48–66.
8. Sampson, *English for the English*, p. 44.

9. H. Caldwell Cook, *The Play Way: An Essay in Educational Method* (London: Heinemann, 1917), p. 4.
10. Ibid., p. 18.
11. Ibid., p. 17.
12. Department of Education and Science, *National Curriculum Proposals for English for Ages 5 to 16* (London: HMSO, 1989), paras. 7.8–7.10.

What I mean by Cook's contemporary pertinence can be seen, for example, in the following comment. Viewed within the context of a statutory national curriculum, and a program for English teaching which threatens to become even more sharply prescribed, Cook's words acquire a telling wisdom:

> The teacher may have a beautiful system, a course of work schemed, graded and ordered in admirable shape, and thoroughly approved by his or her chief, and by his Majesty's inspector to boot. But what if the child's mind does not work orderly?—which happens to be the case. What will his Majesty do then, poor thing? What if a growing mind scorns systematic progress (which is also true) and leaps back and forth ... ? Let us have outline schemes by all means, but leave the details to the hour in which it shall be told us what to do. (*The Play Way*, p. 3)

13. Marjorie L. Hourd, *The Education of the Poetic Spirit* (London: Heinemann, 1949), p. 92. Subsequent quotations are from pp. 95–6, 153, 119, 120, 140.
14. David Holbrook, *The Secret Places* (London: Methuen, 1964), p. 29.
15. Ibid., p. 65.
16. David Holbrook, *The Quest for Love* (London: Methuen, 1964), p. 63.
17. D. W. Winnicott, quoted by David Holbrook, ibid., p. 89.
18. David Holbrook, *Education, Nihilism and Survival* (London: Darton, Longman and Todd, 1977), p. 30.
19. Michael Polanyi, *Personal Knowledge* (London: Routledge and Kegan Paul, 1958), p. 58.
20. Holbrook, *Education, Nihilism and Survival*, p. 82.
21. Holbrook, *The Secret Places*, p. 70.

A Relish for the English Word

Roger Knight

The neutering of English: "planned amnesia"?

The scene is an ordinary primary school classroom. What is going on looks familiar enough. A group of six ten-year olds have just acted out a short play. What is new is that they are being formally assessed by their teacher; as they have to be, constantly, in the National Curriculum. The teacher is pleased—and relieved. (Parents have to be kept informed of their children's progress). The play has been done with obvious enthusiasm, verve, and pride. These children have clearly met one of the national "standards of attainment" in "English": "to plan and participate in a presentation, e.g., of the outcome of a group activity, a poem, a story, dramatic scene, or play."

But wait; have they? Or rather, has each one of them? Assessment in the National Curriculum is the new minefield. That is why there are so many "experts" on hand to advise and guide her. For the most authoritative advice she turns to the School Examinations and Assessment Council.[1] Her heart sinks. They tell her very precisely where she has gone wrong. They do it through examples of familiar classroom activity. It could be her group they are talking about. In their example too, there is one child who "contributed little to the group discussion" and was "content to participate as directed by others." There's another who "dominated both the planning and presenting." But then there nearly always is. Does she have to worry about that?

Emphatically she does. She discovers, from the SEAC, that these children are *problems*. She is used to encouraging the shy and restraining the overexuberant. Now though, for purposes of assessment, they must be *policed*. For, in the words the SEAC use about similar children in their example, *"their degree of involvement was suspect and open to question* (my italics) in terms of interpersonal skills and group interaction." The teacher is disturbed by this way of talking about children. She is dispirited to find that she should have been "assessing language behaviours rather than actual output." She has yet to master what the SEAC in its bizarre jargon calls "Observation of Process." In other words, what was really important was not whether her children displayed understanding and imaginative energy, not whether their play was any good, but how they got on with one another. That's what she should have been assessing.

There is worse to come. For now, say the SEAC, she must take the shy one and the confident one separately aside and explain "in child's language" that each is "suspect and open to question" and "how progress might be made." For a teacher who thought that she knew what she was in teaching for, this is a role as absurd as it is melancholy. The idea of persuading her particular shy lad, in any language, that he's "short on interpersonal skills" and inadequate in "group interaction" is both laughable and offensive. She knows him to be intelligent and painfully self-conscious. What's more, there are two children in that group of six he doesn't like. No SEAC-style inquisition is going to change that.

In the deadly philosophy of the SEAC, the human image of the teacher trusted by her pupils is obscured by that of the behavioral scientist coldly engaged in "observation of process." You have to keep reminding yourself that it is flesh and blood to which the jargon refers. Teachers, we hear, "organize individual needs in the classroom"; they "monitor" "learning behaviour" and check "product." This neutered, mechanistic language is rife in education. It enables those who use it to persuade themselves that there is nothing teachers cannot precisely observe and nothing they cannot objectively test. With the National Curriculum, Assessment threatens to become the new tyranny; its servants the teachers, its victims the children.

Flesh and blood children don't of course come tamely to heel. To the SEAC real children are a bit of an embarrassment, almost at times the enemy. As the teacher creeps up on them, "observing process," the children "may become obsessed" with what she is doing with her "assessment devices": her clipboard and checklists. Obviously: children aren't stupid. Which is more than can be said of the tactic advised by the SEAC: "minimize the intrusion of the device . . . . fit it inside a familiar notebook or file." So it is a war game: a memorable image for a brave new world.

English for Maturity: Helping Us to Remember

When *English for Maturity*[2] appeared in 1961 such scenes could have been imagined only by a humorist of a particularly sardonic turn. By the time of *English for Meaning*[3] (1979), which appeared four years after the Bullock Committee's *A Language for Life*,[4] the philosophies of knowledge and learning that would lead to such grossness were already in the ascendant. Now, with the SEAC we seem to be in the condition George Steiner calls "planned amnesia." An established mode of moral understanding is in eclipse, along with the vocabulary that enshrined it. There is little room in the new vocabulary for the idea of a school as David Holbrook could still see it in *English for Meaning:* often "the one center of humanness in children's lives, perhaps their one experience of care and gentleness, of human values;[5] perhaps their best opportunity of experiencing what Dickens called 'a childhood of the mind no less than a childhood of the body.'" The phrase is from *Hard Times*. Dickens's profound understanding of the 'childhood of the mind' (which Gradgrind's daughter Louisa never had) and of the forces that denied it in his own time is Holbrook's witness and example as he analyzes those that threaten it in our own. In 1979 Dickens's phrase was invoked as a warning; in 1992 it can without exaggeration be used to describe a denial of childhood that is being deliberately planned. For SEAC's view of children, of learning and of language, is in many ways closer to that of Thomas Gradgrind than it is to the tradition that links Dickens with Holbrook.

There must of course still be many teachers whose feeling for children and the work they wish to do with them finds a strong echo in that tradition. Now, however, they have little choice but to submit to an idiom that denies it; the National Curriculum has given it prescriptive force. Clearly SEAC's self-conscious policing strategies, destructive of trust, have no place in the "loving context" that Holbrook says is essential if a child's imagination and, thus, his language are to flourish. That "loving context" will include the nurturing of trust and, on the teacher's side, a proper humility. For "the child's 'living principle' in dealing with the world, including language use, is an unfathomable mystery, taking its own pace and developing at its own rate."[6] In *English for Maturity* Holbrook had noted the delusions of the "communications experts" who "so often fail to see the mystery of the flesh that can think and be aware of its existence." They are amongst the "modernists" who would "bring what Yeats called 'all the complexities of mire and blood' into schemes and catalogues." Their expertise merely hides an "intolerance of the infinite intractability of language and personality."[7] It is a prescient critique; a critique energized by a powerful, instinctive but of course cultured understanding that reductiveness of the kind with which SEAC now confronts us is at the expense of what makes us human. What is in eclipse is the idiom through which that cultured understanding expresses itself. Thirty years ago Holbrook knew where to look for its safekeeping: to "the best members of the teaching profession [who] have cherished and used that independence which English tradition leaves them."[8] Now, that tradition is as good as dead. Your own experience, your own culture and literacy may tell you that SEAC's view of "English" is barbarous. It is of no avail. SEAC isn't interested in your culture. What it offers you is a substitute, an apparatus that will (if you allow it) give you the illusion of control over the growth of your pupils' "competence." Our efforts to "control" the growth of "competence," said Holbrook in *English for Meaning,* are bound to be self-defeating if we forget that "we are dealing with complex human beings who are living," if in those words of Yeats that he is fond of quoting, we lose sight of "the whole man, blood, imagination, intellect all running together."[9] SEAC's advice to teachers is an incitement to forget. The continuing value of David Holbrook's writing about English is that it helps us to remember.

To anyone setting out to teach English in the sixties, *English for Maturity* was a challenge and an inspiration. It was passionate, combative, and practical. Its energy was that of an intense and articulate responsibility towards both the English language and those who would inherit it. What should English be for? What vision of the subject could include the education of secondary modern children in particular—"three quarters of the nation"? It was their "sensibility" that the teacher was "helping to train." As Holbrook outlines his view of the way English may "develop that richness of the individual being which releases sympathy and creative energy in community", "sensibility" takes on a rich and productive definition. The English teacher's responsibility was not technical but cultural:

> This is achieved by the arts: and it was to them civilised and leisured communities of the past gave their effort—to coming together in submission to embodiments of the human spirit. It is by these men that come to possess their traditions and values—possess them in their thought and feeling, rather than as acquired fragments of knowledge about them. And we possess our traditions largely through and in *the word*. What D. H. Lawrence called 'spontaneous-creative fullness of being' is, paradoxically, achieved only by what Mr. T. S. Eliot has called the obtaining of tradition: 'It cannot be inherited, and if you want it you must obtain it by great labour.' The obtaining of tradition is

largely a matter of possessing our native language, using it responsibly, and maintaining its vitality. The Englishman develops a fullness of being only in as far as he possesses the English language more deeply and extends his responsiveness to it. Keeping the English word alive, therefore, is crucial to any future flowering of English civilisation: and crucial to our own need for positive attitudes to life. As Keats said, 'English ought to be kept up.'[10]

"Sensibility," we have been told more recently, is "a word made virtually obsolete by its clear class overtones"[11]—a remark that sharpens one's sense that with the above passage, as with *English for Maturity* as a whole, Holbrook could still count on a substantial measure of shared values amongst his readers. The practical program to be found in *English for Maturity* (whether on poetry, drama, reading, marking or "drills") are shaped by those values. Teachers are offered a vision of how, practically, these values may be passed on, how we may "possess the English language more deeply and extend our responsiveness to it." It is the strength of that vision that it yields the simplicity of Holbrook's advice on the cultivation of literacy: "The way to develop one's mastery over English is to live within a rich context of its lively use, by reading, listening and talking."[12] *English for Maturity* shows us what that "rich context" might be and how "a real discipline" lies within it. This latter phrase does not advertise a spurious rigor. It is in no way theoretical. *English for Maturity* gives it body, articulate and usable form. As Holbrook demonstrates how a teacher might take a class through a discussion of de la Mare's *Song of the Mad Prince* or Edmund Blunden's *The Mole Catcher,* we see how a concern with language must go beyond language, how careful attention to English in the hands of the best writers confirms the intimate connections between thought, perception, and feeling. Trying to see the flavor and meaning of the work "speculating" (in Edward Thomas's *Thaw*) "helps us to deepen our relish for the English word."[13] It is Englishness, with all that that implies of what binds together those who inherit a common language, that he speaks. The "relish" that he would have us share with our pupils is the relish upon which his own work as a poet and novelist is built. If a man "speaks the English language his will be an English civilisation." The roots of Holbrook's power with words lie indeed in a profound knowledge of the English that has shaped that civilization. Their persuasiveness is thus the consequence of a rich endowment. It is, accordingly, of the first importance in his view that teachers are themselves educated in the best that the culture has to offer; that teachers themselves appreciate the true link between a continuous acquaintance with imaginative work (that "rich context" has to be "a context of its imaginative use") and the individual's own growing powers. The growth of those powers cannot be precisely planned; the process is mysterious. What a teacher can do is to create the conditions for it. Given the conditions, literacy will grow; without them no amount of linguistic knowledge will produce it.

Holbrook's confidence in his reader's willingness to assent to these propositions is rooted then in shared cultural assumptions. Amongst these assumptions is a respect for educated subjectivity (another way of describing "sensibility"). Holbrook expects his readers to reflect on the development of their own power with words, on the roots and the growth of their own literacy. It is a form of civilized appeal fallen into disuse. Nowadays vast sums of public money can be spent on a project (The Language in the National Curriculum Project) to train teachers to teach children "knowledge about language." Is the director of the project convinced that such "knowledge" will lead to "a development of competence in the use of language"? He cannot say. No "evidence" is available. The kind of evidence that might be produced by an appeal to experience, observation, and common sense is not considered. The appeal is to what the director admits we do not have: "evidence of the kind required by extensive longitudinal studies."[14]

The Real Discipline

To minds satisfied only by that kind of evidence Holbrook must now appear to be addressing his readers from an altogether alien mental country:

> Poetry has great value as a civilising art-form because it is written in the language we use for everyday purposes. The rending of poetry can help restore life to our language habits because it is language used at its richest and most accurate, in defining and enlarging experience.[15]

It is a sign of our present predicament that the "language habits" that shape "official" English are almost entirely out of sympathy with this idea of literacy. The inadequate idea of human relations and of being that dominates SEAC thinking cannot survive the scrutiny of anyone who is alert to "language at its richest and most accurate." If we agree with Holbrook in seeing metaphor as an attempt "to extend our experience over the abstract, the spiritual, the intractable, starting from the known" we are bound to feel repelled by the behavioristic universe of the SEAC, from which such mysteries are excluded. It is significant that Holbrook frequently returns to the poetry of Wordsworth and of Edward Thomas. In both there is so often a sense of what lies beyond language, of something that we strive through words to embody but that remains obstinately out of reach. Indeed it is as he discusses instances and classroom demonstrations of language "at its richest and most accurate" that we see into English as a "real discipline." If we want to know *how* "poetry has great value as a civilising art-form," or in what way Shakespeare is "a present spiritual force," if we wish to understand what is meant by saying that "it isn't what a man knows that makes him able to live without giving up, but what he is deep down in his being," we can answer: "The very Culture of the Feelings." Chapter 4 of *English for Maturity* takes J. S. Mill's phrase for its title. With great feeling and delicacy of attention Holbrook explores King Lear's "Thou rascal beadle hold thy bloody hand," Wordsworth's *Surprised by Joy* and the English folk song *The Turtle Dove*. The "real discipline" is enacted in these demonstrations; they show how poetry may be "the ordering of experience," how through Shakespeare "we may come to have a renewed grasp on life, to undertake how to live in this post-Renaissance era." We feel, reading Holbrook's account of *Surprised by Joy* ("the movement of the experience is registered in the movement of the poetry: it is felt in the blood and felt along the heart") that it would be an unresponsive reader indeed for whom the poem did not "propagate sympathy" "by making us more aware of the inward life of others." Holbrook's theory is also a theory of tradition and culture (though the word "theory" won't do; what he gives us is an experience which pushes us to share his convictions). In remarking that Lear's language is "close to that of the common people, the metaphorical and proverb-like balance of the phrases belonging to popular saw, to the liturgy, the Authorised Version and the popular sermon," he makes the point that "the pondering of life with metaphor" is not restricted to high art.[16]

"The Very Culture of the Feelings" alone makes an excellent case for English. It acknowledges and documents a history of the language that is also the history of a culture in which a nation has been in various ways united. Being born to English we grow with a language through which we may make over into our own lives the insights carried in its idioms, its arts and literature. They may become part of our responsive consciousness, shape our identity, what we value and the way we live. How that happens is ultimately as mysterious as the process is natural. As Holbrook memorably puts it: "the word—the complex, sinewy, subtle and evasive word—is at one with our life."[17] It is a note not often heard these days when English is discussed. Holbrook speaks as a creative writer whose fascination with words has deepened through his own original work and his study of the English tradition. There is in his work a palpable and justified pride in that tradition; it is what gives his writing at its best its energizing and persuasive force. Such a pride has become unfashionable. The contemporary tendency (in a "multi-cultural society") is to emphasise the constraints rather than the privileges made available through a particular cultural inheritance; to see it as imprisoning perception rather than enriching and enlarging understanding. Those who argue along such lines offer illusory freedoms. Repudiating the "reverential notion of literature" as "the best English," a chief examiner at A Level rejoices in "the alternative construction of the English curriculum into language modes": this "offers a much wider conception, drawing attention as it does to universal behaviour, rather than to a particular cultural heritage."[18] The offer of greater breadth is spurious, the phrase "universal behaviour" merely empty grandiosity; for no behavior can be studied except within "a particular cultural heritage." The desire is to turn away from words as "our chief source of insight," to make them objects of study and thus to drain them of the moral and spiritual energies that make them "at one with our life." And if words are only objects, all too easily people will seem so too. This indeed is SEAC's view. As they offer to pin one label on children's "speaking and listening skills" and to bully them into qualifying for the next they are deaf to the cautionary words that thirty years ago Holbrook offered about "the Communications experts":

> What too often they leave out of account is our communication with ourselves, in the inward world with which we must first learn to deal, before we can deal with the outside world.[19]

Such "experts," he said, "really seem to act as if human beings are a form of rather inefficient thinking machine; they "often fail to see the mystery of the flesh that can think and be aware of its existence."[20]

English for Meaning

Little more than a decade later the failure had been embodied, as Holbrook saw it, in official writ: The Bullock Report (1975). *English for Meaning* (1979) was Holbrook's strongly felt and closely argued retort. In finding Bullock "pathetically inadequate on literature," "limp and apologetic" on poetry in particular, he expresses great dismay that the committee could have abandoned "the recognition that teaching is an art, that teaching English is especially an art rooted in intuitive powers." The dismay becomes personal. Had he not himself "made incontrovertibly clear that the most effective way of training children to use English is through imaginative disciplines (and that) abstract rules and theories are of minimal use"? Bullock's approach was "positivistic and functional"; it had "consigned the imaginative approach to oblivion."[21] It is hardly an exaggeration. *English for Maturity* had been an answer, for the modern age, to Keats's "English ought to be kept up." It is itself shaped by and continuous with a traditional way of thinking about language, culture, and education. Holbrook explicitly acknowledges George Sampson's *English for the English* ("which I cannot hope to emulate"). Alongside Sampson we might think of Newbolt's inclusive definition of English as "not merely the medium of our thought" but "the very stuff and process of it . . . . the English mind, the element in which we live and work."[22] We might call to mind Coleridge's wonderful description of "the blessed organ of language" as "a magnificent history of acts of individual mind, sanctioned by the mind of the country."

These are profound and inspired words, the voice of a tradition that leaves little mark in Bullock, on the quality of the ideas or of their expression. The sense of solid achievement, of insight, wisdom and practical guidance having been willfully thrown aside is thus very strong in *English for Meaning*. "When it comes to literature the Bullock Report ("like the New English Bible") is illiterate . . . . a catastrophic *bureaucratic* act of hacking away our best connections with the past" in favor of "a new obsession with "morphemes" and *mechanistic concepts* of processing and structures rather than *living mysteries,* speakers and writers as human beings, children or men."[23]

The words italicized indicate the basic problem, the shift towards the misapprehension that Bullock embodies and that subsequent publications have reinforced. Bullock's overmastering stress is upon language as an objective study rather than as a process of which we are indissociably a part. From Bullock onwards we find a tenacious insistence (notably in the Kingman Report, 1988)[24] that *explicit* understanding, knowledge *about* language, itself provides the conditions for the growth of literacy. Continually it has been maintained that teachers do not know enough, that children in consequence do not know enough either and that this is a lamentable ignorance that must be corrected if standards are to be raised.

English teachers are in a sense thus dispossessed, their own culture and "intuitive powers" discounted. They are led (or invited) to discredit or disbelieve in forms of knowledge that cannot be codified in the manner of Bullock and Kingman. Both committees advocated comprehensive and complex courses in linguistic studies for teachers in training. To Holbrook such courses are "wasteful and futile." Any teacher who has been well-trained "*knows* what disciplines and forms of understanding are valuable in practice. They are developed from experience of the tacit, intuitive and imaginative processes of encounter in the classroom." Such teachers no more need to "know about" language in the Bullock sense than Sissy Jupe (who had been brought up amongst circus riders) needed Bitzer's aridly encyclopaedic definition of a horse. Holbrook's telling use of *Hard Times*, of Sissy's intuitive knowledge and Gradgrind's ignorance is central to his reaffirmation in *English for Meaning* of those "forms of knowledge" that belong most distinctively to the arts. Bullock is indifferent to the "childhood of the mind." It repudiates a powerful and coherent tradition of understanding and of teaching in favor of a "knowledge about language" whose true home is the very restricted company of adult linguists: "Only a few linguists need to study the rules, for the sake of truth and not in order to prescribe. The rest of us can simply do English, enjoying plays, poems and stories—and improve our language powers through art."[25]

The case against Bullock made in *English for Meaning* has never been answered. Holbrook's key criticisms are crisply made and substantially documented. The alternative, "real discipline" of English is there in the book too, in a variety of practical accounts of work with children and adolescents. His critique has not, however, acted as a check on subsequent developments. On the contrary, those developments have given it a sadly prophetic force. In observing that the Bullock Report "sets up a false analogy between computers and the human mind," Holbrook remarks that "the mechanistic cybernetic model is so deeply entrenched that people tend to become bemused when the question of doubts about it is even raised."

The entrenchment has deepened immeasurably since those words were written, so that the task of reestablishing a human idea of language has become all the more difficult and necessary. Holbrook noted that the emphasis was not on "training response to meaning" but on "theories "about" the structure and function of language. The dominant assumption is that literacy is to be inculcated by a set of rules and procedures derived from linguistics and psychology." He notices the dehumanizing tendency of the terms in which relations between teachers and taught are characteristically described. His principal objection is that with its talk of teachers "controlling the growth of competence" and needing to "examine the verbal interaction of a class or group in terms of an explicit understanding of the operation of language," Bullock "turns a natural process into a mechanical theory." It is in this connection that Holbrook insists on the "unfathomable mystery" of the "living principle"—of which language use is one manifestation—"taking its own pace and developing at its own rate." There, prophetically, is the answer to the schematic pretensions of the National Curriculum and of the SEAC, to the insistence on analyzing human learning into fixed and describable stages, in the development of competences. What has been lost sight of is the wisdom of negative capability: "We must simply live with these truths: it is self-deceiving to believe we can control rather than foster competence, while it will not do to see competence as a mere function apart from his whole emotional life."

English Mechanized

The mechanistic models of language that Holbrook so persuasively analysed and found wanting in *English for Meaning* have advanced relentlessly into the center of English teaching. So relentlessly indeed that it becomes increasingly difficult to persuade people (even English teachers) that there is anything wrong. Holbrook himself saw that when the overmastering philosophy of knowledge entrenched itself sufficiently deeply, people found it difficult not to see it as natural: "In our commonplace thinking about the world and ourselves, our view, whether we are aware of it or not, embodies a metaphysic, and very often today it is a thoroughly mechanistic one." This is a distressingly accurate characterization of the current conventional wisdom about English. We can, for instance, discern a clear line of continuity between the mechanistic conception of "listening and speaking" in the oral communication component of the GCSE syllabuses, the "knowledge about language" prescriptions of Bullock, Kingman, and the National Curriculum and the latest series of advice to teachers emanating from SEAC.[26] The "metaphysic" uniting these various authorities is predominantly mechanistic and behavioristic; it turns its back on the tradition articulated and defended by Holbrook, is insensitive to the conception of literacy as a partly inscrutable process of growth and throws up an approach to learning the native language that is built on the accumulation and measurement of "knowledge" and "skills."

Increasingly now the cultural view of literacy is being displaced and, with it, trust in the educated judgment of the teacher—who is left with the spurious authority that comes from executing central orders. The "commonplace activity" responsible for what has happened frequently excludes what would not long ago have been seen as the merest common sense. For instance; in suggesting in *English for Meaning* that "perhaps much of our work in the secondary modern school should be oral work," Holbrook was mindful of two key facts: first, that "from, say, the Middle Ages until, say, 1870 our children's ancestors followed oral, not written patterns of culture: and that their own is an oral verse culture"; second, that while "for many reading and writing are difficult acts of abstraction . . . . listening and speaking come to them by nature."[27] He could hardly have foreseen that "what comes by nature" would fall victim to the relentlessly mechanistic systematizings that accompany the attempt to make very precise measurements of "oral and aural skills." Only the absorption of the mechanistic model into "commonplace thinking" can explain the absence of concerted protest when teachers were compelled to assess their pupils in "oral communication situations" at GCSE level; or when, typically, a GCSE board insisted that in "dialogue situations" pupils must exhibit and be assessed in "paralinguistic skills (including appropriate body movements)." Similarly, so firmly in place was the computer model that there was no obvious outrage when teachers were instructed to be mindful of "the complexity of the data which we process whenever we evaluate spoken language."[28] Such perversions of understanding had become the common intellectual stock.

Regularly and predictably in recent years we have had cause to reflect on Holbrook's rejection of Bullock's "language for life": "what the committee means by language is not what I mean by attention to language, a full responsiveness to the meaning of words." That "full responsiveness" cannot be cultivated through language study of the kind that preoccupied Kingman and Cox. The dutiful bows towards the literary tradition are with each committee transparently at odds with the unfounded confidence each displays in linguistic study. To be inward with that tradition is to feel at once the shallowness of much of the committee's own language. Kingman's formative metaphors, for instance, derive from the familiar technological lexicon that presents language simply as an object. According to Kingman it is "just as important to teach *about* our language environment as *about* our physical environment . . . . to teach *about* the structure of English as about the structure of the atom"[29] (my italics). English as a "real discipline" is inescapably in touch with language as "a rich source of insight," as a potent moral and spiritual source. With Kingman we descend into mere moralizing. Its aspirations are as vague and unrealizable as its expression is feeble: schoolchildren should "make some systematic comparisons with other languages learned or used in schools and in present day British society." Why? "So that an interest in linguistic diversity might be encouraged."[30]

"Interest in linguistic diversity" is a hollow phrase. Interest in itself contains no criterion of value. And we must have some idea of value if we are to decide what is worth studying. Without it there is chaos. Even now children are paying the price of this sloppiness. It must, for instance, have required an improbably sustained suspension of disbelief to anticipate that adolescents would benefit (within the National Curriculum) from "a knowledge of organizational differences between spoken and written English" by "talking about the fact that speech is interactive, spontaneous and informal while writing is more tightly planned." Could there be more astonishing proof of the failure both of imagination and of memory than the supposition that children need explicitly to be taught that "speech ranges from intimate or casual spontaneous conversation e.g., *jokes, anecdotes, banter, gossip, argument* through discussion, documentary and debate to more formal forms—lectures, sermons and more formulaic utterances such as *toasts, oaths and sermons.*"[31] If a man speaks the English language, says Holbrook, "his will be an English civilisation." Our forebears, illiterate though they were, spoke that language and were part of a civilization in which, if only through ale house on the one hand and church on the other, they would have known such "facts" on their pulses.

The futility of so many such prescriptions for "knowledge about language" is that they are culturally ignorant. For all that we now speak of a National Curriculum, the indissoluble connections between national history, language and present-day consciousness are as often as not felt to be an embarrassment. Holbrook's own use of English is healthily in touch with realities we can grasp. We know and he can demonstrate what it means to "possess our traditions" through and "to deepen our relish for the English word." With the Cox report such confidence and clarity has been displaced by evasiveness and vapidity. "In our multi-cultural, multi-lingual society," children need to develop "a firmly based but flexible and developing linguistic and cultural identity."[32] These are the words of a committee that doesn't know what it wants to say. The vagueness is part of that general tendency to disparage the native English traditions of literature and its study; to free English indeed from that "responsiveness to the meaning of words" which, if it has one at all, must be its raison d'être.

Notes

1. *A Guide to Teacher Assessment—Pack C: A Source Book of Teacher Assessment* (London: School Examinations and Assessment Council, 1990). Quotations from this document in the section which follows will be found on pp. 32, 41, 46.
2. David Holbrook, *English for Maturity* (Cambridge: Cambridge University Press, 1961).
3. David Holbrook, *English for Meaning* (Windsor: National Foundation for Educational Research, 1979).
4. *A Language for Life,* Report of the Bullock Committee (London: HMSO, 1975).
5. Holbrook, *English for Meaning,* p. 18.
6. Ibid., p. 37.
7. Holbrook, *English for Maturity,* p. 31.
8. Ibid., p. 37.
9. Holbrook, *English for Meaning,* p. 42.
10. Ibid..
11. Len Masterman, *Teaching About Television* (London: Macmillan, 1981), p. 18.
12. Holbrook, *English for Maturity,* p. 23.
13. Ibid., p. 64.
14. Ronald Carter (ed.), *Knowledge about Language and the Curriculum:* the LINC Reader (London: Hodder and Stoughton, 1991) p. 16.
15. Holbrook, *English for Maturity,* p. 69.
16. Quotations in the preceding section are taken from Holbrook, ibid., pp. 43, 48, 49.

17. Ibid., p. 38.

18. M. Jones and A. West (eds.), *Learning Me Your Language* (London: Mary Glasgow, 1988) p. 141.

19. Holbrook, *English for Maturity*, p. 31.

20. Ibid., p. 31.

21. Holbrook, *English for Meaning*, pp. 9, 11, 12, 32.

22. *The Teaching of English in England*, Report of the Newbolt Committee (London: HMSO, 1921) p. 20.

23. Holbrook, *English for Meaning*, p. 13.

24. *Report of the Committee of Inquiry into the Teaching of English Language* (London: HMSO, 1988).

25. Quotations in this and subsequent paragraphs, unless separately noted, are all from Holbrook, *English for Meaning, passim*.

26. *Key Stage 3 Pupils' Work Assessed: English* (London: SEAC, 1992). The authors of this publication fully accept the notion that provoked Holbrook's incredulity in the Bullock Report: "Bullock takes it seriously that the quality of language may be measured by its syntax."

27. Holbrook, *English for Maturity*, p. 22.

28. *English: GCSE, A Guide For Teachers* (Milton Keynes: Secondary Examinations Council in collaboration with the Open University, 1986), p. 41.

29. *Report of the Committee of Inquiry into the Teaching of English Language* (London: HMSO, 1988), p. 4.

30. Ibid., p. 30.

31. *English in the National Curriculum* (London: HMSO, 1990) pp. 27, 41.

32. *National Curriculum: English For Ages 5–16* (London: DES, 1989) section 2, paragraph 12.

A Moral Approach to English

Gordon M. Pradl

What connection exists, however tenuous, between the reading and writing of literature and the quality of private and public lives? As soon as we view English as something other than an instrumental skill to get something done in the social world, we are inevitably drawn to some moral claim for the workings of the imagination. Yet once we overstep the boundaries of a merely practical curriculum, we risk entering unpredictable and disturbing zones of meaning and value. For when feelings and conduct, motives and actions, become a primary focus in our concern with literary texts, both in their making and unmaking, we suddenly are faced with competing sensibilities and judgments. When we seriously entertain how work in English contributes to the personal growth and maturity of students, we see that our subject is as much about relationship and identity as it is about information and knowledge. And fundamental to such a shift in ethical concern within the English classroom has been the tireless voice of David Holbrook.

Matthew Arnold's Moral Argument for Literature

One way of accounting for the intense energy behind David Holbrook's educational thinking is to view it in the context of the intellectual stance initiated by Matthew Arnold. Responding to a society and a landscape forever changed by the industrial revolution, Arnold struggled with the question of what was to form the abiding values and mores of a greatly expanded middle class, since the rise of science and industry had eroded religion's exclusive domination of the culture's world view. Through his influential writings, such as *Culture and Anarchy,* Arnold helped set in motion the idea that literature might replace religion as a proper source of authority over the *"inward* condition of the mind and the spirit."[1]

In his essays, Arnold argued that criticism, obeying the rule of "disinterestedness" in order to follow the "law of its own nature", represented the "free play of the mind on all subjects which it touches." By refusing to be trapped in practical matters, the criticism Arnold envisioned would discover a true morality in "the best that is known and thought in the world."[2] But it was in poetry that Arnold found a real understanding of human existence, and by tying criticism to it, he arrived at this most direct of moral equations:

> that poetry is at bottom a criticism of life; that the greatness of a poet lies in his powerful and beautiful application of ideas to life—to the question: How to live. Morals are often treated in a narrow and false fashion; they are bound up with systems of thought and belief which have had their own day; they are fallen into the hands of pedants . . . We find attraction, at times, even in a poetry of revolt . . . in a poetry where the contents may be what they will, but where the form is studied and exquisite. We delude ourselves in either case; and the best cure for our delusion is to let our minds rest upon that great and inexhaustible word *life,* until we learn to enter into its meaning. A poetry of revolt against moral ideas is a poetry of revolt against life; a poetry of indifference towards moral ideas is a poetry of indifference towards *life.*[3]

Although Arnold is chiefly remembered for his writings on literature and culture, his daily career as an inspector of schools and his consequent visits to the continent produced some educational reports that, despite their class bias, were ahead of their time in advocating more humanistic approaches to the curriculum. Borrowing from his social analysis and his debates with Thomas Huxley and others who saw science as ousting "letters" from their preeminence in the schools, Arnold argued for an education which emphasized the development of character: "The fault of the teaching in our popular schools at home is . . . that it is so little formative; it gives the children the power to read newspapers, to write a letter, to cast accounts, and gives them a certain number of pieces of knowledge, but it does little to touch their nature for good and to mould them."[4] Arnold's inspiring rhetoric served as a major touchstone for a moral tradition in English because his concern for literature and the quality of social living involved an awareness of the primary importance of the individual's inner being. His cultural equation, however, was based on elitism, a contempt for common everyday people and their *popular* culture, and an undue reliance on the efficacy of the state to establish the reign of aristocratic values of conduct and sensibility. The real challenge was how to honor civilized values in a non-hierarchical democratic society, how to foster an individual's development from the inside rather than dictate it from without.

At the beginning of his career Holbrook too shared Arnold's faith in the benefits of culture:

> In my early cultural work, I found great sympathy in myself with Matthew Arnold, and his insistence on sweetness and light, and on the beneficial effects of culture. I believed with Arnold that the quality of a man's life depends upon what he reads during the day, and so forth. I thought that perhaps if only we could spread culture widely enough, it might have the effect of humanizing individuals so that they would become more loving and brotherly, and that peace might be possible. I felt that where states and authorities were oppressive and tyrannical, one could find also that they were terrified of men finding one another's essential humanity—"what it is to be human"—and that this was political dynamite: good dynamite![5]

This attitude became modified considerably as Holbrook gained experience through actual educational work in the local community. He was, for instance, shocked one day to discover the irony of a passage from one of Arnold's letters that he had used to head the Introduction to *English for Maturity*—"And, unattractive as the raw Englishry is, it is good stuff, and, always supposing it not to deteriorate but to improve, its spread is the spread of future civilisation." This quotation in context referred to a British defeat in Africa, and thus "Englishry" was the "English soldiery." For the second edition, this was changed to read, "unattractive as the raw Englishry is, it is good stuff . . . always supposing it not to deteriorate but to improve . . ." As Holbrook comments, "Arnold's sweetness and light obviously required the subjugation of the Zulus, and, one suspects, a good deal else that we would now see as alarmingly inhuman. Could we see the *army* as bringing a spread of civilisation?!"[6] Thus, although Holbrook continued to share Arnold's enthusiasm for literature, he gradually stopped endorsing any direct cultural solution to the problems of social living:

> I find, when I read Arnold now, that his concepts of "perfection" and "culture" are terribly narrow—classical and literary education. I enjoy his irony, but he seems to be too parochial, and propagandistic, and his emphasis is too heavily on culture as a source of moral good—and

as a way of making people polite, elegant and cultivated, rather than "mean, or vulgar, or hideous."[7]

F. R. Leavis and English as a Discipline

The other major inspiration behind Holbrook's moral approach to English includes the writings and teaching of that consummate outsider in academic literary criticism, F. R. Leavis. Although his championing of the novel and his marking out of "the great tradition" have proved crucial in establishing new criteria for the reading of English literature, Leavis's direct personal influence on his students may have had more impact in spreading the force of his ideas. As D. J. Enright recalls, "Leavis was one of the very few teachers I came across who actively and deeply *wanted* his pupils to follow what he was saying and treated them as something approaching equals, without a hint of condescension."[8] By functioning as a commanding presence at Downing College, Cambridge, and continuing his running battle with the cozy literary establishment, Leavis was able to impose a stance of seriousness toward literature that prompted H. M. McLuhan to assert, "He ended the idea that English was a subject."[9]

Many have faulted Leavis for not giving "anything like adequate recognition to those aspects of art which are gratuitous, which arise from high spirits and the impulse to play."[10] However, as McLuhan has noted, his "method is that of an artistic evaluation which is inseparable from the exercise of a delicately poised moral tact,"[11] and so a critical judgment, for Leavis, can be nothing less that a "moral" judgment:

> A poem in itself functions dramatically, not strategically or persuasively. It is for contemplation, and functions for the spectator or reader as a means of extending and refining moral perception or dramatic awareness. Where Mr. Leavis sees the function of poetry as the education or nourishment of the affections, Richards and Empson tend to regard it pragmatically and rhetorically as a means of impinging on a particular situation.[12]

Here McLuhan has pointed to an important distinction between Leavis and the new critics: the difference between the subjective life of the feelings and the objective life of action. Leavis's insistence on the former mirrors his characteristic refusal to separate form and content because this would in turn involve separating language and the experience it was intended to convey. Consequently his criticism and teaching came to depend upon close reading so as to properly identify the quality of the emotion invested in a poem: "the discovery of an interest in ambiguities and shifts is very far from making less necessary a due concern for relevance, and a due perception that such a concern involves a training in sensitive and submissive integrity—and integration—of response."[13]

Living in the midst of what he took to be confused and chaotic modern times, literature for Leavis became what it had been for Arnold, a criticism of life, the one remaining repository of the values which make good living possible. As social critic, Leavis bitterly condemned England's fragmented industrial culture and set against it a vision of standards growing out of the wholeness of some lost organic community. Accordingly, Leavis held the writings of D. H. Lawrence in the highest regard, because Lawrence "knew every day of his life in intimate experience the confrontation, the interpenetration, of the old agriculture England with the industrial; the contrast of organic forms and rhythms and the old beauty of humane adaptation with what had supervened."[14] This sensibility embodied, for Leavis, the kind of intelligence missing in modern life: "the power of recognizing justly the relation of idea and will to spontaneous life, of using the conscious mind for the attainment of 'spontaneous-creative fullness of being.'"[15] Such intelligence stressed the values of individualism which work against the effects of collectivism in contemporary society, that "life is a matter of individual lives, and that except in individual lives there is no life to be interested in or reverent about, and no life to be served."[16]

Leavis's earnest stance toward culture and literature, and finally education itself, inevitably came at the expense of any broad-based appreciation for popular culture and the self-creative innovation and renewal of the "masses." Bombarded every day with a wide variety of stimuli—the cinema, mass journalism, advertising, television, and now digital technology—average people, Leavis maintained, had no way of discriminating the good from the bad, and consequently their emotional and creative lives had become impoverished and their existence devoid of meaning and significance. Alarmed at what he saw as the corrupted state of literary culture and how this was intensifying the emotional squalor he interpreted around him, Leavis countered with an aggressive proposal that the study of "English" should naturally lie at the center of any education and, accordingly, he worked out a plan for such an "English School" in *Education and the University* (1943).

The facts of the matter have never supported Leavis's contention that once there was an age with a truly discriminating reading public, one that extended the values of a firmly established literary culture to all members of society. Order and authority were always at someone else's expense and while Leavis never merely stood for Victorian gentility, he unfortunately concluded that only a select few were capable of the kinds of judgments necessary to sustain the vitality of literature and culture:

> The minority capable not only of appreciating Dante, Shakespeare, Donne, Baudelaire, Hardy (to take major instances) but of recognizing their latest successors constitute the consciousness of the race (or of a branch of it) at any given time. For such capacity does not belong merely to an isolated aesthetic realm: it implies responsiveness to theory as well as to art, to science and philosophy in so far as these may affect the sense of the human situation and of the nature of life. Upon this minority depends our power of profiting by the finest human experience of the past; they keep alive the subtlest and most perishable parts of tradition. Upon them depend the implicit standards that order the finer living of an age, the sense that this is worth more than that, this rather than that is the direction in which to go, that the centre is here rather than there.[17]

Such talk sanctions a cultural elite and ends up imposing judgments rather than nurturing them. It does, however, hold great appeal to many English teachers: those who feel they are being overwhelmed by the unwashed as they work in a time when the language is being debased, when it seems hard to strive beyond functional literacy, when mass culture seems never to rise above the lowest common denominator. And this presents a clear danger for a moral approach to English, for it can easily end up validating the teacher's morals over all others as the teacher keeps trying to save the public from itself.

Despite the many good suggestions about how to develop critical readers, Leavis's proposals reinforced a serious division within education. While education for creativity and the imagination might initially undergird the development of critical sensibility, increasingly minority culture came to stand for a defensive posture within the curriculum, one seeking to inoculate students against the evils of mass civilization. As Leavis outlined it in *How to Teach Reading,* English in his terms meant confronting "anti-life" trends in all directions:

> A serious concern for education in reading [at the school level] cannot stop at reading. Practical criticism of literature must be associated

with training in awareness of the environment—advertising, the cinema, the press, architecture, and so on, for clearly, to the pervasive counter-influence of this environment the literary training of sensibility in school is an inadequate reply. Here is raised the whole question of the relation of reading to education and culture, a question . . . of the utmost importance, having obvious bearings on the question of the status and function of literature.[18]

In *Culture and Environment*, written with Denys Thompson, Leavis gives a fuller view of how an education centered on language discrimination might serve to promote a general critique of industrialized and urbanized society. While the emphasis here is always on instances of how "culture" influences the mature development of individual lives, the picture of what might count as quality and "life" remains consistently narrow and increasingly out of touch with the reality of everyday existence given the spread of democracy and the fact that more people might actually have some say in their own affairs. If Leavis's values of "individuality," "wholeness," and "life" were to assume any real authority, the attitudes expressed in *Culture and Environment* needed to be offset by more careful attention to the inner culture of the child waiting to be expressed as it begins to grow and connect with the symbolic forms surrounding it.

It is in the work of David Holbrook, who had been a student of Leavis during the early 1940s, that we find a more positive synthesis emerging. While Leavis conveyed to Holbrook "a deep sense of the value of creative literature, in bringing insight and human understanding, and in establishing a sense of civilized values," it became increasingly difficult for Holbrook to rationalize "Leavis's emphasis on minority culture as a source of values which must be preserved at all costs (even perhaps at the cost of democracy)." Such a position attempted "to *control others for their own good*" and so revealed insufficient trust in human nature and creativity. Furthermore, Holbrook began to see the necessity for wider notions of symbolism and culture. These were not the moral prerogative of any one group, but, rather, were elements that affected one's sense of being real and consequently one's ability to accept being weak, moral, and human. Because of events in his own personal experience, Leavis could not "tolerate weaknesses of any kind." This caused him to have "a very anti-creative influence" and prevented him from undertaking any wider epistemological journey into the realms of psychoanalysis and philosophical anthropology, the intellectual voyage that Holbrook chose in his effort to move us toward a more sophisticated notion of the moral function of literature in education.[19]

Poetry and the Struggle for Personal Significance

In order to locate the essential voice of poetry, Holbrook has gone back to folksong and children's imaginative work. In the case of folksong, he has pointed to passages and etymologies to indicate how the concreteness of its language is closer than modern poetry to sensuous experience. Six principles capture what this poetry embodies: (1) "Human life is short and subject to change, time, suffering and death." (2) "In the face of these conditions ... *Love* is the most meaningful and enduring experience, as the assertion of vitality and fertility. Good love is that in which there is a flow of true feelings and *constancy*." (3) Love itself is subject to many *betrayals*—unintended alliances, jealousy, infidelity, fatherless children—and "the folksongs, unconsciously and anonymously, select those truths of survival of the race which our civilization arrives at slowly and painfully by conscious understanding through the study of the human mind and human nature such as the relationship between love and family life." (4) "Love itself is also subject to many assaults both from weaknesses within us and because of the tragic evanescence of all human experience." (5) "Paradoxically *constancy*, romantic love and the security of the family depend upon a robust delight in physical lovemaking, and yet on courtesy, delicacy, and social consent too." (6) "Yet again love depends for its development on a delicate courtship so as not to impair the relationship conducted with neither lustful crudity, nor yet hesitancy. . . . compatibility . . . needs to be discovered before marriage, and with this paradoxically we are all faced, either to risk it . . . in premarital anticipation, or come to terms with it after."[20]

The wisdom of folksong "is unhypocritical, profound, and essentially life-promoting: it is mature. It seeks a positive hold on life. It portrays a genuine community which is adult, and comprehends the wise, the courteous, the erotic and bawdy without apportioning blame to those who suffer or 'go wrong' in any oversimplified form. . . . The folk songs emerge from a people whose bodily life was accepted with satisfaction."[21] In contrast these values are absent from most popular culture, Holbrook asserts, and although summarizing them in this way risks nostalgia for a lost "organic community," they do represent, obviously, important ideals of love, marriage, and identity defined in terms of interpersonal relationships and social living.

In the case of children's creative writing, Holbrook views poetry as "one chief means to self-realization."[22] Employing metaphorical processes inherent in poetry the child is able to explore certain dark areas of existence that would otherwise go unexamined. This process of development includes exposure to "nursery rhyme, saw, hymn, chant, game-rhyme, poem, and creative composition of its own, from nonsense jabber to the languishing poems of the sixth former."[23] It allows children to escape from the isolation of their own world by assuming other roles and participating in the shared experience of the community.

Mature poets order language "consciously" in contrast with the "unconscious" use of language in folksong and children's utterances; thus they "must train" themselves "to cooperate with unconscious phantasy" and this in turn "requires a profound sense of moral responsibility"—which, as Holbrook insists, is anything but the simple undertaking of the moralist who is easily shouted down:

> I hope I will not be taken to mean by "moral" that poetry must be didactic, or that its moral impulses should exhort us to do good. But essential to a civilized people is the constant pondering in the spirit, in the feelings, of the nature of life, of possible patterns of living, possible attitudes to life, possible significances in it—How to live? And poetry is one essential means of maintaining continuity in the pondering and reconsidering in concrete, felt terms this "why?" and "what for?" of human life.[24]

As a creative writer, both poet and novelist, Holbrook himself has been prolific in using the resources of language to explore and extend his understanding of the human condition, and so it is in this capacity that he speaks to us most directly about the contradictory life-conditions that we struggle with every day. In some of his poems, Holbrook pursues the problem of morality, not simply the grieving over a recent death, but in terms of the raw untamed natural world continually breaking in on the carefully constructed world of civilized conventions. In "The Flies," for instance, he juxtaposes art and the reality of physical existence.

> Down by the woods there is not history, nor histology
> There is only the dank moment, the flies biting,
> The frantic itching and flaps that inhibit thought,
> The pointless chasm of mere breathing existence,
> Body and flies at odds, dark hints of night and breaking storm.[25]

The flies evoke all the phenomena of existence that do not fit neatly into place. The integrity of art lies in its immediate confrontation with the complex wholeness of life. It must continually attempt to establish meaning and order while simultaneously avoiding false and easy solutions; still, the solutions which keep out the flies are at best transitory.[26]

To read Holbrook's poetry is to eavesdrop on a personal search for the boundaries of identity, one conducted with an obvious and almost embarrassingly direct honesty. Holbrook himself speaks of the place his poetry has maintained in the midst of his ongoing educational and cultural endeavors:

> Meanwhile I have gone on writing poetry, in the hope that by this discipline I can maintain touch with what Winnicott calls "the true self." If one can listen to one's inward rhythms, then perhaps one can maintain a sense of "what it is to be human," and cherish that, in oneself and others. I write so often about family life because I believe that its turmoil enforces upon one an uncompromising confrontation with "inner reality." So, I have sometimes written about the world seen through the downy film of a baby's hair. Seen this way, it looks, I believe, no larger than life, but yet hopeful—since one discovers that the essential yearning in everyone is to survive, and to realize the possibilities they have within them.[27]

This quest for his personal humanity is carried out with a characteristically restless energy and enthusiasm. But the vision that reflects Holbrook's own roots is essentially a rural and domestic one, and this naturally places the created voice outside of the mainstream of popular modes, the shrieks and cries of the very public private voices of much of modern poetry. By acting as an important source of confirmation and affirmation, Holbrook's poems, as evidence of his symbol-making power at work, have helped to keep his own "center" together and his love flowing. Because the symbolic processes inherent in poetry have played such a significant role in his attempt to fathom the transitory nature of human experience, Holbrook believes that poetry should be central to everyone's education. In his own use of poetry to "make sense" out of living, Holbrook has enacted on a personal level what the moral concerns of English might be.

Creativity and Reparation

The English program Holbrook envisioned, and personally worked toward whenever he was involved with children in a classroom, has at its center *creativity*, "which is the approach to inner dynamics through symbolism, as a primary preoccupation of human beings in the preservation of identity."[28] In "The Wizard and the Critical Flame," Holbrook expands on this notion of creativity by considering "implications about moral growth from the work of D. W. Winnicott." The central work Holbrook draws upon is "Morals and Education," a lecture Winnicott gave in 1962, reaffirming the first principle of moral education: "moral education is no substitute for love."[29] Here Winnicott is emphasizing that the first stage in developing a moral sense involves the facilitating environment (proper mothering) that allows the child to gain a feeling of reliability and consistency. Winnicott emphasizes, however, that this inner maturity—constituting trust—is not implanted; rather, it is dynamically developed as the self grows amid the stimuli of inherited cultural surroundings. Winnicott tells, for example, of a father

> who refused to allow his daughter to meet any fairy story, or any idea such as that of a witch or a fairy, or of a prince, because he wanted his child to have only a personal personality; the poor child was being asked to start again with the building up of the ideas and the artistic achievements of the centuries. This scheme did not work.[30]

The point is decisive as Winnicott ends his lecture:

> By the time the child is growing up towards an adult state the accent is no longer on the moral code that we hand on; the accent has passed over to that more positive thing, the storehouse of man's cultural achievement. And, instead of moral education we introduce to the child the opportunity for being creative that the practice of the arts and the practice of living offers to all those who do not copy and comply but who genuinely grow to a way of personal self-expression.[31]

Creativity, in Winnicott's terms, acknowledges that children are "going concerns," that moral development, with its goal of mature adult dependency, only occurs when the child's inner world is permitted to transact with "the storehouse of man's cultural achievement."

Holbrook extends this central contention of Winnicott's to teachers:

> Our role is that of fostering a life flame which is already going, and this we can do by offering the child all kinds of cultural resources which are "lying around" in our civilisation. These he will make use

of as he chooses, as he finds them relevant or not, to take his personal culture and employ them there, in the quest for an identity. Many of these artefacts will be the products of man's reason: but many will be symbolic and mythological expressions of "inner reality," including both bodily existence, and the signs and meanings of emotion, of meeting, and relationship, to use Buber's terms.[32]

As children grow within the family and outward from it, they experience a primary need to participate in these creative acts of the imagination. These processes allow children to accept the hate and destructiveness felt from within and thus make "reparation in such a way as to embrace and modify these," for as Melanie Klein demonstrated, the inner world continually utilizes fantasy situations in positive ways;[33] this in contrast to Freud's viewing fantasy only in terms of deprivation and wish-fulfillment. This reparation makes the child (adult) feel more "integrated" and is "the basis of personal richness and fulfillment."[34] Furthermore, as Holbrook continues, this "reparation" should be an integral part of the child's schooling:

> In the school situation in which a sympathetic adult is being "given" reparative creative effort by the child, the essence of what is happening is a symbolic engagement with "destructive impulses and ideas" within. Creativity belongs to the effort to exert love over hate, by coming to terms with one's own human nature, including its weaknesses. In this way education can become ... a contribution to peace by the engagement with hate towards establishing a balance which helps resolve aggression. That is, creativity reduces the likelihood of aggression being used at the expense of others as a means to establish identity when the individual feels weak and threatened with annihilation, depersonalization or inanition. The individual who has found satisfaction in creativity has learnt that gains over these fears can be achieved by exploring the "inner space" of his own humanness.[35]

Symbolic processes of communication with oneself, whereby individuals seek order in, and come to terms with, dynamics in their personality, lie at the core of the creativity Holbrook proposes. He finds support for this position not only among the British psychoanalysts who pioneered "object-relations" theory, but also in other sources such as Marian Milner's *On Not Being Able to Paint*, and in the work of Susanne Langer, whom he quotes in "Creativity in the English Programme":

> there is a primary need in man ... the *need of symbolization*. The symbol-making function is ... the fundamental process of his mind,

and goes on all the time. Sometimes we are aware of it, sometimes we merely find its results, and realize that certain experiences have passed through our brains and have been digested there.[36]

Symbolization is used by the individual (both consciously and unconsciously) to work on problems of both the inner and the outer world. Any English program that denies this personal "need of symbolization" by dealing with only the "larger" practical concerns of a subject matter will, Holbrook asserts, achieve little; the child's basic struggle for identity must be the first concern of English. Moreover, because Holbrook also recognizes "that it is possible for forms of symbolic utterance to have a harmful effect by seeming to confirm primitive fears, and inculcating primitive solutions"[37] to the problem of living, the symbolization process itself must be connected to positive values and meaningful relationships with others.

Although many things contribute to foster the inner lives of children as they grow toward maturity—family love, social intimacy, confirming experiences with external reality, participation in artistic processes—English can aid in this growth because of what should be its fundamental concern for language, for the word, the medium not only of all education, and of thought and feeling, but also the chief mode for extending and deepening the individual's perception of inner reality while she continues to probe outer reality. Yet, as Holbrook notes, English can only function where healthy development is already taking place; it is no substitute for primary interpersonal attachments:

> But we can only achieve this [reparation] at all if we are "healthy" up to a point (which is the point of being able to be "usefully depressed"). If we are not integrated, then we can achieve integration only very slowly. Even our most successful creative achievements do not "stand for health itself." That is, creativity by way of "true reparation" can do a great deal for us, but even the most satisfying creativity has only a minute and slow effect on the intractable area of the "inner world," and if there are crippled elements there they will remain so, unless some profoundly effective therapeutic relationship is experienced, as in psychoanalysis. We are here up against the intractability of psychic reality, even while recognising that symbolism is the means by which this reality is sustained in its viability and growth, in normal individuals.[38]

Nevertheless, "with most people, effort made by normal symbolic creativity is enough to maintain integration, to preserve a sense of identity, and to feel real."[39]

Holbrook has richly illustrated the importance of creativity for the inner life by providing throughout his writings numerous examples of how children use words, their own and others', to work on psychic ontological problems. In one poem, for instance, 12-year-old Florence invests a tree with symbolic significance.

> The lilac tree stood over the gate
> Its young leafs moved in the breeze
> The little green flowers not probly out
> Heafely ladan it sways this way and that
> Soon my little lilac tree we'll be out
> Each day it gets whiter and whiter brighter and brighter
> Very soon it's like a crown.
> A crown worn by an angle
> An angle in white the best to be seen.[40]

The aspirations here are expressed more metaphorically and less self-consciously than in some bald utterance such as, "I hope to grow into a beautiful woman." The teacher, of course, should not second-guess the child; rather she should be attempting to see what the poem, in fact, means to the child. If "creative" poems such as Florence's are to be written in the classroom, feelings will need to flow naturally, and any adult who has ever worked openly with children in such a way understands that "creative" expression will emerge endlessly, even while it will not all be of the same quality or significance.

Similarly, as Holbrook argues in "Creativity and Education," reading literature "engages children with great subtlety in psychic problems which are eminently theirs."[41] He considers *Charlotte's Web* by E. B. White, for example, as offering in manageable form the important themes of death and continuity. Regarding the opening in which Fern identifies with the runt pig about to be slaughtered, Holbrook remarks:

> We can see why children are at once gripped by such an opening: They too are small and weak. They know too well what lurks behind the phrase "do away with it," because they have known how in phantasy "the object disappears when not wanted." They know, in phantasy, a terrible talion father who threatens to do away with them. Will they "amount" to "anything"? Are they good enough to survive?: the problem now is to persuade the father to be far more human than the talion one—which Fern manages to do.[42]

Just as Fern with the help of Charlotte the spider saves the pig (the "weak" self threatened with extinction), so children who can identify with the experience of these characters have the opportunity of symbolically facing the guilt and anxiety associated with death because they have at times wished (internally) to annihilate their own persecuting object. This is a tenuous step toward maturity and one's realized humanity:

> such a really creative book helps the child, by its symbolism, to feel greater inward strength—to overcome the feelings of fear associated with the destructiveness of the father and fear of death of the mother. It is "real," and so brings relief. It humanizes (as Batman doesn't) and reassures, leads toward a sense of continuity, and gives a feeling of resources and strength of identity, despite the destructiveness in the world and in oneself.[43]

The process Holbrook points to here is essentially intuitive and indirect; a child never says, "Now it's time to work through my death anxiety!" but the danger of such explicitness exists when adults misconstrue the true methods of creativity. Again Winnicott's notion of the "facilitating environment" helps us to see what is involved in the dynamics of psychic growth: things are *allowed* to be worked through in a culturally stimulating environment; they are not forced or compelled. If left solely to their own devices, children will not reach maturity in life (or in the English classroom); however, neither will the positive (moral) values of personal symbolism affect the child's growth if creativity becomes translated into dominance, regulation, and rational consciousness. The creative work Holbrook advocates, "can only be spontaneous, and the teacher works best when he works with opportunities as they arise."[44] In this sense the teacher must be willing to tolerate many kinds of behavior:

> A teacher who can trust human nature and "natural" morality can afford to "hold the ring" for self-exploration, and self-organization, through creative work. I tried to suggest in *English for the Rejected* how this could be done, without rejecting children for "wicked" utterance or disturbed utterance, or for anti-social behaviour, and without moralising. I believe there can be in such an approach an implicit high valuation of human nature, and a respect for the natural ordering processes of the human psyche. Such high valuation and respect often seem to me strangely absent from "religious instruction." As Winnicott says, such manifestations as moralizing may merely convey to the child that its parents or teachers may lack "confidence in the processes of human nature and are frightened of the unknown."[45]

Furthermore, creativity is never solely a means of facilitating "self-expression"; rather, it seeks to establish "links between the civilization which is growing in each child with the inheritance of civilization on the shelves of libraries and in the English tongue itself."[46] Thus the continuing task of English (and the school) must be both individual and community oriented.

Unfinished Business

Holbrook's study of psychoanalysis and phenomenology proved to be crucially influential in his formulation of a non-authoritarian moral approach to English because it allowed him to find a deeper basis for his intuitive judgments of what happens in children's creative work. Besides refining the connections between therapeutic theory and "creativity" in English, his educational writings—from *English for Maturity: English in the Secondary School* (1961) to *Education and Philosophical Anthropology: Toward a New View of Man for the Humanities and English* (1987)—have attempted to influence educational policy by exposing the "anti-life" aspects of contemporary acquisitive society as they tend to shape negatively both children's growth and the school curriculum and by providing materials and teaching strategies to aid English teachers faced daily with translating theory into the reality of encounters with children.

Never one to avoid or deny the mess and muddle, the frustrations and conflicts, of every child's struggle to develop a meaningful and positive sense of reality, Holbrook has remained cautious about any easy solutions to the profound problems of human development, even while he has joined, without rhetorical restraint, the great debate against what he sees as the philistine outlook in education spawned by the stranglehold of trendy commercial interests—and the reason why his message so often seems to fall on deaf ears. As he wrote in 1967: "I had come to distrust the self who made such sweeping statements about the beneficial relationship between English work and personal growth, yet on the other hand I wasn't prepared to give ground to those who wished to cling to beliefs that the English teacher's work had nothing to do with the development of individual personality, but with a subject or 'structure.'"[47] Yet despite his despair with the increasing trend toward a vocational ethos in the schools and the bald political manipulation of educational policy for narrow "conservative" ideological ends, Holbrook has remained an unyielding champion for the moral value of the arts, because they develop "that richness of the individual being which releases sympathy and creative energy in community"[48] and do not simply teach students to be dissatisfied with their environment or pander to any solipsistic forms of self-expression.

Through his insistence that literature genuinely matters, Holbrook encourages English teachers to create opportunities for students to imaginatively dwell within the possible symbolic worlds evoked by the words on the page, both their own and those of others. For it is these words finally that chart the very real contradictions of human existence that each of us must come to terms with. Still, just as we cannot deny the wisdom of Holbrook's educational analysis, we cannot escape the serious challenge it continues to pose for us: if children's lives are to develop positively in environments that celebrate the reparative power of the arts as a crucial way of human knowing and being, how are teachers to proceed without in some fundamental way working to change those conditions which serve to exacerbate the "anti-life" characteristics of western culture?

Notes

1. *Culture and Anarchy*, in *The Complete Works of Matthew Arnold*, vol. V, ed. R. H. Super (Ann Arbor: University of Michigan Press, 1965), p. 95.
2. "The Function of Criticism at the Present Time," in *The Complete Works*, vol. III, p. 271.
3. "Wordsworth," in *The Norton Anthology of English Literature*, vol. II, ed. Abrams et al. (New York: W. W. Norton, 1962), pp. 939–40.
4. *Cross Commission Report* (May 1886) in Paul Nash, *Culture and the State: Matthew Arnold and Continental Education* (New York: Teachers College Press, 1966), p. 245.
5. Personal correspondence from the author, 30 June 1969.
6. Ibid.
7. Ibid.
8. Quoted in *Contemporary Authors*, 21–22, ed. Barbara Harte and Carolyn Riley (Detroit: Gale Research Company, 1969), p. 312.
9. Personal correspondence from the author, 19 July 1968.
10. Lionel Trilling, *Beyond Culture* (New York: Viking Press, 1965), p. 151.
11. "Poetic vs. Rhetorical Exegesis," *Sewanee Review* 52 (April 1944), p. 272.
12. Ibid., p. 276.
13. F. R. Leavis, "Advanced Verbal Education," *Scrutiny* 6 (September 1937), p. 214.
14. F. R. Leavis, "Mr. Eliot and Lawrence," *Scrutiny* 18 (June 1951), pp. 69–70.
15. Ibid., p. 72.
16. F. R. Leavis, *D. H. Lawrence: Novelist* (New York: Alfred A. Knopf, 1956), p. 116.
17. F. R. Leavis, *Mass Civilisation and Minority Culture*, Minority Pamphlet No. 1 (Cambridge: Gordon Fraser, 1930), p. 4.

18. In F. R. Leavis, *Education and the University* (London: Chatto and Windus, 1943), p. 138.

19. All material quoted in this paragraph is contained in personal correspondence from the author, 30 June 1969.

20. David Holbrook, *Llareggub Revisited* (London: Bowes and Bowes, 1962), pp. 45–6.

21. Ibid., p. 46.

22. Ibid., p. 41.

23. Ibid., p. 42.

24. Ibid., p. 72.

25. David Holbrook, *Old World, New World* (London: Rapp and Whiting, 1969), p. 42.

26. Like Leavis, Holbrook has avoided theory and, despite an annoying tendency to be too quick with categories and labels, he has stood very much for the concrete experience of particulars. In this regard, Holbrook's sense of the contradictory and impermanent nature of human existence is remarkably compatible with the thinking of Mikhail Bakhtin who "held self-hood to be intrinsically 'dialogical': the self cannot be understood or expressed except in relation to an audience whose real or imagined responses continually shape the way in which we define ourselves" (Aileen Kelly, "Revealing Bakhtin," *New York Review of Books*, 24 September 1992). Such a position encourages an individual's moral freedom since each of us is seen as being responsible for our ongoing self-determination; this is seldom a popular view, however, because of the way all too many social institutions insinuate their authoritarian doctrines into our lives.

27. *Poetry Book Society Bulletin* 63 (Christmas 1969), p. 2.

28. David Holbrook, "Creativity in the English Programme," in *Creativity in English*, ed. Geoffrey Summerfield (Champaign, Ill.: NCTE, 1968), p. 7.

29. D. W. Winnicott, *The Maturational Processes and the Facilitating Environment* (London: Hogarth Press, 1965), p. 97.

30. Ibid., p. 101.

31. Ibid., p. 105.

32. David Holbrook, "The Wizard and the Critcal Flame," *Moral Education*, I, 1 (1969), p. 23.

33. See, for example, J. D. Sutherland, "Object-relations Theory and the Conceptual Model of Psychoanalysis," *British Journal of Medical Psychology* 36 (1963), p. 113.

34. Ibid., p. 29.

35. Ibid.

36. Susanne Langer, *Philosophy in a New Key* (Cambridge: Harvard University Press, 1957), pp. 40–1.

37. Holbrook, "The Wizard," p. 31.

38. Ibid., p. 29.

39. Ibid.

40. David Holbrook, *The Exploring Word* (Cambridge: Cambridge University Press, 1967), p. 131. For a seminar discussion of this poem see pp. 216–32 in the same volume.

41. David Holbrook, "Creativity and Education," *Universities Quarterly* 21 (September 1967), p. 473.

42. Ibid., p. 481. ("Talion is from the Latin *lex talionis:* retributory, revengeful, of an 'eye for an eye' kind": Holbrook's note.)

43. Ibid., p. 482.

44. Holbrook, "Creativity in the English Programme," p. 14.
45. Holbrook, "The Wizard," p. 34.
46. Holbrook, "Creativity in the English Programme," p. 14.
47. David Holbrook, *English for Maturity,* 2nd ed. (Cambridge: Cambridge University Press, 1967), p. ix.
48. Ibid., p. 18.

The Tradition of Poetic Humanism and the Teaching of the Arts

Peter Abbs

The Tradition of Poetic Humanism

David Holbrook's various and once influential writings on education from *English for Maturity* (1961) to *English for Meaning* (1979) belong to a particular English tradition of educational thinking. The more time passes, the more easy it is to see this tradition clearly; it has a moral vision of education and a vision of the English teacher as a cultural transmitter, an agent of the articulate life of consciousness in an age in which civilization itself is in question. This tradition can be seen to run from Blake and Coleridge to Matthew Arnold, from Matthew Arnold to George Sampson, from Sampson to F. R. Leavis and Denys Thompson, and from Leavis and Thompson to David Holbrook, Raymond Williams, and Richard Hoggart, and then to a small group of writers (both educationists and critics) still working and extending, in the most hostile circumstances, the tradition today. It has never been called the tradition of English poetic humanism but, all in all, I think that would be a fitting title.

It is certainly true that the tradition has much in common with classical humanism. Matthew Arnold's "disinterested play of consciousness" sounds very classical yet it has qualities which both distinguish it and make it distinctive; for example, its emphasis on the exploratory rather than the mimetic nature of literature, its commitment to intuition and imagination with its concomitant scepticism, if not hostility, to the power of reason and abstract thinking. Along with these unclassical virtues there is a further unclassical commitment, namely to the English language, as shaped by its speakers and particularly by the Authorized Version of the Bible, Shakespeare, and the truly significant writers through the centuries who have made English a subtle language of resonance and sustaining echo. As Leavis put it: English is "a product of an immemorial *sui generis* collaboration on the part of its speakers and writers. It is alive with promptings and potentialities, and the great creative writer shows his genius in the way he responds."[1]

The titles of books are nearly always indicative of their central preoccupations. Thus if we glance at some of the titles of David Holbrook's educational work—*The Exploring Word, The Secret Places, English for Meaning, English for Maturity*—we can immediately sense something of the poetic humanism I am trying to define. In the classroom the English teacher, according to this vision, is there to release in his pupils the exploring word, which has power to enter the secret places of their lives to disclose their latent meaning and, in so doing, to induce a greater maturity of understanding, judgment or, another key word in much of the tradition of poetic humanism, discrimination. My use of the word poetic in this context is, of course, broad. Poetic, first of all, is best understood negatively as the antithesis to all that is prosaic, literal, mechanical, factual, all that remains untouched and unredeemed by the transformative powers of individual sensibility and transpersonal imagination. But, of course, it also has a positive charge of meaning and this involves a profound recognition of, to quote Wordsworth, "a dim and undetermined sense of unknown modes of being"[2] together with the apprehension that we are implicated in a world which requires our recognition, our contemplation, our symbolic acts to complete it.

The Wordsworthian sense of dim apprehensions—of other forms of knowing, relating and being—is defended throughout Holbrook's educational writing. What is involved here is a recognition of preconceptual, almost bodily processes of rhythmic half-articulation and absorbed reverie which are often the foundations of creative work in the arts and which need to be understood and respected by the teacher. In *English for the Rejected*, Holbrook defended what he called "the poetic function" and defined it as "the capacity to explore and perceive by the exercise of the whole mind and all kinds of apprehensions, not only intellectual."[3] This entails a more refined epistemology than we have at the grim moment in our schools and one that I will return to later in this essay. The second positive connotation of poetic (closely related to this notion of various apprehensions of meaning and value) is best illustrated—for it cannot be finally argued or fully conceptualized—by a quotation from Leavis's scathing polemic against C. P. Snow. Referring to that lack of depth which marks civilizations when creative questioning has atrophied, Leavis went on to defend what he saw as the crucial value of literature:

> In coming to terms with great literature we discover what at bottom we really believe. What for—what ultimately for ? what do men live by—the questions work and tell at what I can only call a religious depth of thought and feeling. Perhaps, with my eye on the adjective, I may just recall for you Tom Brangwen, in *The Rainbow*, watching by the fold in lambing-time under the night-sky: 'He knew he did not belong to himself'.[4]

Religious here clearly does not denote any doctrinal belief but rather the apprehension of *being engaged beyond oneself*, being bound into something larger than the ego. The connection established, with a Tolstoyan intensity, is the connection between art and living, between aesthetics (not a word used in the tradition I am defining) and ethics, between book and belief—a connection which during the last decade has become deeply unfashionable.

One other characteristic of the tradition of poetic humanism must be mentioned. It is *oppositional* in nature. It is the anxious and, at times, febrile voice of critical dissent. In this tradition both teacher and artist have little choice but to act as the alert critics of their own society, of a society driven predominantly by material and mechanical imperatives. Produce—consume; consume—produce. In *English for the English*, a seminal book in the tradition of poetic humanism, a book which is consciously repeated and rephrased throughout Holbrook's early volumes, George Sampson is emphatic about the need to prepare pupils not for their jobs but *against* their jobs, not for earning a living but for living itself.[5] Once again these have become deeply unfashionable commitments in our own conformist and consumer age. This resistance to the dominant society and its standard iconography (to advertising, to art as entertainment packaged in terms of extrinsic marketing rather than intrinsic meanings) permeates poetic humanism. It gave birth to the first critical classroom reader on mass culture. (*Culture and Environment* by F. R. Leavis and Denys Thompson was published in 1933). The general nature of the cultural challenge and the implications for the teacher of English are brought out in the following characteristic passage from *English for Maturity*:

> What is missing from the music of our young people, from their entertainment, and from their social life together is the germ of positive vitality. They have few cultural sources of succour to develop posi-

tive attitudes to life, and develop human sympathy. The home is afflicted by the influence of the mass-media, by the pressure of advertising and by the new illiteracy. As Richard Hoggart points out, such traditions as standing by one another, or of passing on traditional wisdom, have declined in working people's lives under these influences. Thus it remains to the school—and mainly the secondary modern school—to supply new positives.[6]

Ironically, as the whole of the media in Britain has become more and more subject to mindless market forces and the ideology of profits, in the last decade this voice of critical opposition inside the life of schools and universities has become more and more a hesitant whisper, a half suppressed stammer expressing an almost taboo notion of the student as active critic and creative agent, rather than satisfied client and well-adapted consumer. The poetic tradition of humanism is a tradition of dissident thinking, of moral and prophetic formulation, against established values and the general drift of collective life in our times. It is a tradition which, like any other, has its own canonical texts: its key manifesto was Matthew Arnold's *Culture and Anarchy*, its selected work of polemical fiction was Charles Dickens's *Hard Times* and its favored conversion narrative was that given in Chapter 5 of John Stuart Mill's *Autobiography* where, under the title of *A Crisis in My Mental History One Stage Onward*, the author described his discovery of Wordsworth's poetry and outlined its transformative effects upon his own excessively regimented and overanalytical consciousness.

Some Limitations in the Tradition

These quickly etched and somewhat unsubtle descriptions are intended merely to indicate some of the basic features of the tradition to which David Holbrook's work substantially belongs. A number of sharp and telling criticisms can be brought against that tradition. It often held—particularly in its Leavisite version—an all but whimsical view of a lost organic society and of a dignified oral culture which was envisaged as existing before the social alienation engendered by the Industrial Revolution. It was, for the most part, peculiarly insular in reference and disposition, failing to encounter the whole mental and imaginative life of Europe, especially with regard to literature before Chaucer (virtually nothing on Homer, Virgil, Dante, Petrarch) and any literature after D. H. Lawrence. It had a number of blind spots (for example, it missed the distinctive genius of Virginia Woolf) and it was poor at seeing the other arts disciplines as the essential, interacting and equal partners of literature—thus critical and celebratory work on drama, dance, music, art, and architecture is minimal. Something of the *verbal* bias of the tradition comes out well in Matthew Arnold's much quoted phrase "the best that has been thought and known," where the emphasis falls on the intellectual and cognitive and not on what has been (like architecture) constructed or apprehended through the nonverbal, nonconceptual symbolism of dance, mime, music, paint, and sculpture. And as I have implied, *even within literature* the range was often narrow and puritanical in tone. The tradition of poetic humanism was also, at least in the case of Leavis, absurdly negative about the value of philosophy and the place of creative work within the program of English studies. In spite of all the rhetoric about creative engagement, Leavis seemed to rely all but exclusively on the well-worn academic essay for the evaluation of his students.

In a number of important respects the work of Holbrook served to correct some of these severe limitations (as did the work of Raymond Williams and Richard Hoggart, especially with regard to its political and historical limitations). As a serious poet and an amateur painter, Holbrook knew intuitively from his own practice the value of imaginative work and the way in which it immediately connects the maker with a tradition of achieved work and tested technique. He was, thus, with an inner authority, able to insist on the importance of seeing pupils and students as artists and explorers in their own right. He was able to broaden the program of activity so that it included creative activity—poetry, drawing, art, drama—and a broader recognition of the multiform ways in which feeling and impulse can find expressive configuration. In this, as we shall see, he was aided by the work of psychoanalysis and philosophical anthropology. And here, again, we can detect in Holbrook's writing a dramatic expansion of the Arnold-Leavis tradition, a courageous moving out into new ground, an opening up to other humanist traditions of enquiry and speculation.

Psychoanalysis and the Creative Act

After *English for Maturity* Holbrook sought for a more comprehensive understanding of the origins of symbolism and the creative act which makes it possible. In *Human Hope and the Death*

Instinct (another key title neatly encapsulating the dialectical preoccupations of nearly all his discursive work on symbol and culture) Holbrook evaluated the post-Freudian psychoanalytical theories of Melanie Klein, W. R. D. Fairbairn, Harry Guntrip, D. W. Winnicot (whose influence on Holbrook was to be as great, if not greater, than that of Leavis) and many others. He argues in that volume that their work demonstrated that Freud's underlying assumption that man was an animal creating culture symptomatically out of sublimation was misconceived. What was more true, and amply demonstrated by the work of the post-Freudians, was that man had *a primary need to create culture and to seek relationship and meaning in a community of being, first established in the profound matrix of the mother-child relationship.* Here then in object-relations psychoanalysis there seemed to exist another tradition which offered a biological and psychological justification of many of the values and practices of the poetic humanist tradition. The discoveries of the psychoanalysts, particularly the formulations of D. W. Winnicot, grounded it, and, at the same time, gave it a broader base. It took the debates of embattled literary coteries out of privileged enclaves and placed them in the daily dynamics of ordinary life and the general human struggle to secure a cultural shape for an inherently precarious existence. In *English for the Rejected* Holbrook talked about the "nourishing of imaginative power, and psychic vitality by sympathy and creative work in all children not excepting those who are least endowed with intellectual capacities."[7]

The conceptions of psychoanalysis offered—or so it must have seemed to Holbrook—a number of principles on which the Arnoldian tradition could more firmly stand and more easily move out into the democratic life of culture, unencumbered by academic exclusiveness or any kind of literary preciousness. Later, he was to join to his evolving argument various notions taken from phenomenology, existentialism and philosophical anthropology. It has to be said, at once and unambiguously, that in creating this broader orientation within the tradition of poetic humanism, David Holbrook was often less than convincing. Too often the style of writing deteriorates and forfeits the lucidity of the earlier work. Many sentences become clotted with jargon or, if not with jargon, with regimental lists of approved names. Too much of the argument is not made through logic or example but simply through quotation: *as Winnicot says: as Marjorie Grene says; as Buytendijk says.* Too often, the interpretation of symbols and expressive images, inherently polymorphic, are too simple or too reductive. Indeed, it would seem a characteristic difficulty of a psychoanalytical approach to art that it tends to narrow the radically plural life of metaphor in the interests of its own more limited and more focused view, whereas metaphor in art frequently means more than what can ever be discursively said about it.

One can only surmise that a sense of messianic urgency overruled the prudent interior voices of the author which call for revision, for selection, for that individual shaping of language which makes an argument (whatever its content) at first reading compelling to the receptive mind. The result was a torrent of work—much of it diffuse and repetitive—which alienated many of those who, if the work had been more accomplished, would have been the first to welcome and support it. Yet it is important to recognise that within the work there *are* fine moments of analysis (the analysis of Edward Thomas's *Old Man* and *Tall Nettles* in terms of philosophical anthropology in *English for Meaning* is, for example, both moving and entirely convincing;[8]) and that, furthermore, the ambition to embrace these broad philosophical and psychological movements *was*, potentially, productive and illuminating. Holbrook's attempt was, perhaps, not altogether dissimilar from that of Coleridge to relate the poetic insights of English Romanticism to the architectonic philosophy of Kant at the beginning of the nineteenth century. It can also be no accident that one of the best art critics of the last two decades, Peter Fuller, sought to connect aesthetic experience to psychoanalysis using, once again, the seminal work of D. W. Winnicott. It must, surely, be the case that any criticism which becomes highly specialized, which no longer refers art to the life of relationship, reflection and encounter is not only bound towards intellectual sclerosis but, more importantly, misses what art is most essentially about: the intimate elaboration of consciousness and understanding. To explore the dynamics which inform the creative act can only remind us, again and again, of this urgent existential element. In this respect, in spite of its blemishes and bludgeonings, Holbrook's work of grounding poetic humanism by connecting it with other forms of inquiry has been more than challenging, it has forged an essential key for further work across the arts and, even more broadly, across the philosophy of education. To conclude this tribute I would like to elaborate the way in which the philosophers and thinkers, whom Holbrook has labored to bring into the arena of educational thinking, can sharpen and animate the way in which we understand the nature of knowledge, especially in relationship to the teaching of the arts.

On the Primacy of Culture

David Holbrook has insisted that all those committed to the creative teaching of English and the arts should attend to the work of Marjorie Grene who claimed that the whole structure of the embryo, and, indeed, the whole rhythm of its growth, was directed, from first to last, to the emergence of a culture-dwelling animal.[9] Certainly, it would seem that a propensity to symbolize—a propensity to create image, narrative, and expressive configuration is innate. Our involuntary acts of dreaming (for we do not *learn* to dream) demonstrate as much; and in the dream one can identify many of the elements later given expression in the collective art forms of mankind: narrative, character, and image, for example. It is as if at birth we already possess a number of *genres* for shaping and telling "reality." Anthony Stevens, in his study of archetypes, has spoken of the infant's ability to find its mother's face as depending on the capacity to rediscover in reality the object which corresponds to what is present in the child's imagination.[10] Such thinking, while deeply alien to the fashionable theories propounded by Deconstructionists and Post-Modernists, parallels that of both a number of philosophical biologists—one thinks not only of Marjorie Grene but also of Mary Midgley[11] and many ethologists (particularly Konrad Lorenz)[12] who sought to provide a biological origin for the a priori categories of Kantian philosophy. Culture, from this perspective, is a wholly natural phenomenon and the analogical imagination a biological gift which can only be released and developed, in all its potential variety, within a particular society, within a specific culture and span of historical time.

As Holbrook persuasively argued, this conception of life has many implications for education and the teaching of the arts. To begin with: if we are *born* cultural beings we do not have to be *made* cultural members of society; nor are we ever mere "vessels" or "tabulae rasae"; blank sheets for professionals to write on. It cannot be the unambiguous function of education to socialize children or to transfer "communication skills" (as the current jargon would have it), simply because children already possess innate social aptitudes as they also possess the ability to create images, narratives, and the rhythmic patterns of speech. These are not new insights but they remain axiomatic and now gain a further weight by the recent evidence, tabulation, and explication of biologists and philosophers. Furthermore, during the current takeover of education in England by a handful of politicians and a leaden medley of managers and bureaucrats, they have a further and somewhat daunting urgency. For if this view of the child as cultural agent, born with the schemas and aptitudes necessary for cultural creation, is true, then the concepts of education as "delivery" and "socialization" are seriously mistaken and can only dangerously repress the deep inner sources of creativity. That is the negative side; that is the indictment of the educational status quo in England. The positive side is an affirmation of teaching as the social art which culturally connects, releases, amplifies, develops. Good teaching becomes the task of relating; of bringing together the natural form-seeking energies of the individual pupil *and* the inherited cultural forms of creation and enquiry; real teaching seeks an encounter between the two and their constant refinement and expansion. Educational experience, thus, lies neither exclusively with the individual (it is not "self-expression") nor with the culture (it is not indoctrination) but in that vast, conscious and unconscious, web of categories, metaphors, narratives, arguments, icons, and interpretations which draw them indivisibly together creating ever new possibilities of thinking, imagining, speculating, apprehending, and judging. This view might be usefully called, in contrast to the progressive and the traditional view, the symbolist conception of education. But the symbolist view of education not only recognizes education as encounter, it also seeks to broaden our understanding of the nature and range of symbolic activity. Holbrook has urged us to consider the arguments of Ernst Cassirer and Susanne Langer, for it is their work particularly which has created the necessary terms for this broader recognition.

Art as a Form of Cognition

It was one of the major contributions of philosophical anthropology to demonstrate analytically that there are many forms of coherent understanding and that conceptual thinking is but one way of coming to knowledge or, rather, one *kind* of (provisional) knowing. Yet the idea that knowledge is essentially a matter of concepts has held such sway in western civilization that other forms of intellection, through, for example, analogy, through dance, through the sequencing of sound, and through narrative, have become widely misconstrued. For the most part, the arts in education have been conceived during the last hundred years as activities which are therapeutic and cathartic, to do with private release and personal discharge of emotion, as now they are becoming the means of leisure, entertainment, and relaxation (linked to tourism), rather than acts of attention concerned with the great task of understanding human existence. It is true that the bogus notion of art as self-expression has retreated and withered in the last few years, yet still the National Curriculum embodies a very inadequate understanding of the arts—for only two of the six[13] have been elected as full foundation subjects (the visual arts and music) and these, unlike all the other foundation subjects, terminate at the age of fourteen. Yet, as Holbrook claimed thirty years ago, 'Metaphor is not, as we were taught at school, a figure of speech. In language it is the means by which we extend our awareness of experience into new realms.'[14] And the same is true, one must quickly add, of the metaphor created by the nonverbal arts.

Susanne Langer's work has been particularly eloquent in establishing the pluralistic nature of knowledge. In all symbolism, she argued, there is an act of intellection, an import of meaning. "Wherever a symbol operates there is meaning"[15] she claimed and went on to declare that she was after "a theory of mind whose key note is the symbolic function ... whose problem is the morphology of significance."[16] The symbolism of the artist is not merely about the expression of an emotion but about *its conception*. In *Feeling and Form*, her seminal book on the arts, Langer put her position as follows:

> How can we capture, hold and handle feelings so that their content may be made conceivable and presented to our consciousness in universal form, without being understood in the strict sense, ie by means of concept. The answer is: we can do it by creating objects wherein the feelings we seek to hold are so definitely embodied that any subject confronted with those objects and emphatically disposed towards them cannot but experience a non-sensuous apperception of the feelings in question. Such objects are called works of art and by art we designate the activity that produces them.[17]

One might want to take issue with a number of specific words in this passage—why, for example, allow the "strict sense" of understanding to be determined by "concepts" and why not a *sensuous* "apperception" of feeling?—but, even so, the central hypothesis is loud and clear. Art embodies the invisible logic of the life of feeling and sentience and, in so doing, brings it to conception and consciousness. Once this is clearly recognized, the common educational distinctions between cognition and affect, between meaning and expression, between objective and subjective, between public and private, break down and give way to what would seem a more valid differentiation between kinds of knowledge, between kinds of intelligence, between kinds of symbolic forms, between kinds of public language.

It is on this understanding that it may be possible to build a more coherent philosophy of arts education, and some of the elements of its good practice can still be derived from the best of Holbrook's writing on education. In *English for Maturity*, in defending his approach to creative work in the classroom, he offered the following three principles:

> First, I wanted to encourage the expression of feelings, in an atmosphere in which such expression was regarded as seriously as the expression of facts. I wanted to make the child explore his own feelings, whether he realised he was doing so or not, and to have between him and me—in a public world, outside ourselves—a statement of them.
>
> Secondly, and complementary to the first point, I felt the only way to achieve this expression was by using as stimulants poems, passages, and themes which the child already recognised as means to the depersonalising of his individual emotion—a way to that "third ground" which is a meeting-place between the 'mind' of a community and his own.
>
> Thirdly, I was concerned to maintain attention on the poem or tale as poem or tale: it was assumed between us that the content, the emotions and thought expressed, were to be respected. And if they are to be respected, they must not be taken outside the pattern whereby the child has realised them. This is the reason for the need for emotional sparseness in the poetry lesson—and in the teaching of imaginative composition: to be "emotional" is to betray the child into having to consider explicitly something he could only grasp implicitly.[18]

Thirty years later, they remain good principles and serve to extend Langer's philosophy of art into a classroom practice. What is more, with a few changes, they could be adapted to fit the teaching of the other great art forms. The notion of entering "the third ground," that place where the creative energies of the individual and the creative energies of the culture meet, is here quite crucial. It is precisely this, as I argued earlier, which characterizes the symbolist conception of education.

Creativity and Tradition

Some of the agitated disputes which Holbrook's prolific and uneven writing stirred up—the question as to whether the teacher should or could act as therapist, the question as to whether original work by children should be corrected—did much to eclipse the essential sanity and balance of the approach. It is pertinent to note *now* that Holbrook explicitly attacked the notion of "self-expression" and Herbert Read's notion of "pure expression."

> Creation cannot, I think, be as spontaneous as Sir Herbert suggests: the creation can only be made through technical conventions which because they are involved in a tradition "outside" the individual, provide a kind of control. This "control" is not "suppression;" it may be a means to creation that seems "spontaneous."[19]

Creative fullness of being, he went on to claim, could only be achieved by the obtaining of a tradition. It is precisely this insistence on the paradox of creativity which stands in need of reclamation. No doubt it was this commitment to the collaborative nature of creative symbolism which first drew Holbrook to the writing of D. W. Winnicot. For it was Winnicot who, examining the origins of culture in the interaction between the child and the mother, wrote:

> In any cultural field it is not possible to be original except on a basis of tradition.... the interplay with originality and the acceptance of tradition as a basis for inventiveness seem to me to be just one more example, and a very exciting one, of the interplay between separateness and union."[20]

We find our own voices in and through the voices of others; we find ourselves in and through the reflections of other selves; we become creative individuals the more we become members of a cultural community infinitely larger than the self. In educational activity in the arts we have to recognize the self with all its potentiality (its innate creativity) and the broad inherited culture (that evolving procession of styles, techniques, living works, exemplars). The task is to bring the two into vivid and perpetual conjunction.

It would seem virtually uncontentious to say that those who are now actively shaping the curriculum of our schools are blind to both elements. They neither cherish the creative individual, nor the inherited culture. That is the scandal of the age and it is our predicament. At such a time to lose contact with the work of David Holbrook and the various intellectual schools it brings together, to lose touch with the long tradition of poetic humanism, would be tantamount to losing contact with education itself.

Notes

1. F. R. Leavis. *Thought, Words and Creativity* (London: Chatto and Windus, 1976), p. 27.
2. William Wordsworth. *The Prelude*, Book 1 (1850 version), lines 392–93 (London: Penguin Books, 1971), p. 57.
3. David Holbrook, *English for the Rejected* (Cambridge: Cambridge University Press, 1964), p. 10.
4. F. R. Leavis, *Two Cultures? The Significance of C. P. Snow* (London: Chatto and Windus, 1962), p. 23.
5. See George Sampson *English for the English*, edited by Denys Thompson (Cambridge: Cambridge University Press, 1975), chapter 1.
6. David Holbrook, *English for Maturity* 2nd ed. (Cambridge: Cambridge University Press, 1967), p. 17.
7. Holbrook, *English for the Rejected*, p. 10.
8. See David Holbrook, *English for Meaning* (Windsor: NFER Publishing Company, 1979), chapters 4 and 7.
9. See Marjorie Grene, *Approaches to a Philosophical Biology* (London: Basic Books, 1968).
10. See Anthony Stevens, *Archetype: A Natural History of the Self* (London: Routledge and Kegan Paul, 1982).
11. See, for example, Mary Midgley, *Beast and Man: The Roots of Human Nature* (London: Harvester Press, 1979).
12. See, for example, Konrad Lorenz, *Behind the Mirror: A Search for a Natural History of Human Knowledge* (London: Methuen, 1977).
13. By "the six" here I mean: art, drama, dance, music, film, and literature. These six disciplines of the imagination can be seen to form the generic community of the arts. See particularly, Peter Abbs (ed.), *Living Powers: the Arts in Education* (London: Falmer Press, 1987) and other titles in *The Falmer Press Library on Aesthetic Education*.
14. David Holbrook, *English for Maturity*, p. 69.
15. Susanne Langer, *Philosophy in a New Key* (Cambridge: Harvard University Press, 1980), p. 293.
16. Ibid.
17. Susanne Langer, *Feeling and Form* (London: Routledge and Kegan Paul, 1953); see chapter 3, *The Symbol of Feeling*, pp. 24–41.
18. Holbrook, *English for Maturity*, pp. 114–15.
19. Ibid., pp. 13–14.
20. D. W. Winnicott, *Planning and Reality* (London: Tavistock, 1971), p. 49.

Working on One's Inner World

John Paynter

The Charm of Impossibilities

A full stop at the end of the world. It's a comforting thought; not only shall we not slip off the edge but also things won't come apart. Existence will be *contained*.

Believing that geography could have an authenticated end was always likely to provoke a desire to find it. The Greek navigators of the fourth century before Christ were precise in their description of Ultima Thule: an island of volcanoes, in the northern seas, "six days sail from the Orcades," where day and night were always equal. Whatever the reality they had in mind (Iceland, perhaps?), as a poetic allusion the image still had currency in the early years of the seventeenth century; for example, in a madrigal of Thomas Weelkes:

> Thule, the period of Cosmography,
> Doth vaunt of Hecla, whose sulphurious fire
> Doth melt the frozen clime and thaw the sky;
> Trinacrian Aetnae's flames ascend no higher.
> These things seem wondrous, yet more wondrous I,
> Whose heart with fear doth freeze, with love doth fry.[1]

Although the conceit is primarily that travellers' tales of farthest Thule are as nothing compared with the simultaneous freezing and frying of a lovelorn heart, there could be also a suggestion that the full stop at the end of the world, somewhere over the rainbow, will not be discovered by voyages through the world or even through the universe because that kind of "finality"—answering the ever-present, nagging questions of existence—is actually to be found within oneself; in the "yet more wondrous" inner world of feeling and imagination.

The flow of human history is marked by many powerful symbols of the desire to understand "reality." Columbus's voyages were, in the widest sense, spiritual journeys, as important in that respect as the search for spices, trade routes, and territories; and Neil Armstrong's "one small step for a man, one giant leap for mankind" is clearly confirmation of much more than purely scientific achievement. However far back we trace mankind we find very similar dilemmas being raised by the diversity and temporaneousness of experience. Glimpsing the possibility of a different order somehow, somewhere, "beyond," humanity responds with models of space and time; images of what might be, to make sense of life as it appears to be.

In their technical realization, the immense spaces of the gothic cathedrals offered medieval Christians foretastes of eternity; light filtered through colored glass, the full height of the soaring vault only dimly visible, and yet the whole manifestly controlled by the unshakable strength of the huge stone pillars. Today, the cool objectivity of high-profile technology is just as likely to produce a public reaction which is in large measure "spiritual" or "artistic": multi-million dollar space probes are as much symbols of a graspable and contained universe as were the contrived and fully equipped "worlds" of the Egyptian pyramids, neolithic and iron-age round- and long-barrows, and the Viking burial ships.

Objects and ideas; the examples could be multiplied endlessly. All tell the same story: in our search for an ultimate coherence, what speaks to us—what moves us—is *form;* new structures, the product of imaginative speculation, again and again revealing hitherto unnoticed relationships and "some sense of possibility beyond the words."

A Capacity for Inward Symbolism

In all of this the work of poets, painters, musicians, sculptors, dancers—indeed every kind of creative artist—is crucial, principally because they all try to come to terms with what is sensed, what is felt, rather than with what is merely measured or calculated. Isaiah Berlin[2] described artists as people "blown through" with the spirit of their time and place and society; each work of art conveying "a total human experience, a world." Sigfried Giedion, in *Space, Time and Architecture*[3], reminds us that, but for this, much of our world would "lack all emotional significance" because the artist's chief mission has always been "The opening up of such new realms of feeling." And Wilfrid Mellers shows that there is indeed no end to this activity: the potential is there in each one of us, so that, in a healthy society, all people "should be artists to some extent and in some way, in proportion to their capacity to live creatively."[4]

It is evident now that, in addition to those people we are accustomed to think of as artists, there could be many more who would welcome opportunities to explore their own creative ideas. This is as important for them as being on the receiving end of artistic enterprise. The surprising thing is how long it has taken us to recognize this—and its implications for formal education.

From time to time in the 1920s and 1930s exceptional teachers would find opportunities to present new points of view about the arts in schools.[5] But it wasn't until much later that we began to see a wider professional acknowledgment of the contribution the arts can make to everyone's general education. The 1951 Festival of Britain had successfully punctured the post-war gloom, and, in spite of continuing austerities, heralded a renaissance; at last there was room for innovation and initiative. By the mid-1950s a growing number of teachers who were themselves active as poets or composers or who were working creatively in dance and drama began to question the established methods, and to look for new ways of educating what, twenty years later, Robert Witkin was to call "the intelligence of feeling."[6]

Changing Attitudes

Inevitably there were pockets of suspicion and, perhaps, resentment. Persuasive advocacy was needed; and in David Holbrook we had the pioneer. Although he may not have intended to do so, in effect he spoke for all arts teachers, producing—in *English for Maturity* (1961), *English for the Rejected* (1964) and *The Exploring Word* (1967)—the evidence of children's creativity and the justification for encouraging it in the classroom. The doubters began to be reassured.

In *Children's Writing* (1967) he establishes the universality of the context:

> When anyone is really working on his inner world, he becomes excited—for he is making important discoveries and gains, as between his ego . . . and threatening shadows within. He sees connections and relationships, and possibilities of structures, patterns, richness of content: and in these, joy and beauty. Expression will convey the bodily feelings of experience, and the "inscape" of an inward effort.[7]

Then, bluntly, he addresses the problem:

> The least piece of writing, if the teacher has established the context for proper "giving," will be a "meant" gift. Of course, it depends on what the teacher's attitude is to human beings. If he cannot believe that every human being has an inward need to find himself, in a struggle with love and hate, and between the subjective and objective worlds, then he probably won't get given poetry. But how can anyone read poetry and not see that these problems are universal? Of course, you can deny the whole area with which art deals. A colleague was told by a scientist in his staffroom, "Children from decent homes don't write poetry." This man meant that it was possible to live without "working on one's inner world." But it isn't![8]

For those of us who had been trying to move in new directions *Children's Writing,* with its inspiring Introduction and its unique approach, offered just the encouragement we needed. It was such a surprising book, taking us far beyond anything we might at first have expected from its matter-of-fact subtitle, "A sampler for student teachers." Music education in particular benefitted immeasurably from this brilliant study of how teachers can handle meaning in children's creative use of language.

In passing, we may note a nice irony in the tangential link with *language;* for the phrase "the language of music" has been something of an obstacle to the development of children's musical creativity.[9] A forced equation between expression and notation (not notation in general but just one form of notation) has been especially unhelpful; quite apart from which, similarities between music and language are hard to justify. Of far greater significance are the crucial ways in which music and language differ.

Constructing Experience

There are no logical models for music; in fact, to a large extent every piece has its own "grammar" which must be defined as part of the process of composition. Then again, music is nonconceptual, and in spite of an amazing expressive diversity it lacks entirely the power of description (other than in a very crude fashion, and then only by association). Every piece is self-justifying; it does not need to be explained. It cannot be paraphrased or shortened: either you have it all or you have nothing. Whilst, in language, a single word retains its meaning(s), in music a single note (or even a group of notes) has no meaning at all aside from its relationship with the larger, and autonomous, musical context.

In other words, music is pure form, as Langer has maintained:

> Music . . . is preeminently non-representative even in its classical productions, its highest attainments. It exhibits pure form not as an embellishment, but as its very essence; we can take it in its flower . . . There is no obvious, literal content in our way.[10]

At root surely that is true of every work of art in every other medium? All art is "abstract" in that its elements are abstracts from a perceived order presented as statements of a "felt" ideal. And the prime concern of every artist must be the variety of ways in which structural forces can be made to work together to produce coherent forms to embody these statements. Indeed—and not least in an educational context, as David Holbrook so convincingly demonstrates—even when *language* itself is the medium, it is as necessary as with any other medium to be reminded that the principal creative consideration is the relationship between ideas and form:

> Once the point of a "creative" approach to children's work has been grasped, a teacher becomes concerned with the germ, the gist of a piece—its content, *first*. Of course, matters of spelling, punctuation, layout and handwriting are important.
> But the most important thing to get is the message.[11]

> To study their [children's] work confirms the impression expressed by Sir Herbert Read that each human soul is impelled to seek order and beauty within by what he calls "ikons" . . . Thus, creativity is a matter of relationship with oneself . . .[12]

Children as Composers

The things that stimulate children to improvise and compose music are essentially those things that motivate all composers: personal experiences, things seen and heard (including other works of the imagination: literature, poetry, paintings and sculpture) or heard about; significant events past and present, things of joy and things of tragedy; sounds themselves; shapes and patterns. Eventually the piece, as it begins to grow through working on the ideas, takes over and dictates its own directions. In a sense, then, starting points are not all that important. What is important is that they should stimulate *musical ideas* of distinctive character that can be worked upon and developed (i.e., made to "go on" in time). Experiment with ideas will reveal their potential for variation or transformation or combination with other ideas to drive the musical form on to the point where it is memorable as a coherent sound pattern. That is really what music is "about," regardless of images that may be evoked by a starting point or a title.

We can see how this works by examining some music made by children at a primary school in the Yorkshire dales.[13] It started with a walk near their school on a windy autumn day. Back in the classroom the teacher talked with them about what they'd seen, and they wrote about it.

> We have been outside to see what the birds were doing in the wind. They seemed to be dancing on the wind. They flew in a pattern, they glided for a while and then they flapped to keep themselves up in the air. The gulls were wheeling in the sky. They went a little way gliding then they rocked. To turn a corner they banked like an aeroplane. The little finches were being driven back. They flapped their wings rapidly. The wind made the finch jerk and it seemed as if it was teasing the finch by making it hop.
>
> Wind constantly rushed into me. Birds manoeuvered gliding then darting. Gulls flew on like aeroplanes then banking and finishing by steadily rocking. The ferns blowing seemed as if they were stuck in ice and the wind was in vain trying to pull them out. The spring rippled in the wind. Wind whistling through the trees was like the sea. Another kite-like bird flew on—it was a rook. A small finch, rapidly beating its wings, then gliding in a small way, then flapping again, seemed to hop along.

The children had enjoyed the clear, bright atmosphere of the day, and were excited at feeling themselves carried along by the wind, almost as though they were flying like the birds.

> As soon as we came back we talked about the manoeuvering birds. Then we acted the birds. At first we acted the rooks. Some thought that they wobbled some didn't. Some thought that they went high, some thought they went low. The seagull I liked best. The seagull had more movement than the rooks. We banked and wobbled, we turned round we went low and high. It was nice to be the seagull for once. The finch was nice, it hopped, it swooped, it dived. But we did not see it much. We talked about making some music. Someone suggested that we would have tambourines to be the beating of the rook's wings. We agreed. We thought what we would have for gliding. Someone

tried top c and g [on recorders]. It goes c then the tambourines, then g and so on. The leaves were falling all the time. The leaves were the xylophone. We had to think of something for the banking of the seagull. Pamela thought four notes on the piano, I thought it was an excellent idea. As well we had recorders and a drum for the wind. I played a part in the finch music. I played the swooping of the finch. Guy played the flapping of the finch by tapping the drum. I had the piano. Then we replayed the first line.[14]

As we shall see, possibly the most important part of this account is the very last sentence. It had been entirely the children's idea to repeat the opening of the piece, presumably because they felt that this literally "rounded it off" and strengthened the impression of it being fully contained by its form.

The music was built up in a series of group "improvisations"; working over each until everyone agreed it was right, gradually developing the sound texture by adding layers, repeating sections or creating new ones. One child described the fast swooping movements of the rooks, and tried to capture the sensation in a musical idea played on a recorder; but another thought a double bass would be better "if we had one!" (He seemed to have some idea of a string glissando). That prompted someone else to describe the kind of music he would make "if he had a harp." The teacher showed them the strings inside the piano, which of course looked like a harp; and stroked, with the sustaining pedal held down, produced the effect the children wanted. There was a lot of discussion about the music for the finches; something was needed that would adequately represent the short, jerky movements. Someone suggested tapping a drum lightly with the finger nails rather than with sticks, although he couldn't control the sounds well enough to his own satisfaction. But another child did succeed. And in this way—trying out each other's ideas—the music grew.

The classroom discussion had begun with the overall impressions of the walk they'd taken. Then, guided by the teacher's questioning, attention began to focus on the birds they'd seen, and the movements of the birds. When it came to making music, the children's first aim seemed to be to "copy" those movements musically. Thus, the musical ideas became symbols of each style of movement, following the action—flapping, hopping, swooping or gliding. Nevertheless, *they were inventing musical ideas;* and we must ask now why those ideas take the forms they do.

At the start the rook-tambourines flap their wings, transferring to recorders to "soar" on the notes d'-G-d'. But while the rooks

BIRDS FLYING

"Birds Flying," John Paynter, 1976.

*piano: glissando with finger-nail across the strings; sustaining pedal depressed.

flap and "manoeuvre" the leaves are falling "all the time" to a pentatonic ostinato played throughout on a glockenspiel and effectively holding the entire piece together. This is particularly interesting because musically it is very different from the obviously imitative symbolism of the bird ideas. Nothing in this pattern of eight bell notes repeated over and over could, of itself, suggest "falling leaves." True, there is the continuity: apart from one short section where the glockenspiel is silent, this idea is present "all the time," like the falling leaves. But why *these* notes rather than others? The child who thought of this figure had not been told about 5-note scales or ostinato patterns, yet, playing on a chromatic glockenspiel[16] with all the possibilities of that full range of notes, he selected a "white key" pentatonic set and used it to make a phrase of considerable character which works splendidly as an ostinato. The aspiring third plus fourth falls back lightly, first to the G and then through a yearning downward sixth to the low C, from where it neatly curls upwards by step to ease the repetition of the phrase.

The loud, strong opening gives way to what ultimately became a middle section in two parts. The first of these (inspired by the banking and gliding of the gulls) contrasts dramatically with the start of the piece. This is simple but beautiful music: rocking back and forth in surprisingly gentle consecutive seconds on the piano, and then "floating" on the recorders' smooth octave Cs against the background of a quietly rolled drum, rising and falling like the hum of the wind. This leads into the second part: the finches with their curious hop and swoop and the return of the "falling leaves" ostinato.

Revelation

It was at this point in the process that the musical structures themselves took over. The children were wondering how they could continue; they'd run out of birds to imitate and no one had suggested either further elaboration of the existing ideas or the addition of new material. It was then that they hit upon the very satisfying idea of repeating the opening section. It is important to realize that this was their idea: the teacher did not suggest an ABA form! Indeed she had not prompted them at all in the shaping of the music other than to ask questions such as "what should happen now?" Instinctively they felt they had to bring back the glockenspiel as an accompaniment to the "finches" (letter C in the score above). That was a clever musical judgment because not only did it make a subtle link with what had been heard earlier, accompanying other material, but also—and this was the point of revelation—it would link perfectly with a straight repeat of the "rooks" music that began the piece.

They were immensely impressed with this discovery and the evident wholeness it produced when they played the piece through. No longer need they cast around for other ways of continuing, but—and much more importantly—the repetition was clearly "right." They reinforced their conviction about this by adding two features of purely musical structural significance: a tiny crescendo figure on the drum (immediately before letter A in the score) which lifts the middle section forward into the reprise, and a single loud drum beat at the end. A more decisive "period" to the "cosmography" of this piece is hard to imagine, characterizing—literally at a stroke—the completeness of this little world of sounds they had created.

Widening Musical Horizons

An important feature of David Holbrook's work has been "to train students in being able to see opportunities for links with literature, as children's poetic needs become apparent from their own expression." Time and again in *Children's Writing* he asks, "What do you do about following this up by other literature?" or "Say what literature (poems and stories) you would give the children" or "what will you read to the class to match this pupil's interests?" and "What then can we supply for Paul from literature?"[17] In just the same way we might now ask, à propos of *Birds Flying*, "What can we supply for Pamela, Christopher, Guy, and their friends from the literature of music?"

Possibly the first thing would be to match the overall atmosphere of the piece (with, perhaps, a special reference to the glockenspiel ostinato). In which case we might play to the children Martin Peerson's *The Fall of the Leafe*.[18]

Later it could be useful to listen to music that uses direct imitation of natural sounds; birdsong, for example. Here we're spoiled for choice because bird songs and bird calls appear in so many works. Noticing how Delius, in *On Hearing the First Cuckoo in Spring*, makes the bird's two-note call a musical motif from which a longer melody is spun and developed, would be a reasonable

The Fall of the Leafe.

MARTIN PEERSON.

"The Fall of the Leafe," Martin Peerson, from *The Fitzwilliam Virginal Book* Vol. II, Dover Reprint of 1898 Edition. Dover Publications Inc., New York.

place to begin. (Incidentally, it would be essential to listen to the work in its entirety; extracts can never tell us what a piece of music is about, and merely to point out the cuckooing clarinet would be totally inadequate.) There's also a cuckoo piece for harpsichord by Daquin; and, among a number of harpsichord pieces by Couperin in which he imitates natural sounds *("les sons non-passionnés"),* there is a *Nightingale in Love.* (There's also a gnat!) A mechanical or recorded nightingale takes its place in the orchestra for Respighi's *The Pines of Rome;* and the nightingale, quail, and cuckoo make an ensemble appearance at the end of the slow movement of Beethoven's *Pastoral* symphony. Messiaen used stylized forms of birdsong as the basis of very many of his works; going far beyond simple imitation, the resulting motifs becoming important structural features of the music.

This is precisely where we should be heading. The simplistically imitative examples make musically superficial "matchings"; and David Holbrook quite rightly insists that "matching needs to be done sensitively, governed by an understanding of the deeper implications of a child's work, not its mere explicit meaning."[19] The deeper implications in every piece of music are to be found not in correspondence between ideas and stimulus but in the structural features of the musical ideas and their development within the timespan of the piece; that is to say, in what the sounds themselves *do.*

In *Birds Flying* we have a pentatonic ostinato which is structurally the backbone of the whole piece; a strongly contrasting middle section featuring gentle consecutive seconds together with the twitching "finch" figure (finger-nail-tapped drum and finger-nail-stroked piano strings, an interesting combination of unusual sounds); and then a modified reprise of the first section for which we have been subtly prepared by the return of the glockenspiel ostinato in the second half of the middle section. It is these characteristics we need to match: their musical nature and the force they exert by driving the music on to a completed form. All have, of course, been worked out intuitively, so the teacher's task is now to draw attention to why certain features are so successful in creating the overall piece. As David Holbrook might say, "The point is that these children need to discover more pieces which are 'about' similar *musical* ideas."[20] Bartók's *Mikrokosmos* exploits a range of techniques, figures and patterns, and is such a rich source of characteristic pieces that we shall very likely find there what we are looking for.[21] Vol. III, No. 78, "Five-tone Scale" is based on an entirely "white note" pentatonic set; not the same set as that used in *Birds Flying* but Bartók's arching melody lines have a lot in common with the children's glockenspiel "falling leaves" ostinato. From there we might move to *Mikrokosmos* Vol. II, No. 61, "Pentatonic Melody." This uses yet another "white" five-note set, and the first nine measures have an ostinato figure as the lower part. Although that doesn't continue throughout, other ostinato-like passages appear in both upper and lower parts as the piece goes on.

Mikrokosmos Vol. V, No. 132, "Major Seconds Broken and Together," provides a useful link with both the musical ideas and the dreamy, slightly unreal, atmosphere created by the middle section of *Birds Flying*. Bartók's piece opens with a slow, wandering melody in the lower part; a gently meandering line, moving by steps never larger than tone or semitone, accompanied above by quiet "cluster" chords which are also built of tones and semitones and which gradually resolve on to a unison G (structurally very similar to the way in which the rocking consecutive seconds in *Birds Flying* resolve on to the purity of the recorders' sustained c'-c" octave). A middle section lifts the whole texture up into a higher, brighter register, the meandering melody now in the upper part and the accompanying cluster-chords below. Then—a useful comparison with the overall form of the children's piece—the opening ideas return in a modified reprise: as always in Bartók, he never repeats anything exactly.

A Revolution in School Music

A leading article in *The Times Educational Supplement* for 8 January 1965 observed that "The failure to draw out the creativity in each one of us is now spread as widely as the mass media spread the creativity of others." It went on to urge that we "provide the conditions for the fostering of all creative talent"; but even as those words appeared things were happening.

We've come a long way in the twenty-six years since that small group of children in Yorkshire composed *Birds Flying* and other pieces like it. The creative arts have been brought more and more into the educational debate as those responsible for curriculum planning have recognized that, whilst it is of course important to see that everyone has good basic communication skills, we must at the same time ensure that they realise how much they do indeed have to communicate.

In this respect music as a school subject has been totally transformed. In the 1960s and 1970s two major projects under the auspices of The Schools Council[22] looked at ways in which creativity could be encouraged; and in the 1980s the new examination at 16+—the GCSE—provided the essential formal framework within which to develop these ideas. Now, for the first time, we had an examination rooted in classroom work and for which candidates would have to submit original compositions. The impetus has carried forward to the implementation of a National Curriculum where music—fundamentally practical and including both performing and composing—figures as a foundation subject from the start of a child's schooling.

The education pendulum will continue to swing, producing the inevitable changes, orthodoxy becoming heresy and vice versa.[23] But we've had the revolution in music education, and the achievements of the past thirty years, together with the influences that triggered them, will not easily be forgotten. Even so, it has never been more necessary than it is now to keep such things in view. Increasingly human potential for thought and reflection is being destroyed; young minds dulled and desensitized by unremitting noise and ever more frequent images of violence. Opportunity for what Dewey would have called "significant experience" may not counter entirely the battering of sensitivities we have to suffer in the modern world, but it could nevertheless be the very thing that pulls us through.

It was Schiller's view that the elements of a successful work of art are incapable of effecting anything: only through form are we *wholly affected*.[24] Form is wholeness; and we learn the truth of that by exercising our own inventiveness. Music with all its subtleties and possibilities for nuance is an especially apt medium because the sounds themselves are our only guide.

One thing that everybody knows about music is that it comes as "pieces": forms which satisfy us precisely because each is "all of a piece." Whenever we make music there will be a moment when it is necessary to decide whether the piece is indeed complete: "Is this now really what I *mean?*" The decision is a crucial one because at that point in the process we come full circle. Here, in a sense, we get our first glimpse of farthest Thule, and know with reasonable certainty that the music we have made is safely contained; it won't come apart, and our efforts are no longer in danger of collapsing. A satisfying and comforting moment. A full stop at the end of the world.

Notes

1. Thomas Weelkes, *Madrigals of 6 Parts* (London: 1600), ed. E. H. Fellowes, rev. T. Dart (London: Stainer & Bell, 1968), no. 7.

2. Quoted in Herbert Read, *Art and Society* (London: Faber and Faber, 1945), p. vi.

3. Quoted in C. A. Patrides (ed.), *Aspects of Time* (Manchester: Manchester University Press, 1976), p. 82.

4. Wilfrid Mellers, *Music and Society: England and the European Tradition* (London: Dennis Dobson, 1946), p. 10.

5. For example, Marion Richardson, in the preface to the catalogue of the Children's Art Exhibition at County Hall, London in 1938, wrote, "The artist discovers in the world around . . . relationships, order, harmony. This cannot be done by the conscious scheming, *planning* mind. Art is not an effort of will but a gift of grace—the simplest and most natural thing in the world."

6. Robert W. Witkin, *The Intelligence of Feeling* (London: Heinemann Educational Books, 1974).

7. David Holbrook, *Children's Writing: a Sampler for Student Teachers* (Cambridge: Cambridge University Press, 1967), p. 3.

8. Ibid., pp. 8–9.

9. My comments have, of course, no bearing upon or reference to the ideas expounded by Deryck Cooke in his distinguished and influential book *The Language of Music* (Oxford: Oxford University Press, 1959). His use of this idea is of an altogether different order. Rather I have in mind the woolly thinking of those who, ignoring the ways in which major cultural differences produce substantially different musics, glibly talk about music as "a universal language." Often the very same people confuse things further by using the term "musical language" as a synonym for "rules" of what is also widely and mistakenly described as "music theory" (=certain conventions of western classical style distilled into bland and anonymous "examples" that have little or no connection with musical reality). In fact there could not possibly be a single theory of all music; it would, though, be quite correct to talk about "the theory of *a* music" (e.g., the theory of Javanese gamelan) or "theories of music*s*."

10. Susanne K. Langer, *Philosophy in a New Key: A Study of the Symbolism of Reason, Rite, and Art*, 3rd. edn. (Cambridge: Harvard University Press), p. 209.

11. Holbrook, *Children's Writing*, p. 115.

12. Ibid., p. vii and p. 2.

13. This piece is a group composition dating from 1966. Although the methodology of classroom composing has been considerably developed since then and many excellent and more recent examples of children's compositions are now available, I have chosen this one because it is more or less contemporaneous with the books by David Holbrook discussed here which had such a powerful early influence upon music education. I have written about this, and other pieces by the same children, elsewhere (John Paynter, "The role of creativity in the school music curriculum," in Michael Burnett [ed.], *Music Education Review Vol. 1* [London: Chappell & Co., 1976]), but have taken this opportunity to revisit it and to think my way afresh through its implications. That in itself has been an interesting and worthwhile experience.

14. Readers who are familiar with *The Exploring Word* and *Children's Writing* will no doubt be feeling that these examples of children's writing contradict all David Holbrook's principles of "engagement with 'felt' meaning." ("It is not mere *vocabulary* we wish to develop—but perception and the capacity to explore and organise experience, from inward sources, symbolically.") Clearly there is an uncomfortable 'sameness' of vocabulary (e.g., the birds "manoeuvre"). But the work described took place a year before the appearance of *Children's Writing*,

so that the teacher had not had the benefit of reading Holbrook's comments on "Mr Rowe's approach" (pp. 17–21). I do not doubt that, had she read them, she would have acted upon them. For although there is not the scope here to explain in greater detail the background to *Birds Flying*, I feel I should say that, notwithstanding the apparent "insincerity" of these pieces of writing by her pupils, this very experienced teacher, then quite close to retirement, was one of the most remarkable educators I have known. She really did encourage the children to generate and develop their own ideas, and to do so in several ways more or less simultaneously; that is to say, they talked, they made pictures, and they worked out their ideas in dance and drama and music.

15. The score printed here is a transcription from a tape recording. It has to be remembered that the composing process was empirical, the music created through improvisations that were then worked upon until the structures were defined and could be remembered by the whole group. When it was completed the children made their own score on a large sheet of paper, a mixture of pictograms and staff notation surrounded by bird pictures (of the children's own making). Not everything that children invent musically can be notated in the standard "staff" system, but even if they have to devise their own signs it is worthwhile; notation gives a sense of permanence to a piece of music.

16. The reference to "xylophone" in the child's description of how they made the music is an error. They found it difficult to remember the difference between the two instruments!

17. Holbrook, *Children's Writing*, pp. x, 17, 36, 37, etc.

18. Martin Peerson (1571–1651), *The Fall of the Leafe*. This impressionistic piece appears in that great early seventeenth century collection of keyboard music, *The Fitzwilliam Virginal Book*, edited by J. A. Fuller Maitland and W. B. Squire, reprint of 1898 edition (New York: Dover Publications Inc., 1979).

19. Holbrook, *Children's Writing*, p. 15.

20. Ibid., p. 16.

21. Béla Bartók, *Mikrokosmos: 153 progressive pieces for piano* Vols. I–VI, 1926–39 (London: Boosey & Hawkes, 1940).

22. The Schools Council Curriculum Projects, *Arts and the Adolescent* (University of Exeter 1968–1972) and *Music in the Secondary School Curriculum* (University of York 1973–1982).

23. Cf. Charles Carter et al., *Swings for the Schools: an Essay on Demographic Waves in Education* (London: Policy Studies Institute, 1979).

24. J. C. Schiller, *On the Aesthetic Education of Man*, ed. and trans. E. M. Wilkinson and L. A. Willoughby (Oxford: Oxford University Press, 1967), p. 155.

Part III
Critic

Introduction

David Holbrook's critical writings engage with an enormously diverse range of subjects. There are the books of literary criticism, beginning with the first of his excursions into the work of Dylan Thomas (the revisions to which John Ferns discusses in Part IV of this book). Among works in this category belong two books which certainly achieved very substantial recognition: *The Quest for Love* (1965) and *Sylvia Plath: Poetry and Existence* (1976), the latter a seminal work to be taken into account wherever Plath's work is discussed.

In more recent years, however, Holbrook's focus of interest seems to have moved increasingly towards novels and novelists—perhaps paralleling a recent surge in the publication of his own novels from the late eighties to the present (though his first fictions were published more than twenty years previously). Whatever the reason for this shift in concentration, within the last several years he has published a study of the novel form, *The Novel and Authenticity* (1987), and individual studies of Edith Wharton, Charles Dickens, and D. H. Lawrence (to whom Holbrook has returned from his first treatment in *The Quest for Love*).

In addition to literary subjects, ranging from Chaucer to writers of the present day, Holbrook produced in the early seventies a series of critiques of contemporary society. Such work, aimed at countering the nihilism, as he saw it, of many cultural products and the degradation of pornography, includes *The Masks of Hate*, and *Sex and Dehumanization* (both 1972). These were preceded, however, by another work of psychosocial criticism, *Human Hope and the Death Instinct* (1971), in which Holbrook's existentialist, post-Freudian psychology is fully expressed. Its influence was such that one contributor to this book remembers reading passages from it to his wife; and, upon this admission to a colleague at another university, was "relieved" to be told that he too read from the book to his own wife!

Just a few years later, Holbrook applied his phenomenological method, together with those insights derived from psychoanalytic theory, to a new—and perhaps unexpected—subject. *Gustav Mah-*

ler and the Courage To Be (1975) is thought by some familiar with his work to be Holbrook's finest single work of critical interpretation. And in addition to all these facets of that questing spirit which searches positive affirmations of life, there are those other critical works especially concerned with the investigation of philosophical anthropology.

The essays gathered in the following section explore some of the key themes and issues across these several fields of inquiry and speculation. Margaret Weldhen addresses herself to the nature of knowledge or "knowing" as a form of experience which results from and is central to the reading of literature. In so doing she elaborates some of the intimate connections which exist among language, symbol, and imagination. For Holbrook, the literary work's ultimate function is to alert us to "that which is beyond the words, in life"—a view which, derived most explicitly from some of his "educational" works, nonetheless remains as a constant implication throughout the total *oeuvre*.

For the whole drive of Holbrook's critical work, as Andrew Brink expresses it, is to look at the artist's world as an expression of "relational life" as experienced, "to see whether this amounts to an affirmation or denial of life's possibilities." Brink demonstrates how Holbrook's phenomenological approach to criticism, founded on psychodynamic theory—"an entirely new critical enterprise"—leads us to fresh, and sometimes disquieting, discoveries about literary texts.

In their contribution, Ann and Barry Ulanov take further one particular aspect of the *animal symbolicum:* that "special symbolism of the true self" which explores the sense of what it is to be truly human. The "true self" implies an authentic relationship between ego and the subjectivities of self and others so that a psychic wholeness is forged. They show how, in Holbrook's scheme of explanation, culture and the arts contribute to the continuing nurturing of the individual; and how such healthy development demands the recovery of what, in psychoanalytic terms, may be called "the feminine mode of being human."

Within these terms Holbrook views woman as both the symbolization of and the "focus for our awareness that we need to be in touch with being." But if feminine modes of being are equated uniquely with "what it is to be female," then there is the danger, as Pamela Taylor argues, that woman can be seen as "the other"— "forever moving in a foreign state of being"—and thereby "problematic." Taylor takes issue, therefore, with several of Holbrook's conclusions, objecting that there are alternatives to his interpretations of female fictional characters and their authors. At the same time, however, she acknowledges that without the "brave and illuminating light" shed by Holbrook, "the question of how writers portray women at the subconscious level might not even be considered."

In the final contribution to this section Roger Poole offers his appraisal of Holbrook as "an existentialist philosopher of our time," and speculates why he should have received so little acknowledgment. Holbrook's philosophical themes and interests are derived in the main, he argues, from a European existentialist-phenomenological tradition which still remains largely alien to British intellectual life. And there is the fact that Holbrook has opposed all reductive thinking in his search for wider, unifying principles of living; a holistic determination which engages such terms as love, empathy, understanding, and hope. Given the urgency of such redemptive themes, Poole presents a detailed case for a major appreciation of Holbrook's work as long overdue.

Language and the Experiencing Self

MARGARET WELDHEN

English: A Lost Direction

"English has lost its way." This is the title of the introductory chapter to David Holbrook's influential book *English for Meaning*,[1] in which he bewails the general failure of confidence in English Studies from the university to the primary school. This failure of confidence, he feels, was what was lying behind the Bullock Report in which he saw

> the retreat to utilitarianism . . . the feeling that at a time of economic trouble, we must turn to the "more practical subjects" and make English more "basic" and "realistic" . . .[2]

However, as he points out, what is forgotten in these developments is that English, like the other arts, has to do with the fostering of our powers of symbolizing. In agreement with both Dilthey and Cassirer, Holbrook views the symbol as necessary to the development of both perception and full being. For he sees language, particularly the richly textured language of poetry, not as a merely utilitarian tool as Bullock makes it, but as an exploration both of our own experience and of the real world:

> English as an imaginative discipline [is] concerned with the whole being and growth of effective personal capacities.[3]

He takes to task the writers of the Bullock Report for their rejection of the great principle of Coleridge, that of the primacy of the imagination in human development.

Although Holbrook commends the writers of the Report in their attention to the question of literacy, he casts doubt on what they mean by "language." Their main concern seemed, to him, to be with "mechanistic" concepts of "processing and structures." Their view of language, unfortunately, does not mean "a concern for the whole rich poetic subtlety of words." But, in addition to this, there is their failure to see that English as a discipline is concerned not only with language but with meaning—"that which is *beyond the words,* in life."[4]

While Holbrook agrees with the Report, that we should look at the form and structure of language, he feels that we should not limit ourselves to this as the Report seemed to do. As well as the "rich poetic subtlety of words" we should look at "what lies before and after the words":

> in the complex interaction between the individual and his world, with all those complicated processes of the identity and the inner life to which we give the term "life."[5]

In sum, for Holbrook, the importance of English Studies as one of the "imaginative disciplines," with English literature at its center, is that it fosters the relationship between mind, symbol, language, and world. This is the relationship I want to discuss in this essay. What is the nature of the knowledge yielded by the "imaginative disciplines"? What kind of meaning, and what kind of truth? Is such knowledge too intangible and elusive to be taught?

Knowledge and Imagination

The question of what kind of knowledge we are engaged in when reading a work of literature is discussed by Ernest House:

> When one reads a novel or a poem, something is learned. If someone were to ask what has been learned, it would be difficult to say. Often the knowledge gained from such reading is not in propositional form. Yet in the reading of such works, experience from the novel or the poem is mapped on to the mind of the reader.[6]

It is being claimed here that the knowledge may not be in the form of propositions, yet "something has been learned," and "is mapped on to the mind." Perhaps it is more appropriate, therefore, to be talking of "experience" rather than "knowledge." And if we can use the word "knowledge," surely it is a special kind of "knowing," quite different from, say, "knowing" a geographical fact?

Helen Gardner in her book *In Defence of the Imagination* makes the important qualitative distinction between "knowing" and "experiencing" a work of literature and merely "knowing about" it:

> We all know there is a world of difference between acquiring information about a book and experiencing a book in our reading of it, as there is in reading about a country and actually visiting it, or better still living in it for a while.[7]

But it would be too extreme to confine meaning in a work of literature to "experiencing" in Helen Gardner's sense in this statement. Indeed, she would have been, as an eminent textual scholar, the first to argue that there is a great deal to "know about" literature. And, in fact, what she argues in this book is that this "knowledge," in the sense of "knowing about," can only *enhance* the reader's "experience" of the work.

Holbrook, in an article in the *Cambridge Review*, refers to the importance of the "knowledge" component of literature as "providing a sense of cartography," and as "putting up signposts," arguing that it is the duty of the teacher or tutor to provide these. But in this article he is clear about priorities: for he writes that "unless the works are read and possessed there is nothing to talk about":

> The significant contours and features of the map can only be erected insofar as literary works of art have been experienced, and through them the minds and sensibilities of authors: . . . Ours is a phenomenological subject, as well as an encyclopaedic one.[8]

Our understanding of the meaning of a work of literature, both Helen Gardner and David Holbrook would argue, depends on this dual aspect.

How exactly is this meaning conveyed to us? Is it a very esoteric process, or is it a part of our ordinary, everyday experience? H. P. Rickmann, in his book *Understanding and the Human Studies*,[9] accepts the distinction made by Dilthey, and followed by Weber, between the "human world" and the "natural world," and he agrees with Dilthey that what distinguishes human beings from other forms of creation is their capacity for symbolic activity. In this line of thinking, which includes Cassirer, the symbol is seen as one of the main vehicles for meaning, and is viewed as needing "interpretation" to bring about "understanding."

Poetry and Experience

I agree with the phenomenologists that how we come to understand anything is part of our everyday, common sense experience. Thinkers such as Husserl and Heidegger have argued that at birth we are "thrown into" a social world which is made up of a web of already existing meanings and interpretations embedded in language. In order to move about in this social world we learn to interpret speech, gestures and actions. We "pick it up" as we live. But to interpret speech, gestures, works of art, we have to "get inside" these various forms of expression. In social life we learn to "read between the lines." Reading a poem we have to re-create within ourselves the experience of the poet. We thus come to make sense of our world by what is a natural, commonsense process.

In *English for Meaning* Holbrook is clearly sympathetic to this phenomenological approach. He criticizes the Bullock Report because of its emphasis on what he calls its "theoretical" and "external" approach to language: it was learning about language "from the outside" in an "abstract and explicit" way. The student, it was said, was to study language as "rule-governed behaviour":

> The emphasis was not on developing the natural processes of language, neither its exercise nor its practice as a way of gaining experience of a rich and subtle enjoyment of words such as must be central to English.[10]

The Bullock Report had put forward, he thought, a mechanistic model of language-use in relation to experience. It was a "positivist, functionalist approach," and this had been, he felt, chosen deliberately, while the "imaginative" approach had been disregarded. The whole Report he criticizes as suffering from:

> a somewhat over-simplified and crude application of scientific analysis to processes of perception, thinking and the nature of behaviour.[11]

From a reading of *English for Meaning* we see that Holbrook makes a fundamental distinction between an external, mechanistic, and technical model of language, and an internal, natural, and poetic kind of language. He makes it clear in his various books on education that he sees poetry as being central to English Studies. In the introduction to *English for Maturity,* writing about the "thin-ness of our culture," he writes of what he thinks should be the aims of the teacher of English:

> Our work is with poetry, the pondering of life by metaphor. And it is the poet who asks, How to live? The more we read literature ourselves, the better sense we should gain of how rich life may and could be.[12]

And in *English for Meaning* Holbrook is scathing of the Bullock Report's limited view of the value of poetry in English Studies: poetry was to be allowed in, but it was to be "realistic" and "relevant"; the teacher had to show that poetry "speaks directly to children, as to anyone else, and has something to say which is relevant to their living here and now." The use of the word "relevant" has the result of raising an angry response from Holbrook as it does from me:

> The magic word "relevant"! The poetic processes of the imagination are the primary basis of *all human powers:* our very relationship with the world is sustained by a continual process of creative formative effort in the inner world of fantasy, dream, day-dream, play, game and cultural artefact. Poetry is "all that we are." Poetry is thus indeed "relevant": but not in the sense Bullock means. What they mean is "narrowly related to immediate explicit interests of social and other kinds."[13]

Thus Holbrook's answer to Bullock is very clear. Since poetry is "all that we are," then poetry is clearly "relevant," and this is the main justification for its centrality in English Studies. But, further, poetry is vital not only for maintaining, but enriching civilization. And it is precisely because it is a *natural* language usage that it has this capacity for renewing and enriching:

> Poetry has this great value as a civilising art-form because it is written in the language we use for everyday purposes. The reading of poetry can help restore life to our language habits because it is language used at its richest and most accurate, in defining and enlarging experience.[14]

Additionally, there is the point mentioned at the beginning of this essay about poetry as being concerned with the expansion of our consciousness and the extension of our awareness. C. S. Lewis, in his book *An Experiment in Criticism,* wrote of this power of literature:

> we seek an enlargement of our being. We want to be more than ourselves . . . We want to see with other eyes, to imagine with other imaginations, to feel with other hearts, as well as with our own.[15]

But if poetry extends the imagination and enlarges our sympathy, it also, paradoxically, fosters a sense of identity. For our explorations with words bring us back to a renewed sense of selfhood. As C. S. Lewis put this in the same book:

> Literary experience heals the wound, without undermining the privilege, of individuality. There are mass emotions which heal the wound; but they destroy the privilege. In them our separate selves are pooled and we sink back into sub-individuality. But in reading great literature I became a thousand men and yet remain myself.[16]

In *English for Maturity* Holbrook emphasizes that poetry is not "writing about," in an external kind of way, but "exploring experience metaphorically"—

> bringing aspects of experience with which we have not yet come to terms into our personal integration. In this sense poetry goes in advance of ordinary human consciousness.[17]

All this provides ample justification for Holbrook's view of the centrality of poetry in English Studies, and for education in general. Perhaps the most important point of all is his view that the language of poetry is both a "natural" language, using everyday words, *and* that it is language used at its richest, having both texture and resonance. Above all it is the metaphor which is able to bring about this paradox.

Literature and Values

Throughout his many books, Holbrook emphasizes metaphor as the essential element of poetry. He sees metaphor not as a figure of speech adding decoration to language, but as the fundamental internal working of language, and the main means by which our language is formed and developed. In this he would agree with W. M. Urban, in his book *Language and Reality,*[18] that metaphor is nothing less than a natural metaphysic of the mind. Urban views the metaphor as the basis of a creative perception which sets up new relationships between things, so bringing about new meaning. One of the main arguments in Urban's book is that the metaphor not only carries an emotional charge in its sensuous imagery, but is also cognitive in that it is the bearer of values. It is thus a form of knowledge, and not merely a peripheral decoration added to language. In metaphor, mind, language, and "world" come into relationship, giving us a sense that we possess a "world." Holbrook accepts, with Urban, the central importance of the metaphor and how it is vital to the development of mind. We find him writing in *English for Maturity:*

> In language it [the metaphor] is the means by which we extend our awareness of experience into new realms.[19]

Both Urban and Holbrook are firmly placed on the side of those who argue against various developments stemming from structuralism, in believing that language is not a self-contained structure but refers to things in the world. In these debates there are, broadly, those who hold that words do refer to some kind of "reality" or "world" beyond language itself, and those who hold that language is an autonomous phenomenon in which literature is seen as a network of literary texts enmeshed in, and parasitic on, other literary texts. I have argued elsewhere[20] that this debate is not just a literary one, but involves two opposed views of the nature of reality. For one side, the very being or essence of literature lies in the system of signs—how words are related to other words—and *not* in the "message" or content; and in this view language does not represent a "reality" said to be existing beyond the words, for it is language itself which is seen as "constructing" the world. The other side deny that language is such a self-contained structure, and hold that it points beyond itself to "life," "reality," or "world."

Holbrook certainly holds that through the experience of literature we are enabled to see the world with new eyes, never doubting the relationship between "words" and "life". We also find that he is in agreement with Urban that the metaphor has not only an emotional but a cognitive aspect, and that therefore it is essential to the development of both language and mind. In *English for Maturity* he writes of the metaphor that:

> The movement is from the known to the unknown, and from the concrete to the abstract. The word "metaphor" comes from words

meaning transfer: to carry across, as it were, the meaning of something known into experience which until that moment is unknown.[21]

It follows from Holbrook's view of the metaphor as a fundamental aspect of language and mind, and from the view that poetic language has to do with the development of the person, that he does not see English Studies as morally neutral. In *English for Meaning* he writes:

> It [English] is a moral discipline, since it engages inevitably with values, because these are bound up with meaning: and it changes us as we study and work.[22]

Clearly, such moral values in literature may not be explicit. As Helen Gardner put this point in her book *In Defence of the Imagination:*

> Since imaginative literature gives us images of human life and records human experience it is inevitably full of moral ideas and moral feelings, strongly engages our moral sympathies, and tests our moral allegiances. But its effects upon us, as a source and a reinforcement of moral values, are often most powerful when indirect and in inverse ratio to the explicitness of an author's moral purpose.[23]

The point is, as she argues, that we are, in literature, involved in a world of moral choice and moral values. We can quite well see how Holbrook, as an educator, feels about the importance of poetry, not only to English Studies in particular, but to education in general. "The pondering of life by metaphor," as he puts it, is making sense of our experience; expanding our perceptions; building up a sense of personal integrity—poetry is central to all these living processes, and is in itself a natural activity and part of our everyday experience, even though rather overlaid by the predominance of technical language. And in his book *The Exploring Word*[24] he shows how all these living processes can be fostered by the good teacher.

Poetry and "Truth"

How do these views link up with Holbrook's own practice as a poet? We should not expect his poetry to be "difficult" as Eliot warned modern poetry would necessarily be, or expect it to talk of esoteric kinds of experience. I see his poetry as a celebration of daily and even mundane experience, in a language which makes us perceive more sharply our ordinary acts of living. In his poetry our awareness has been extended by the use of non esoteric yet richly textured language made possible by metaphor. Perhaps one can say of Holbrook's poetry what Hardy wrote of William Barnes, that he aimed at "closeness of phrase to vision." This surely is an example of the Coleridgean principle of the power of the "primary imagination" in all perception, and is surely one of the best descriptions of poetic truth.

David Wright, in his introduction to the *Selected Poems of Thomas Hardy*, said of that poet:

> He tells truths, without pretending to "the truth," which in the matter of relationship between people is more than illusion.[25]

Poetic truth seems to be more like a series of "truths," with language closely related to perception, largely through the power of metaphor. Holbrook aims at that "closeness of phrase to vision" in the celebration of ordinary, everyday acts of living. In his poem *Reflections on a Book of Reproductions* he writes that although life is made up, on the whole, of little, seemingly trivial events, yet they all add up to the creation and celebration of order by art. Of these ordinary events he says:

> Yet this is the family food of the aspiration
> To celebrate order: Bach's elation
> Was nourished on soup and hearth . . .[26]

There is no need, he writes, to underestimate the banal or simple. They are the necessary ingredients of that ordering of experience which art can achieve. The language used is simple and unsophisticated, yet the ordinary words of our commonsense world are made to work hard to wring out meaning. They are not words merely pushed about like counters, or used as tools, as technical language would be. Poetic language, as in this poem, can make the mundane significant, and relate the small things to the huge mysteries. In the last part of this poem he writes:

> So we are not demeaned by simplicity or banality,
> By our cars, electric kettles, or lamps; the finality
> Of our death, even, in the mass-produced chest. . . .

Certain cultural implications follow from Holbrook's view of language. As we have seen, he not only views the metaphor and poetic language as essential to the development of mind and identity, but he sees it as a natural and not an esoteric activity. Further, the way we try to make sense of our ordinary, everyday experiences, is the nourishment of that poetic activity. As an educator, he emphasises again and again, in his books, that the imagination needs constant nourishment by immersion in works of literature. While we should have a concern for the "whole, rich, poetic subtlety of words," yet at the same time we have to look at "what lies before and after the words," to "that which is beyond the words, in life." For mind, symbol, language, and world are bound into a coherent whole by the particular kind of knowledge which comes from the literary work.

Notes

1. David Holbrook, *English for Meaning* (Windsor: NFER Publishing Co., 1979) in which Holbrook discusses the Bullock Report, *A Language for Life* (London: HMSO, 1975).
2. Holbrook, *English for Meaning*, p. 9.
3. Ibid., p. 11.
4. Ibid., p. 25 (Holbrook's emphasis).
5. Ibid.
6. Ernest House, *Evaluating with Validity* (London: Sage Publications, 1980) p. 279.
7. Helen Gardner, *In Defence of the Imagination* (Oxford: Clarendon Press, 1982), p. 6.
8. David Holbrook, "Against a Curriculum for English Studies," *Cambridge Review* 109, no. 2276, 1983, p. 5.
9. H. P. Rickmann, *Understanding and the Human Studies* (London: Heinemann, 1967).
10. Holbrook, *English for Meaning*, pp. 31–32.
11. Ibid., p. 44.
12. David Holbrook, *English for Maturity*, 2nd ed. (Cambridge: Cambridge University Press, 1967), p. 9.
13. Holbrook, *English for Meaning*, p. 62.
14. Holbrook, *English for Maturity*, p. 69.
15. C. S. Lewis, *An Experiment in Criticism* (Cambridge: Cambridge University Press, 1961), p. 137.
16. Ibid., pp. 140–41.
17. Holbrook, *English for Maturity*, p. 69.
18. W. M. Urban, *Language and Reality* (London: Allen and Unwin, 1961).
19. Holbrook, *English for Maturity*, p. 69.
20. See Margaret Weldhen, "Living Inside or Outside the Text: Two Versions of English Studies," *The Use of English* 37, No. 2 (Spring 1986).
21. Holbrook, *English for Maturity*, p. 69.
22. Holbrook, *English for Meaning*, p. 117.
23. Gardner, *In Defence*, p. 37.

24. David Holbrook, *The Exploring Word* (Cambridge: Cambridge University Press, 1967). In this context, see especially chapter 9.
25. David Wright, ed., *Selected Poems of Thomas Hardy* (London: Penguin Books, 1983), p. 27.
26. David Holbrook, *Selected Poems* (London: Anvil Press, 1980), p. 19.

Psychoanalysis and the Humanities: The Toronto Experience

Andrew Brink

Literary Criticism and Moral Vision

David Holbrook's literary and cultural criticism is a beginning point, not an eccentric end. It firmly establishes psychoanalytic criticism as a moral discipline and belongs to the British moral tradition in criticism, having little or nothing in common with the recent French trends towards decentering authors and valorizing texts as sufficient in themselves. Holbrook is interested in the health of interpersonal relationships, in good child development, and the use of imagination to enrich life. Inspired by post-Freudian developments in psychoanalysis, he has seized the initiative to assess cultural information in the light of the standards of emotional health set by psychoanalysis and underpinned by biological norms described by "philosophical anthropologists." So far-reaching is this enterprise, so encompassing its concepts, and frequently so brilliant its applications that it tends to remain isolated, even ignored, by those who should be paying most attention. Holbrook asks for so complete a change in critical practice that it is little wonder his books should be set aside in favor of the easier-to-take intellectualizations of deconstructionists, who refuse to move outside texts to their referents in the feeling to which human interaction gives rise. I should like to reflect on the strengths and shortcomings of Holbrook's criticism and comment on how teachable it is in the university.

Renewal of moral vision usually occurs with the proclamation of some fresh ideology revising society's perception of itself. Such a new order was emerging when in 1644 Puritan John Milton wrote *Areopagitica* to challenge licensing laws, or when in the nineteenth century Utilitarianism prompted John Stuart Mill to rethink the first principles of human freedom in *On Liberty*. The promise of socialism to renew human purpose prompted William Morris to envisage a better social order in *News From Nowhere* and other books. Our century's experience of total war and upheaval of all traditional expectations of life prompts a still more drastic reconsideration of the limits of freedom. In object relations theory, mainly the work of Melanie Klein, Ronald Fairbairn, Donald Winnicott, and Harry Guntrip in Britain, Holbrook sees the groundwork of a new and more realistic account of human nature's possibilities and limitations.

Breaking with Freud on the pessimistic suppositions of impersonal libido (drive theory), Fairbairn in particular saw the maturational process as conditional on the quality of mother-infant interaction. True psychological freedom comes not of rebellion against repressive parental authority but by having moved from infantile dependence through a transitional stage to mature dependence, which makes possible unencumbered natural development of one's genetic gifts. Constraint, lack of freedom, comes of some developmental failure in the maturational process—when the normal course of events is impeded by a trauma (maternal loss or severe impingement) impairing trust between mother and infant. The result is a splitting of the developing ego between an internalized exciting and rejecting object, both aspects of the mother. This split is repressed, and the basic endopsychic situation endures as a guide to all relational expectations, unless there is some corrective intervention, usually psychotherapeutic. The most severely developmentally impaired individuals—those Fairbairn and Guntrip term schizoid—hardly believe they exist and live in fear of nothingness. Depressives fear their rage against, and consequent guilt about, the internalized mother. Neither personality type is in any sense free, yet they issue protestations of radical freedom to stay psychologically alive. This sobering realization puts utopian moral hopes in a different light.

Fairbairn the psychiatrist had been sobered by studying shell-shocked casualties in the Great War, and Holbrook the critic by experiencing battle conditions in the Second World War in which he was wounded. The study of destructive wishes, either against others or by self-immolation, became urgent, and post-Freudian theory gave entirely new concepts by which to understand culturally transmitted information. Value judgments became more informed in terms of the developmental conditions underlying constructive and destructive motivations. While we are all subject to both, it is important to know which developmental conditions are likely to promote a healthy ego and which lead to schizoid, obsessional, and paranoid pathologies—to the projective negations and abuses of power which the psychoanalytically informed critic detects with alarming frequency in contemporary behavior and culture. Holbrook's revolutionizing psychoanalytic learning appears fully formed in *Human Hope and the Death Instinct,* a treatise on human nature as "object rational," elaborating a new view of creativity and culture. One wonders what personal upheavals led Holbrook to depart from the practical criticism of *Scrutiny* to psychoanalysis in order to deepen literary criticism. There is a story to be told about this, and it would draw upon his endeavours as poet and novelist richly reflecting his own experience of the maturational processes. To have arrived at so powerful a set of critical precepts as Holbrook found in psychoanalysis implies facing and resolving personal conflict beyond what most critics are prepared to attempt. Study of his art would throw light on this, but I shall remain with Holbrook's function as a psychoanalytically-informed moralist addressing contemporary culture.

The Humanist Conscience

Summarizing in "The Humanist Conscience," Holbrook writes, "both individual viability in the psychic sense, and the survival of civilization, depend upon activity of conscience—on that 'healthy moral sense' that Winnicott finds, which is bound up with a personal culture as the meeting point between 'separateness and union.'"[1] Psychoanalysis shows us an "inner integrative spring . . . prompt[ing] moral impulses"[2]—in other words, a reparative impulse that urges us to seek correction of bad developmental experiences and to learn to live by the True rather than the False Self. Thus, the "'sacred' area of symbolic creativity should never be violated, exploited or laid waste."[3] A "new kind of conscience," neither authoritarian nor hypomanic but self-knowing, must be developed to counteract the split off projected hatreds and negations of life that too often appear in modern culture.

This conviction put Holbrook in the position of critic of False Self solutions to existential problems, and of exorbitant claims to freedom, especially sexual freedom, made by increasing numbers of writers, filmmakers, and publicists for the counterculture of the 1960s. In the name of healthy ego development, he tried to face down a flood tide of amoral sexuality and schizoid negations of life's creative possibilities. Whereas earlier English reformers had extended areas of moral freedom—Milton arguing for easier divorce, Mill for freedom from society's encroachment on the private realm, Morris for latitude to aestheticize life—Holbrook seemed to be restricting the very freedoms that many of his contemporaries felt were necessary to ease their psychic pain. A superficial reading of his literary criticism can lead to the conclusion that Holbrook is stigmatizing psychological false solutions rather than understanding their origins. It is indeed easy to see his studies *Dylan Thomas: The Code of Night* and *Sylvia Plath: Poetry and Existence* in this way. The attribution of schizoid features to poetry appears to be a kind of rejective labelling that casts out that which is morally disapproved. There is certainly a shock factor in the criticism psychoanalysis led him to write. Through the magnifying lens he first trained on himself he saw that motivations to creativity look very different than they appear to the eye of the critic who takes the artist's word as authoritative. Holbrook's view is that the writer's word expresses something about the quality of relational life he or she experiences, and that we should look to see whether this amounts to an affirmation or a denial of life's possibilities. When Thomas's alcoholic incoherence, amidst bursts of poetic brilliance, is seen to be a slow suicide, and when Plath's poetic struggle with overpowering feelings about her parenting, her marriage, and being a mother lead to a death trend she cannot deflect, fundamental questions about false directions in literature arise. Object relations theory gave Holbrook a powerful hold on such nihilistic counter-creativity, putting him at odds with the *Observer*'s poetry critic, A. Alvarez, for example, who appeared to celebrate "extremist art" without seeing its dire warning for the culture as a whole. In *The Savage God: A Study of Suicide*, Alvarez had revealed that he himself was a failed suicide with little taste for the underlying psychodynamics.[4] Holbrook's view of Plath's predicament has since won support from several psychoanalytic studies, including Alice Miller's "Sylvia Plath: An Example of Forbidden Suffering" in the influential *For Your Own Good: Hidden Cruelty in Child-Rearing and the Roots of Violence.*[5]

Towards a Phenomenology of Criticism

Holbrook's use of psychodynamic theory in psychobiography, backed by the philosophical anthropology he has progressively assembled from European sources, is bold but just. Of course it will be argued that he applied psychoanalysis to the ego states of creative writers before the theory itself had been made consistent, and certainly before object relations theory was widely accepted among professionals—a matter requiring further comment. But he repeatedly identified in faulty parenting the most probable sources of the existential anxieties shown by writers: the general and typical dislocations of attachment that made their products compulsively fascinating for their generation. We get the art that tells us why we fail to feel fully real, but it requires a normative psychodynamic to explain why this is so. Holbrook is less given to detailed psychobiographical reconstructions, such as are found at their best in Phyllis Grosskurth's studies of Havelock Ellis and Melanie Klein, than he is in identifying psychopathology and warning against it.[6] Thus in identifying Dylan Thomas's fear of women as a function of his having been inadequately mothered, Holbrook writes that "he sought at times to involve the reader in the inversion of values, in vindications of hate, and even in his 'death circuit' delusions about the nature and goals of self-destruction."[7] Similarly he raises the problem of "how to respond" to the searing pain and near celebration of suicide in Sylvia Plath's novel *The Bell Jar*—a courageous self-disclosure about "a desperate and inverted 'remedy'"[8] to the intrapsychic consequences of having lost a father and living with an intrusive mother. No doubt this is a hard revision of standards for conventional literary scholars to take, but it is to be preferred for instance to the moralizing attacks on the faults of luminaries from Rousseau to Sartre and Lillian Hellman launched by Paul Johnson in *Intellectuals*.[9] To read Johnson on the duplicity and degeneracy of leading intellectuals is to become depressed about the direction of civilization. Unsparing though Holbrook may sometimes seem, he does not depress but invigorates with the possibility of healthy ego development and with the possibility of reparative imaginative discipline when development has been suboptimal.

Calling his literary studies "phenomenological" rather than psychobiographical allows Holbrook to examine texts for their imaginative and fantasy contents. When the discovery is disquieting by the light of psychoanalytic criteria, of course psychobiography comes more forcefully into play. His formulations are compassionate and fully appreciative of the creative effort to transform the ego's persecutory contents into negotiable aesthetic forms. As he says in his study of C. S. Lewis, *The Skeleton in the Wardrobe*, "I have tried to restrain myself from making use of biographical material to 'diagnose' Lewis because I want to try to make my phenomenological analysis of his symbolism the basis of my criticism of the fantasies."[10] The psychobiographical material bearing on Lewis's earliest relations with his mother is indeed scant, and Holbrook speculates on why Lewis resorted defensively to "diminution of affect,"[11] favoring male company until he married late in life. The problem of splitting and projection of evil in his fables is faced in terms of "the threatening baby inside him [and] his phantom woman who haunts him. . . ."[12]

In *Where D. H. Lawrence Was Wrong about Woman*, Holbrook seeks reasons for the novelist's ambiguously gendered hypersexuality in his having been mothered by a domineering woman mourning for a dead son, Lawrence being the replacement child. The dangers of Lawrence's pejorative and controlling attitudes toward women are understood in terms of his having been "Jocasta mothered," a psychoanalytic concept. This approach sheds new light on Lawrence's entire literary production helping us to resist his "somewhat disastrous" sexual message.[13] A little late in the game to assist the women's movement some may say, but the point about distorted psychosexual development is well-supported throughout this important study and may yet be listened to. Similarly, readers puzzled by obsessive father-daughter incest themes in the novels of Edith Wharton will be enlightened by *Edith Wharton and the Unsatisfactory Man*, a revelation of Wharton's own sexual predicament, which also appreciates the extraordinary achievement of her art. The *locus classicus* of Holbrook's critical method, however, should be recognized in his masterful *Gustav Mahler and the Courage to Be*. Here the composer's childhood, filled with tragic family loss, is used to full effect, especially in exploring the Ninth Symphony's preoccupation with the loneliness of facing death. Mahler's very modern existential anxiety in a Nietzschean godless universe is worked out creatively in the music, voicing a triumph of creativity over meaninglessness. Mahler's strength as an artist was to preserve "his humanness, and his authenticity of being, against violation, even by death."[14] This study is Holbrook's criticism at its most compassionate and constructive, a full vindication of the method. It forces us to see art facing up to the darkest doubts and anxieties that assail us, and thus to the core of social and cultural values.

Pornography and Dehumanization

To consider the rise of pornography, as Holbrook did in the early 1970s, was to feel deep dismay at the deflection of creativity from its use as a way of constructing meaning. Like the psychoanalyst Robert Stoller, who from the mid-1960s published papers leading up to *Perversion, The Erotic Form of Hatred,* Holbrook saw pornography as filled with contempt for women. As Stoller writes, in pornography "there is always a victim, no matter how disguised: no victim, no pornography."[15] Love is driven out by daydreamed, eroticized revenge, usually against the mother, for some early trauma suffered by the child. In *Sex and Dehumanization: In Art, Thought And Life in Our Time* and in *The Pseudo Revolution: A Critical Study of Extremist 'Liberation' in Sex,* Holbrook reacted with dismay to the cheapening of love in such stage productions as *Oh Calcutta!* and Dr. Alex Comfort's explicit magazine on sex, *Man and Woman.* Instead of increasing the possibilities of love, Holbrook argues, pornography and much sexology limits them, constraining the imagination along ever more narrow pathways. The physical sexual act becomes compulsive as relational meaning ebbs away; indeed obsessive sexual adventuring is designed to keep relational meaning out of awareness. Holbrook saw that sex was being separated "in an unreal and dangerous way from human wholeness."[16] He called for reconsideration of the anarchistic emergence of eroticism in popular culture and literature in the light of object relational insights about the sources of love and hate. The books are strongly polemical and tend to demonize the so-called sexual revolution's activists, such as Kenneth Tynan. They hold up as healthily erotic such works as Marvell's "To His Coy Mistress" and Rodin's "Le Baiser," not questioning whether they too may not spring from male sexual pathology.[17] Yet the soundness of Holbrook's argument is increasingly supported, as in the late Robert Stoller's *Porn: Myths for the Twentieth Century* where he points out how many "stars" of porn video films were sexually abused as children and how many entrepreneurs in the porn industry are aging adolescent rebels, the cynical survivors of the sixties pseudo-revolution.[18] Of course Holbrook got very little thanks for his trouble at the time of publishing. An anonymous reviewer in *The Times Literary Supplement* found Holbrook "hysterical": "can he cure the culture of hate by screaming at its victims?"[19] Profiled in the *Observer* as a "disciple of Lord Longford" and an affiliate of Mary Whitehouse, Holbrook is made to look a reactionary.[20] The basic point he was trying to make about the possibility of self-knowledge to take us beyond the need for pornography—about the insights into healthy development by the child-analyst, D. W. Winnicott and others—were ignored. Holbrook had questioned the wisdom of new freedoms, and freedoms of all sorts, including sexual, had been the rallying cry of liberal philosophers from Locke to Mill and Bertrand Russell. Freedom and social constraint had been debated to the point where a consensus was reached that Victorian sexual morality was grossly restrictive and that the fullest possible emancipation was needed. Holbrook saw that true freedom does not arrive with indulgence of sexual wishes but with understanding the psychological origins of their urgency. Yet who was he to stand in the way of new sexual experimentation, even if it sometimes appeared detrimental to the emotional health of consenting adults? Liberal intellectuals, left wing humanists of Holbrook's own sort, did not want to be patronized; they had to proceed with a sexual revolution no matter where it might lead. A group dynamic, fuelled by powerful erotic fantasy, had taken over; did Holbrook err in not fully understanding its origin or calculating its strength? He could not be expected to have done this much; what he did do was remarkable and courageous enough—stand out like Milton's "one just man" in *Paradise Lost*, a seer of light amidst gathering darkness, against the decline of creative imagination, against the perversion of healthy marital relationships and against forced pace in the sexual development of children. There are indeed limits to freedom in relationships set by our growing understanding of human nature gained through psychoanalysis and allied disciplines. Holbrook is in the forefront of gathering and assessing this new knowledge, but it is exceedingly hard to take.

Humanism and the Language of Scientific Psychology

Since Holbrook is startlingly original in using object relations theory from Klein, Fairbairn, Guntrip, Winnicott, and others to ground literary criticism in the realities of human development and interaction, it is curious that he found difficulty with the work of John Bowlby. In *Attachment and Loss,* the most important recasting of psychodynamic theory since Freud, Bowlby claimed consistency with all but Melanie Klein in the group of revisionists named above. His work on the depressive effects of maternal loss on children is basic to psychobiographical consideration of creativity, as Holbrook acknowledges. Holbrook's psychobiographical insight into the fantasies of George Macdonald, who lost his mother when he was eight, owes much to Bowlby. (See Holbrook's introduction to the Everyman edition of *Phantastes,* 1983.) Bowlby is usefully invoked in studying C. S. Lewis's fantasies in *The Skeleton in the Wardrobe* and is indispensable in Holbrook's sensitive study of creativity in *Gustav Mahler and the Courage To Be.*

Mahler's solution, in symphonies and songs, to the problem of mourning early losses of siblings—enlarged to the problem of human mortality itself—is preferred to the "magical" solution of J. M. Barrie to his childhood anxieties in Peter Pan. In the brilliant *Where D. H. Lawrence Was Wrong about Woman* he cites Bowlby on Lawrence's claim that the writer can shed his sickness in books. Bowlby had written of "the intractability of the 'psychic tissue.'"[21]

Perhaps such signs of approval signal a modification of Holbrook's earlier doubts about the value of Bowlby's contribution to humane studies. In "Dr. John Bowlby: No need to nod to positivist dogma" Holbrook had taken him severely to task for an overly scientific approach to human development and interaction. He much preferred Winnicott's warm and often poetic language of analysis to Bowlby's language of experimental observation and "systems theory." "The 'objective' kind of science to which Dr. Bowlby in part inclines is marked by a serious failure to contribute insights into human nature. Why should he, who has contributed such truly valuable insights, defer to such a sterile discipline?"[22] Bowlby responded in the same volume, hoping that mainly hermeneutical psychoanalysis had become as redundant as a positivist one. It looked like a standoff between an ideal of kindly interpretation in the humanities and a hard line determinism in scientific psychology. This was unfortunate, even tragic, as the principal line of advance in post-Freudian psychoanalysis now seems to be through the attachment theory originated by Bowlby and Mary Ainsworth as carried forward by Mary Main, together with a cohort of researchers who work as experimental psychologists and report their findings in statistics.[23] This, however, does not mean that studies using Ainsworth's "strange situation" technique to observe mothers and their babies, or studies of attachment styles using Main's Adult Attachment Interview are dehumanized. An ever present risk of which most investigators are fully aware, the price of accurate, replicable work is a measure of methodological *sang-froid.* The problem is that of the psychologist's need for mindfulness of the underlying purpose of reducing suffering and improving the human lot, while the humanists must increase comprehension of the language of scientific psychology in order to translate it into their own idiom. Holbrook's warning that the "two cultures" not drift apart was timely, but he did not see clearly that the humanities, at this stage in history, are more in need of Attachment Theory than the reverse.

We can anticipate that the parenting conditions for a whole range of psychopathologies—including the mother-induced fear of women and wish to control them which Holbrook finds in Lawrence's fiction—will soon become clearer through attachment research. Let us hope that students of fiction are willing to penetrate the technicalities of scientific reporting to make the applications so essential to understanding the obsessive fear of women which pervasively troubles literature, and perhaps our culture in its entirety. There are signs that this is being recognized in criticism, for instance in Bruce Bawer's *The Middle Generation: The Lives and Poetry of Delmore Schwartz, Randall Jarrell, John Berryman and Robert Lowell* and in John J. Clayton's *Gestures of Healing: Anxiety and the Modern Novel.* Clayton looks at the family psychodynamics, including mother-boundness, of such writers as Joseph Conrad, Ford Madox Ford, William Faulkner, Ernest Hemingway, Henry James, and Virginia Woolf. My own forthcoming *Obsession and Culture: A Study of Sexual Obsession in the Novel* (analyzing H. G. Wells, Hermann Hesse, Vladimir Nabokov, John Fowles, and John Updike) offers a broad psychoanalytic interpretation of the meaning of sexual drivenness.[24]

Psychoanalysis and the Teaching of Literature

We must ask whether Holbrook's methods of applied psychoanalysis have a place in the university teaching of literature under present conditions. The very intensity of his concern may of course be a disincentive to some, and the Jeremiah and neo-puritan labels may also be applied. But what of those teachers who agree with him that English poetry has lost its bearings and that the novel too often urges false solutions to our existential problems? Can the Humanities be regenerated along the anti-Cartesian lines proposed—those urging a return to intentionality and imaginative enrichment through a creativity informed by psychoanalytic self awareness? By probing his own experience in novels and poems, Holbrook shows the way forward for the gifted few; for those more given to philosophy, the studies in "refinding man's moral dimension" in *What is it to be Human? New Perspectives in Philosophy,* an edited conference collection,[25] will be helpful, as will other recent works on education and philosophical anthropology and on the importance of Darwinian evolution in setting a psycho-biological agenda. This leaves the question as to whether

Holbrook's method of detecting psychopathology in literature and popular culture is viable in undergraduate studies.

My experience working with the undergraduate students of literature in the Humanities and Psychoanalytic Thought Programme at Trinity College in the University of Toronto shows there is reluctance to enter upon the inquiry for which Holbrook calls. The present critical climate is so heavily influenced by "Theory" that, while psychoanalytic criticism is acknowledged, its practice is limited. Lacan remains fashionable and students appropriate his terminology thinking that it will serve. As we offer a full seminar in the British School of Object Relations Theory from Klein to Bowlby, a more empirically responsible set of concepts is available. Students in this seminar are enabled to see imaginative processes as strongly influenced by the internalization of objects in the mother/infant matrix. This is indeed helpful, but it does not change the climate of taboo on affects in authors and readers or the dogmatic skepticism of deconstructionists about the function of language. I have occasionally seen brilliant psychobiographical insights—in essays on destructive obsessions in Fowles's *Collector* and in Wilde's *The Picture of Dorian Gray*, for example; but fully to uncover motivation in the conflicted creative psyche is more than most undergraduates are willing to attempt, unless the pathology is so evident (as with the poetry of Sylvia Plath) as to leave little alternative. In "True and False Self" Winnicott hit on the limiting factor in teaching applied psychoanalysis: the intellectual defense, by which the individual attempts "to solve the personal problem by use of a fine intellect," only to falsify his actual inner condition and therefore suffer from the sense of being phony.[26] While cultivation of fine intellects is well understood in universities, the meaning of affect is not. Holbrook calls for a sort of "affective education" which is beyond the capacity of all but a very few university teachers. The rigours and risks of engaging with affect-laden material in authors, and in the students addressing them, are more than most university teachers are prepared for. At Toronto we are fortunate to have a number of professors who by inclination and training are able to do this difficult work; most have been in personal analysis and are able to provide ways to fill this missing dimension in higher education.

Enriching the Critical Enterprise

Holbrook has started an entirely new critical enterprise—but nobody would claim it complete, any more than the critical efforts of Frederick Crews, Norman Holland, and other such pioneers can be said to be complete. Ground is lost as well as gained, and it takes time to decide which lines of inquiry are worth pursuing. Acknowledgement of the critic's own personality as the instrument of inquiry, of his or her own ego dynamics as relevant to the questions posed and answers received, is a long way off. Assumed intellectual omnipotence of dominant critics from Jacques Derrida to Stanley Fish is hard to dispel in the name of intersubjective sensitivity. Holbrook, himself, relies on the collective authority of a new existentialism comprised of philosophical anthropology and humanist psychoanalysis; a cloud of witnesses to his species of truth is invoked. It is hard to see how it could be otherwise and, further, the effects of feeling real and authentic must be personally experienced before the claims of Holbrook's sort of criticism can be vindicated. Psychoanalytic criticism reveals the feelings in our personal being by which we are most fascinated and compelled, but about which we may least want to know in explicit terms. There is tacit agreement in conventional study of literature as to what constitutes a safe or unsafe level of awareness of the core of pain, a core from which writers suffer and write to relieve suffering. For many academics it seems easier to collude in silence about this than to recognize it as a starting point for enriched critical practice. This takes enormous care, skill, and time on the part of mentors, of which universities are yet to see the cost-effectiveness. Students can only do what they are ready for, and to extend capability is to become involved at a level usually not recognized in higher education as we know it.

Will this change for the better? It depends on how worried people in general become about the abuses of imagination which obtrude into their lives. When we see clearly that spousal and child abuse, parental loss and family disorganization, inconsistent care giving and discipline, and so on, are at the back of most distressingly distorted imaginative material entering culture, we will reconsider how education at all levels should be conducted. It may be that universities will be unable to alter their instructional function enough to meet the new challenges of intersubjectivity posed by our students. Can psychoanalytic training institutes overcome dogmatic investments in particular theories in order to meet more fully the need for "affective education" beyond the merely intellectual? In Toronto Freudian, Jungian, and Self Psychology analysts attempt to do this in extension programmes and discussion groups, but the need for reorientation and enrichment of education far exceeds what is available, including the course offerings in the Humanities and Psychoanalytic Thought undergraduate major.

When David Holbrook directs attention to basic questions of cultural health and disorder he involves us in unpleasantness we may wish to avoid. Don't we go to the arts for exactly the sort of stimulation, reassurance and consolation his criticism tends to strip away? Avoidance, however, is to invite through ignorance the disruptive results of bad child rearing. Whatever can be done to prevent violent and disruptive behaviour must be done, and the clues as to its causes coded into the arts need attending to. The fantasies governing sexual relations and child rearing should be monitored and the results made known so that at least ignorance cannot be pleaded. This is a tough assignment, but David Holbrook points the way and we should build on his insights. I, for one, am enormously hearted by his criticism, and consider it a most promising pathway out of the cultural cul-de-sac into which neglect of information about healthy human development has led.

Notes

1. David Holbrook, *Human Hope and the Death Instinct* (Oxford: Pergamon Press, 1971), p. 297.
2. Ibid., p. 299.
3. Ibid., p. 301.
4. A. Alvarez, *The Savage God: A Study of Suicide* (London: Weidenfeld and Nicolson, 1971), p. 225.
5. Alice Miller, *For Your Own Good: Hidden Cruelty in Child-Rearing and the Roots of Violence* (New York: Farrar, Straus, and Giroux, 1983), p. 254f.
6. Phyllis Grosskurth, *Havelock Ellis: A Biography* (Toronto: McClelland and Stewart, 1980); *Melanie Klein: Her World and Her Work* (Toronto: McClelland and Stewart, 1986).
7. David Holbrook, *Dylan Thomas: The Code of Night* (London: The Athlone Press, 1972), p. 6.
8. David Holbrook, *Sylvia Plath: Poetry and Existence* (London: The Athlone Press, 1976), p. 11.
9. Paul Johnson, *Intellectuals* (London: Weidenfeld and Nicolson, 1988).
10. David Holbrook, *The Skeleton in the Wardrobe: The Fantasies of C. S. Lewis: A Phenomenological Study* (Lewisburg, Pa.: Bucknell University Press; London: Associated University Presses, 1991), p. 80.
11. Ibid., p. 81.
12. Ibid., p. 274.
13. David Holbrook, *Where D. H. Lawrence Was Wrong About Woman* (Lewisburg, Pa.: Bucknell University Press; London: Associated University Presses, 1992), p. 362.
14. David Holbrook, *Gustav Mahler and the Courage To Be* (London: Vision Press, 1975), p. 238.

15. Robert J. Stoller, *Perversion: The Erotic Form of Hatred* (New York: Pantheon Books, 1975), p. 65.
16. David Holbrook, *Sex and Dehumanization: In Art, Thought and Life In Our Time* (London: Pitman Publishing, 1972), p. 4.
17. Ibid., pp.180–81.
18. Robert J. Stoller, M.D., *Porn: Myths For The Twentieth Century* (New Haven and London: Yale University Press, 1991), Chapter 11.
19. *The Times Literary Supplement*, 3 November 1972, p. 1346.
20. *The Observer*, 4 February 1973, p. 44.
21. Holbrook, *Where D. H. Lawrence Was Wrong*, p. 43.
22. David Holbrook, "Dr. John Bowlby: No need to nod to positivist dogma," *New Universities Quarterly* 36, no. 4 (Autumn 1982): p. 326.
23. See Mary Ainsworth et al, *Patterns of Attachment: A Psychological Study of the Strange Situation* (Hillsdale, N.J.: Lawrence Erlbaum Associates, 1978). The research of Ainsworth, Main and many others is incorporated in John Bowlby, *Attachment and Loss*, 3 vols. (London: The Hogarth Press, 1969–1980).
24. Bruce Bawer, *The Middle Generation: The Lives and Poetry of Delmore Schwartz, Randall Jarrell, John Berryman and Robert Lowell* (Hamden, Conn.: The Shoe String Press, 1986); John J. Clayton, *Gestures of Healing: Anxiety and the Modern Novel* (Amherst: The University of Massachusetts Press, 1991); Andrew Brink, *Obsession and Culture: a Study of Sexual Obsessions in the Novel* (Madison, N.J.: Fairleigh Dickinson University Press, 1995).
25. David Holbrook, *What is it to be Human? New Perspectives in Philosophy* (Aldershot: Avebury, 1990), p. 3.
26. D. W. Winnicott, *The Maturational Processes and the Facilitating Environment: Studies in the Theory of Emotional Development* (London: The Hogarth Press, 1965), p. 144.

Looking: Subjectivity and the True Self

Ann and Barry Ulanov

"Look!" somebody says to us, immediately arresting our attention.

"Where? What?" we ask, annoyed, fascinated, caught, but, unless it is something that stares us in the face, without any clue as to what it is we have been asked to look at.

Nothing so commands us as this imperious "Look!" and nothing so little informs us about how to look, what to see, or where to go to understand what we have been doing. And yet nothing is so fundamental to the human, to being human, as looking and knowing how to look and where to look and what to make of looking. From the very beginning of our lives, out of a rudimentary looking, we find the postures, the gestures, and even in time the sounds and tastes and smells and touches of our being. But, except in rare cases, we do not find instruction in looking. We must pick up the skill as we do language, out of the air, from watching others do their looking, from an instinctive recognition that we had better look before we fall. Even more frequently, we learn from falling and discovering that if we had only looked we might not have fallen. Even then, unfortunately, we do not bring the discovery to full consciousness. We allow the urge to self-preservation to etch some simple patterns of looking in the unconscious and thus to help us avoid the sillier trippings up, the worst affronts to our dignity. But avoidances themselves can trip us up as, in the effort to maintain our dignity, we develop a pomposity of demeanor that lacks only a few throat-clearing har-rumphs to turn us into figures in slapstick comedy.

How is it possible? How can the informed use of what is clearly the most important of our five senses have so completely dodged us? We cannot help looking out at the world from the moment of waking each day until bedtime, and even in our sleep, in the eyesight we bring into our dreams. Somewhere, sometime, surely, we must have thought how good it would be to know more about how we might look at things, see people, and register the pictures of the parts of the world that confront us. For some reason—some twist of feeling or misadventure of consciousness or inaccessibility of the unconscious—we did not bring the passing thought to fruition. We continued to take looking for granted; it was as much a part of us as our getting up and sitting down, our eating and sleeping, the flow of our blood. It needed no intervention. It would go on working as a proper natural function should. Why bother with it? We saw no reason to develop the phenomenological eye, a name we were not likely to have known and even less likely to have adopted if we had heard about it.

The Phenomenological Eye

Out of a language that the philosopher Edmund Husserl has made his own, we now have this precise name for educated looking—the phenomenological eye. But what that splendidly crunchy term describes was not Husserl's invention. It was rather something he saw with a new and heightened clarity that characterized the art of looking, a way of summarizing that the prodigious observers of all epochs possessed. What it amounts to is a joining of eye and consciousness with much of the unconscious in the pursuit of full awareness of the world of which one is a part and of such of its parts as one might confront. It is a fullness which, it may be, only a few have possessed, but which many have aspired to and approached. It is, at its peak, perhaps, Lao-Tze's "long hard stare," when we stand poised at the threshold of mystical experience. It is that sense of being that a richly endowed looking gathers from all things, no matter how trivial, which in turn spur us to do, to act, and in acting to find our being. It is that opening to action through steadfast looking that led Goethe to the simple solemn words of Faust, *Im Anfang war die Tat*, "In the beginning was the deed," words that for Husserl suggest the infinite range of possibilities that press upon us when we accept the "multiplicities of givenness" that everywhere meet our subjectivity.

The world that is always with us, the lifeworld, is not simply given us, but "pregiven." It is not the world of scientific observation, however much it may be reflected there in the mathematized universe that has been with us at least since Galileo. It is what we perceive and intuit in all the particularities that surround us. We open our consciousness by "intention," to use a treasured concept in phenomenological philosophy, to what is there, to what can be related to, to what really is. And what really is, the tutored observer gifted with the phenomenological eye understands, is in touch with whatever has been and what may still be coming into being. We see out of the present eye not only the present world but all that is gathered up in the "pregiven," all that can be reactivated, all that can follow outer looking with inner observation.[1] To everything that has potentiality for us, everything that we can speculate upon, we give ontic validity. The future comes upon us, in this way of looking, joining what we have appropriated from the past and seen or touched or tasted or smelled or heard in the present in something like a seamless consciousness.

There is for the phenomenologist a ritual approach to this indivisibility of consciousness. It involves the concentration upon phenomena that Husserl calls the *epoché,* a suspension of judgment that removes from consciousness everything that is not in the experience of the phenomena. That is to "see" a phenomenon as an event, an act, of transcendent purity. It is there, outside oneself, for the moment all by itself, and it is there inside oneself, free of interference, unjudged, allowed to be itself. We have looked and we have seen. We have achieved, in this educated way of looking, an exchange of being with the world in at least some of its parts in which we find some of that satisfaction that the Book of Genesis tells us the Creator God knew after each of the days of creation.

Husserl knew such satisfaction in the development of his own understanding of what the phenomenological eye could see. He also knew an anguished dissatisfaction, in his growth over the decades from a philosopher of number and master of logical theory to a phenomenologist of the lifeworld. He looked and he saw in the Europe of the mid-1930s *The Crisis of the European Sciences,* as he called it, which is to say the failure of those who were graced with knowledge. His word for sciences is Wissenschaften, meaning the disciplines of learning, not simply the physical or biological sciences. Their failure was one that had been building over many centuries. Men of learning were no longer in touch with the pregiven world; theirs was the methodologically reduced, mathematized world of scientific "objectivity." An idealized nature had replaced the lifeworld, the world of endless subjectivities, including those of the scientists themselves, for they had excluded their own subjectivities in their truncated looking. Europe offered to the phenomenological eye of the 1930s the *grand guignol* to the totalitarian dictatorships, which was about to turn into a real horror show. But Europe itself simply had no idea of what was the true specter haunting it. It could no longer look at itself as it was, but only at mathematical models of itself. In the last paragraph of the unfinished *Crisis,* Husserl's mixture of horror and contempt are unmistakable in the face of the spectacle. These are the effects of a truncated, scientific looking: "everything is decided in advance as pure mathematics and as nature itself. Such is the dominant hypothesis which has guided natural science through the centuries." But this is surely impossible for all who are part of "a world which also contains spiritual beings"; for such a world and its subjectivities, "this being-in-advance is an absurdity. The idea of an ontology of the world, the idea of an objective, universal science of the world, having behind it a universal a priori according to which every possible factual world is knowable *more geometrico*—this idea which led even Leibniz astray—is a *nonsens.*"

For Husserl, as for many other observers of his dimension, the separation of human subjectivity from its true dwelling place in the pregiven world, in the name of scientific objectivity, was an absurdity of tragic consequences: "For the realm of souls there is in principle no such ontology, no science corresponding to the physicalistic-mathematical ideal. . . ."[2]

The psyche could be investigated, Husserl thought, to bring us some knowledge of how we connect with our own subjectivity and with the subjectivities of others in the world around us which in such large measure consists of subjectivities. In such an investigation we must be on guard against the facile psychologism which only too quickly becomes just another falsifying determinism consecrated to "the physicalistic-mathematical ideal." Fixed psychological laws are as untrustworthy as any others drawn from dubious positivism. And we must add, sadly, so really is Husserl's own attempt through the exercise of phenomenological procedures to produce some certitude of understanding of the human psyche. It leaves us, partly because of his own wisdom, as unsatisfied, in some ways, as the *Wissenschaften* in crisis that he has been writing about. We see, if we look hard enough, that we too are in the difficult position of having to deal with what comes to us through the psyche almost entirely with resources that are also drawn from the psyche and reside in it. We are back with that dilemma that St. Augustine described so winningly, when we are forced to scratch at an itch in a finger with another finger of the same hand and cannot tell after awhile which is the finger that is itching and which the one that is working to end the itch.

Leonardo on the Eye

What the phenomenological wisdom does give us, richly restored in its potential, is the eye. We can look again—and see. We can rhapsodize, at least for a moment, with Leonardo da Vinci over the eye as "the window of the soul . . . chief organ whereby the understanding can have the most complete and magnificent view of the infinite works of nature." With Leonardo, we can accept again the role of the eye as conveyor of light to the soul, leaving the soul as a result "content to stay imprisoned in the human body. . . ." We may or may not be content with the reasoning that leads Leonardo to conclude that "the eye transmits its own image through the air to all the objects which face it"; but surely we must recognize the solidity of his conclusion, which he reports as the result of his elaborate experience of looking: the exchange of memories he has observed between the receiving eye and the objects it receives, each of them ending up with an imprint of the other, in their life together, which he identifies as a *sensus communis*. There is no banishing of human subjectivity from the pregiven world in Leonardo's observations, or of the subjectivity of an object, human or non-human.

As with Goethe some four centuries later, Leonardo was persuaded that the deed was what there was in the beginning. Movement was what he looked for as a painter, but never to end with his observation of the flexing of a limb or the shifting of someone's eyes or any other positioning of a body. "A good painter has two chief objects to paint," he said, "man and the intention of his soul. . . ." It is easy enough to get the first, by which Leonardo means the surface of a body, but not the second, for there spiritual and psychological intention must be gathered from a close reading of a painting's surfaces following the painter's direction in discovering what "the attitudes and movements" of the human body reveal of its interior life. "The knowledge of these," he tells us, "are best acquired by observing the dumb, because their movements are more natural than those of any other persons."

Leonardo's directions for the way painters should look at objects are like Husserl's—they stress intention. "The most important consideration in painting," says the artist, "is that the movements of each figure express its mental state, such as desire, scorn, anger, pity, and the like. In painting the actions of the figures are in every case expressive of the purpose in their minds."[3] If we follow Leonardo where he leads, we may end up seeing more in a movement than the mover intended, but as we come to recognize this way how much a movement may convey, we will be attending to the most important of the pregivens in the world that surrounds us, other people. If we can do so with some understanding edge to our consciousness, seeing this as a preliminary exercise in the art of looking, we will make few foolish final judgments and learn a great deal about the lifeworld that we share with others.

Leonardo's suggestion about the usefulness of observing the movements of those without speech might well be the center of our exercise. We should begin by looking at the whole world around us as if it were mute. That is the way really to see it, unconfused by sounds, undistracted by the complexities words bring with them. It is not easy to do, because, even hanging onto the outskirts of a situation, the trivia of a place or of a time, we can quickly be drawn into conversation and quite forget our original intention. We may have to pretend to be mute ourselves to bring along a sketch pad and warn people off as we make notations on its pages, whatever is necessary to protect the inviolability of our looking.

Is all this necessary? Only if we really want to look and to see, and not simply to look and to see the surfaces of people. The same is true of all the related worlds of nature. Plants and trees are not likely to draw us into conversation, but animals might. To become a true observer, one must practice the looking of quiet. One must put aside everything else, everything that presses from the outside and everything that presses from the inside. To find oneself as an observer, one must forget oneself.

The ego works hard, on these occasions, to assert itself, to remind us who after all is doing the looking, and doing it with such élan. "Look at me looking!" we hear it say. "What a piece of work!" What a fullness of observation! What an eye for detail! Or just as clamorously, it may remind us how woefully we are performing this simple task. "Look out, you idiot!" How could you have missed that bending of the knee, that twisting of the hips, that simpering *moue*? Don't you realize that you're dealing with a come-on? Her—his—sexuality just oozes."

All of that is precisely what must be emptied out, as in the purgative stages of mental prayer. It is not our part in the looking process that matters at this point, but what is looked at, all the way from an oddly discolored blade of grass that seems to demand to be looked at in a large sweep of lawn of which it is a tiny part to the soft, shuffling movements a particular person makes as he pushes into a crowd, looking around nervously to make sure no one notices and thereby assuring that everybody will notice. We come, in this practice of muting out the world, really to see the world, and not just those parts of it that, by such strategies as off-colored grass or nervous attempts not to be seen, draw our attention to themselves. As we become sensitized to detail, as we come, all but oblivious of ourselves, to receive others and otherness with ease, we may begin also to bring ourselves into the picture. If we do this with a Leonardesque or Husserlian assurance, we are bound to become a part of things, not as a central player, perhaps, not with a false ego-emphasis, but as a deliberate participant, one who has earned the role of mediating consciousness by such long and persistent devotion to others. We will have looked so long and so well at the others' subjectivities, including the subjectivities of animals and plants and inanimate objects, that our own subjectivity, simply as subjectivity, will have to take its place in the intersubjective landscape.[4] We know now that the *sensus communis* really exists, and exists this way, by the intentional interpenetration of subjectivities, by the multiple mirrorings of people, and places, and things exchanging images in open and oblique ways, including the animate with the inanimate. This is the way our looking will be rewarded. This is the way we will know that we really have looked and seen, for what we have seen will clearly reflect our seeing.

Listening

What is true of looking is equally true of listening. We learn to hear as we have learned to see, by a rigorously directed listening, from which, at least to begin with, we have excluded our egos. It is not important, when we first begin to listen, that *we* are listening; what counts is *what* we are hearing. All our conscious intention is directed to hearing accurately, to hearing what is there in the multiple voices, say, of some Bach counterpoint, in the staccato rhythms of Stravinsky, in the retrograde or crabwise maneuverings of a Schoenberg tone row, in the dartings away from or back toward the chord progression upon which a jazz improvisation is based. For all the technical difficulties that may be involved for those inadequately instructed in listening to music, most of that is easy compared to what is involved in listening to persons and really hearing them as persons, not only their voices and the words they speak, but their underlying intentions or lack of them, as best we can make them out. We are in Leonardo's realm of soul, and again, as with looking and the appropriate movement from self-detachment to self-reflection, we will in time reach the point of mediation in our listening exercises. We will not only listen and hear what is said, but know who is saying it and some of the reasons why it is being said. We will be able, then, to intercede for the speaker or for ourselves or anybody else who might be listening. We want now to listen, and to look, for the person. We want to use such skill as we may have to make more of the persons we meet, to increase the fullness of their presence, and in so doing to make more of our own presence in an interdependence of presences and persons, of places and things, of all that a fineness of looking can achieve.

David Holbrook's Looking

What we are talking about is well exemplified by David Holbrook. In his life and work, there is a constant seeing of who is there and seeing into what is there. His has been a wide and deep looking that recognizes the interrelation of personal identity and shared life with others in a culture. His is a persistent looking that sees what many in our late twentieth century want to deny. Along with depth psychologists, principally those of the Object-Relations School, Holbrook recognizes the range and depth of psychic reality and with it the inestimable effects of consciousness. We are conscious; we can be conscious; we can help each other to become more conscious. Or, we can attack this definitively human capacity by trying to reduce it or control it. How we enhance or restrict our own consciousness—our own looking and looking into, our own listening, all the intentions of our consciousness—inevitably affects how we treat others' capacity to look and see, to listen and to hear, to be conscious. The refusal to allow a subject to be a subject is the special skill of totalitarian governments, the inevitable result of tyranny over personal freedoms in the workplace and of the control of censorship over the imagination in culture. We annihilate the subjectivities of others as we have annihilated our own in the name of an all-purpose and all-powerful objectivity. As Augustine put it so long ago, *Non quod dabet non quod habet:* You cannot give what you do not have. What is it that Holbrook exemplifies in his looking? This is a looking that combines two habitual ways of beholding the pregivens of the world around us. Marion Milner, the painter and psychoanalyst to whom Holbrook often refers, describes the differences between the two ways as contrasts between female and male ways of looking.[5] The female way combines a wide looking at what is actually there with the more concentrated long hard stare that we associate with the contemplative mind. The result is that we see an object honestly; it is fully beheld as a subject in its own right. Following what our eye actually sees, without the intervention of our thought or will as to what we ought to be seeing, or wish we could see, we contemplate the other in all his or her otherness, and may even plunge into a state of nonseparateness from him or her or it. We say "No" to a spurious objectivity. In our gladly received subjectivity, we come to share something like a mystical union with this other in which we retain a responsive alertness to and a sense of reciprocity with the other that affirms both ourselves and the other in our subjective reality.[6] Under the stress of an extreme objectivization, following that mathematization of everything which has so blighted modern life, we may fear the possibility of total loss of identity in a merger or fusion with the other in which we must all lose our sense of being. In an assured, subjectivity-centered looking, we see and know instead the spontaneous ordering forces of life that proceed without our interference, that stop or go on without our willing them to do one or the other. We recognize and trust the forces of order that lie beyond our control. We see that all is not up to us to make or break in a world. We cease trying to make others into objectivized subjects who can be accounted for and put in their proper places in an objective order that a geometrically tidy universe demands. Whatever this spontaneous ordering is, we recognize that in it parts are brought into wholes by a mixture of order and disorder, made into what psychoanalysts call "whole persons," not stray gatherings of bits and pieces, no matter how many fragments may have had to be picked up along the way to make these wholes. In this kind of looking, Milner's way, we relate inner fantasies and dreams to outer facts, and inner imaginings to the world of otherness that exists there, all around us, unmistakably outside us.

Male and Female Looking

Our more accustomed way of looking, the male way, narrowly focuses our attention so that we can analyze what we see and can think about it deliberately and logically. The result often is a shutting out of any vital, intense, or disorderly experiences in thought or feeling that we might have known, and with them the wholeness of our own subjectivity, one existing in its own right, with its own particular identity and individual nature. Thus omitting our "haloes of feeling," we separate ourselves from what we see. We look *at* it, not *into* it or *with* it.[7] At extremes, this kind of looking so separates a subjectivity from otherness that it may find itself condemned to exist in a schizoid isolation. That is what looking at subjects as objects, with the excuse of scientific objectivity, only too often accomplishes. We have been promised an unbiased and fuller way of seeing, but in fact all we have been granted is the most partial viewing of our relation to our world. For in this way of looking, we see others only in terms of our own expediencies and exigencies, directing them only to our own purposes, which even when they are good purposes can only produce a restricted viewing. Too often, as adults, we rely upon this second way of seeing, this male way, this "objective" way, as the grown-up, tough-minded way of seeing the world as it really is, and then quite thoroughly miss the miracle of looking at things and actually seeing them.

When we stop looking at the world in terms only of our own purposes, we can look instead to that openness to seeing that proposes a "complete transfiguration of the common sense expedient view where objects exist mainly in terms of their usefulness. . . ." We may see again "a world of living essences existing in their own right and offering a source of delight simply through the act of being themselves."[8] This still and active "imaginative concentration," to which we have given ourselves, "gives of itself, of its own essence, to what it sees," and this in turn brings joy, "shouting seraphim . . . 'cosmic bliss.'"[9] Looking at the world in this way is in itself a creative act, one which most of us have known in childhood and too often lost as adults, but can still, with a renewal of the graces, regain. David Holbrook's purpose, as we look at it and see it in his poetry, novels, criticism, and psychological speculation, in his exploration of educational theory and in his paintings, is to enable us to recover a matching firmness of looking and fullness of beholding, which dwell upon being and take fire from it in that species of creative doing that springs from a certitude of seeing. That is what holds open to all of us, regardless of differences of class or educational level or endowment, the possible recovery to consciousness of the life of the imagination, bringing to fruition a wholeness of the person which is affronted neither by the female nor the male way of viewing things.[10]

We arrive at this kind of male and female looking, so full of awe and respect for being, and our constant active response to it, from ordinary "good-enough mothering," to use Winnicott's consecrated phrase for it.[11] We can also be helped in this kind of looking by an educated imagination, or a happy love relation and the mutual looking and beholding that goes on between lovers. What goes on in acts of praise or in prayer or in our feeling of gratitude to something or someone beyond ourselves is equally conducive to such a matching of ways of looking, and equally trustworthy. Holbrook's own trust is in the worlds we are given in ordinary life, for in them the acts of what Milner calls "transfiguration" occur; there the miracles of perception develop through interchanges of the two ways of looking. We see being as it is in its back-and-forth fullness, rich, abundant, unfolding, as if offering itself for the taking across all the divides and conjunctions of the sexes. This looking upon being, founded upon a deep trusting respect for the given potential in each of us for true-self living, is drawn by Holbrook from Winnicott, other Object-Relations theorists such as Fairbairn, Guntrip, and Klein, and his own life as teacher and theorist, writer and painter, husband and father.[12]

Holbrook's contribution is to take this understanding out of the consulting room into its surrounding culture, and most particularly into education and the arts, to see how true-self living is engendered or endangered there. He not only puts before us how in the shared spaces of culture we can nurture in each other an authentic and rewarding living; he also sets himself against the enemies of trust in living in the true self, and especially against the elaborate casuistries and causes that pretend to be advancing life while in fact they seek to evade and cancel it. He has set his sword against pretensions to high art that camouflage attacks on being, philosophies and psychologies that purport to give insight into being but actually work to sabotage it in their narrow, foreclosing determinisms, and such attacks on the self as are to be found in abundance in films that use themes of violence to mask dread and annihilation of the female and of the feminine kind of attention to being.

Psychic Reality

One can see in Holbrook's work a remarkable implication: through this kind of looking that penetrates through surfaces to psychic reality and finds in acts of beholding a great fund of human experience, new criteria of judgment must emerge. We must ask ourselves, does this art, or political position, or philosophy, this kind of symbol or educational method, promote or hinder true-self living in us? The emphasis is on "us," not "me." In the shared spaces of our culture, whether by choice or not, we directly affect each other; in them, we can enhance or wither the kind of looking that brings life. Society is not imposed upon us in order to repress our instinctual satisfactions. Society is our own product much of the time, a conjunction of people and institutions trying to find ways of expressing their basic need—of self for other. Libido is not, in this understanding, simply aimed at pleasure, but rather at effecting relation to an "other." To be a subject, in this undertaking toward relationship, is the only way to meet the need for an object. Finding and living with real people, with love and reparative effort, fosters integration, and helps us find solutions to vexing social problems. Culture, we come to see in this sort of looking, is not a reward for the deprivations society imposes, a sort of consolation prize in the form of sublimated drives, but a complex space in which daily we are offered the opportunity to explore being, to feel real in a real world.

A new criterion for social action arises when in our looking we recover the feminine mode of being human.[13] With it, we recognize dependence as an inescapable part of ourselves. We all begin our life in absolute dependence on woman, a fact Winnicott makes much of, which Holbrook finds celebrated in the archetypal image of the holy mother and child. Love of this sort is what allows us to grow from relative dependence to independence and finally interdependence with others. In love we do not have to deny our dependence, but can see it and accept it and celebrate the ways that in it we are able to help each other, each making up for lacks in the other, and all together building relationship where we can take care of the fullest flow of the libido in each of us and send it forth, in pairings, into the world.

The Nurturing of the Arts

Unlike psychoanalysts who can make us feel that it is all over by the time we are five years old—if we missed that good-enough mothering in our infancy, it is clearly too late now—Holbrook shows us how our culture and the arts can go on nurturing us toward full-hearted living. We can do this for each other on a large scale when we establish a community, with whatever organizing principle, an idea of the joining of persons not unlike that held by the religious who come together as the people of God. Inexorably, Holbrook brings what psychoanalysts have discovered, in practice and theory, into the world of everyday life. We do not have to enter analysis to find the source of creative living. It is there for the taking in paintings, literature, music, film, philosophy, even politics. The one area Holbrook leaves out, except for a few passing remarks, is religion. But we will come to that later.

By focusing on symbolism, Holbrook explores the ways cultures offer us spaces in which we can thrive or be poisoned. For the symbols in which a culture communicates itself can peddle hate, paranoia, despair, even death, dressed up in avant-garde colors as a structure that inheres in the modern or combats it and requires subscription, in a flurry of hyphens, to an anti-value, contra-judgment, all-purpose, anti-purposive post-modernism. Holbrook contrasts true-self symbolism with manic or schizoid symbolism. The difference turns on a simple perception: the looking at or blinding ourselves to our human dependence, which generally means reflecting upon the female element in all of us. Schizoid symbolism springs from a deficit of dependence in love: we could not lean upon another, but were, so to speak, dropped, not held in being. A gap exists in us where there should be a whole fabric, without any breaks, and we fear to fall into the gap, which is to say into madness, forever. We cover the gap over and look with self-loathing at our fear of it, and the threat it holds over us, of disintegration, by reversing values. Lust is celebrated over mutual lovemaking, for example, in the early James Bond film *Goldfinger*;[14] hatred and contempt for the "other," embodied as woman, is prized over nurture and seeing the other really flourish, an attitude of distortion and constriction also, unhappily, reflected in several different kinds of existentialist philsophy.[15] Knowing how to be seen in the right places is the grand appeal made in advertising, altogether effacing the possibilities of actually being in places, right or wrong, and experiencing their people and environments.[16] Splitting male and female ways of looking is promoted as the solution to the struggle to knit them together. The immediate gratification of impulse and the concomitant denial of suffering through an acquisition of riches, or power, or status is sold as the ideal. Violence is vaunted as strength, quite concealing the fact that most often it is the result of a desperate attempt to combat an inner deadness.[17]

The schizoid solution is invariably a false one, a way of not looking at the pregiven world. Its identifying marks are a running away from the heart of being, a determination to escape from vulnerability and dependence, and denying an underlying hate by setting hate loose in the world. In the name of our cause, we bully others. To satisfy the starvation of the unborn self in us, which we deny, we thrust into the world our savage hunger, one that can devour the whole world, a hunger like Hitler's or Stalin's.

In revenge against the love of which we are deprived, we attack its existence in others, reducing it to sentimental softness, or pie-in-the-sky unreality, or an anti-social elitism. Holbrook's good point is that false solutions to life's sufferings are easily collectivized in the form of tyrannical government, social injustice, discrimination against the young, and with particular deadlines, against the female.

The question that remains at the end of such analysis is clear. If manic symbolism substitutes obsessive doing for the being it denies, and schizoid symbolism withdraws from the basic human experience of feeling real in oneself and respecting the reality of others and covers its splitting off by its frenzied opposites, then what does true-self symbolism do?

The Symbolism of the Self

The special symbolism of the true self comes from a large experience of looking at the world as it is manifested to us on the surface and beneath it. Such symbolism explores being as a matter of course and the way it is articulated in the arts, in politics, in religion. These are symbols enlisted in the effort to express what it means to be human, to be a person, to possess a subjectivity related to other subjectivities in a world of subjectivities. Such symbolism does not traffic easily in sentimentality. It may emerge from a psychic agony, such as displayed in Arshile Gorky's paintings, most earnestly in the one called "Agony." Beholding such pain through color, shape, line, composition; entering it and letting it enter us imaginatively, allows us to experience what sorely afflicts us, without having to act it out or in any way feel pressed to act on it. Art does not offer us preventive medicine, though it can keep us from suicide by allowing us to venture into the most dangerous precincts of emotion and the imagination without the literalism of the act.[18] We can understand, then, why we have constructed such elaborate resistance to the arts. For they take us into the vulnerable parts of our being—which are not always so easily identifiable as agony—and we can feel these dissociated or depressed bits of psychic being, both in the artist and in ourselves, in an embodied way, not just abstractly as mental construct or concept. As Jung puts it, the image is the real thing.[19]

Symbols of this kind address the selves we truly are, with all our conflicts and ambivalences, all our dependencies and vulnerabilities, our gladness in creating, our loving as well as our hate.

They feed us, indeed root-feed us, as if we were trees gathering nourishment from the ground up. Such symbols water our earth, plow it, fertilize it, plant our seed in it. True-self symbolism offers shelter for our fledgling egos moving into being and protection for what we have arrived at in our actual becoming. In story or image or dramatic conflict, in instrumental sound or bodily movement, we explore our anxieties and fears, our ambiguous mixtures of feeling, not denying them or putting them onto someone else, whom we can then blame for our misadventures. True-self symbolism helps us own all that belongs to us to live and to discharge. We feel our hunger for positive experience and our anger that we are not fed or seen or valued by others. We do not split them off and intellectualize them in schizoid symbols, or fear that if we acknowledge our needs, we must then incorporate the whole world, as we try to do in manic symbolism. In really listening to music, for example, instead of having it invade us with a repetitious bombarding, or having it lull our fear of emptiness by providing a constant background noise, we feel the inexplicable mixtures of loving and hating, as well as the worldless unity we are capable of with another. Room is made in symbols that in effect look at us as we have looked around us to find traces of our actual being, of our selves as we live them, our guilt, our sense of deficiency, our dependence on others. We do not have to deny anything that may seem to detract from us in a display of omnipotence. Nor are we constrained to deny the goodness of our love, or, in an offering of Uriah Heep-ish humbleness, our energy to accomplish, our willingness to give, our gladness in putting help into the world, our sheer pleasure in the wonder of being. All this can be expressed openly. Bridges can be built, back and forth, again and again, from inner fantasy to outer fact, from psychic dream to social reality. All the different kinds of feelings, thoughts, fears, hopes, pains, plans, needs of which human beings are capable can be allowed to flow in and out of symbols of the truly human self, symbols providing a space in which the self can grow or even diminish if that proves to be the best way to receive the self.

Receiving Being

So much of what Holbrook writes is concerned with receiving being, responding to being, celebrating being, not in a namby-pamby way that disregards the anguish and terror of life, but in a passionate way that embraces all of life. His temper lets loose against those who would shortchange us. We come then to a puzzling question: Why is the transcendent left out of it? When one presents Holbrook's works to theological students, both those already in and those preparing to go into the trenches that comprise the ministry in the late twentieth century, one quickly sees that they are heartened by Holbrook's insistence on putting first things first. They find themselves at one in giving precedence, as he does, to the reality of the human self drawn into community with the selves of others. This seems to such students almost exactly what so much of their religion leads them to believe that the God of Christianity and Judaism, and indeed of other religions as well, commands us to do. Holbrook's work helps them see the value of our culture, how much good dwells there, how much resource the arts offer. They like his ways of looking that permit so much to be seen, in themselves as well as in their work in church and synagogue. Acceptance of our weakness, eschewing an obsessional doing that seeks to certify our all-rightness, claiming the good instead of dreading it and fastening upon evil instead—all this seems very close to religious vision. Why then is a sense of the transcendent, whether beyond us or within and among us, not an explicit part of Holbrook's thought? It certainly is implicit again and again in his work.

These same students grow restive sometimes at the impassioned tones of the pleas for the true self, its living through us, its symbolism. They worry that a new list of rules may be in the wings, a certifying of those symbols which are acceptable and a casting off of those which are not. They feel, some of them, addressed in hortatory tones; they fear a new moralism. We who write this essay are saved from this reading by our own looking, seeing the passion that Holbrook brings into his work. His looking, which we are looking at, bespeaks the transcendent object that lies behind Object-Relations theory, which its theorists claim no more explicitly than he does. Holbrook is in fact, we think, perceiving the big object, the infinite one, that transcends the finite objects to which he directs his looking. What feels like an exhortation to some is in fact a burgeoning passion, a passion that may sometimes seem incommensurate with what it lights upon. It looms; it insists; it magnifies into still another interesting, original, vital project. It is a passion that goes beyond its immediate objects to come strongly at the reader, to persuade and then to convert, at the very least to an emancipated strong-willed looking that will sometime somewhere find an object large enough for its informing energies.

Holbrook himself will surely go on looking and creating many more books, pictures, poems, ideas, imaginings. Explicit acknowledgement of the object larger than life, the transcendent one, the one that has been pushing and pulling him through his long creativity, will, we think, inevitably emerge under its appropriate name. His seminal recognition of psychic reality as the one we share in our culture requires him to go further. The true self, we learn through his looking as with all looking of such distinction, opens to the reality of the whole world, the pregiven world, and that whole world then comes back to us through the psyche. We share this reality together in our culture as it looks beyond itself into another, greater reality. Jung puts it well in words that seem to us to be appropriate to the subject of looking and to fit that exemplary demonstration of looking that David Holbrook provides: "The collective unconscious, it's not for you, or me, it's the invisible world, it's the great spirit. It makes little difference what I call it: God, Tao, the Great Voice, the Great Spirit. But for people of our time God is the most comprehensible name with which to designate the Power beyond us."[20]

Notes

1. Husserl says of the pregiven world, "It is pregiven to us all quite naturally, as persons within the horizon of our fellow men, i.e., in every actual connection with others, as 'the' world common to us all." And again, "The pregiven world is the horizon which includes all our goals, all our ends, whether fleeting or lasting, in a flowing but constant manner. Just as an intentional horizon-consciousness implicitly 'encompasses' [everything] in advance." See Edmund Husserl, *The Crisis of European Sciences and Transcendental Phenomenology*, trans. David Carr (Evanston, Ill.: Northwestern University Press, 1970), pp. 122, 144. The quotation from *Faust* in the previous paragraph is from Part I, line 1237.

2. For this and the previous quotation see Husserl, *Crisis*, p. 265.

3. See *Selections from the Notebooks of Leonardo da Vinci*, ed. Irma A. Richter (London: Oxford University Press, 1952), pp. 110–12, 176.

4. We achieve, within our limits, the kind of response to the natural world—the looking, the listening, the taking counsel with the natural world and all its subjects and objects—with which North American Indians have been so long associated. See, for example, the gathering of "Sacred myths, dreams, visions, speeches, healing formulas, rituals and ceremonials" in *Native North American Spirituality of the Eastern Woodlands*, ed. Elizabeth Tooker, in the Classics of Western Spirituality series (New York: Paulist Press, 1979).

5. Marion Milner, *On Not Being Able to Paint* (New York: International Universities Press, 1979), pp. 81–82.

6. See Ann Belford Ulanov, *Receiving Woman: Studies in the Psychology and Theology of the Feminine* (Louisville: Westminster Press, 1981), chap. 4.

7. Milner, *On Not Being Able*, p. 81.

8. Ibid., p. 21.

9. See Marion Milner, "The Sense in Nonsense (Freud and Blake's Job)," in *The Suppressed Madness of Sane Men* (London: Tavistock, 1987), pp. 178–79. Milner's use of "cosmic bliss" here is from Freud.

10. See, for an extended treatment of these "ways" of viewing things, Ann and Barry Ulanov, *The Healing Imagination* (Mahwah, N.J.: Paulist Press, 1991).

11. See D. W. Winnicott, "Ego Distortion in Terms of True and False Self," in *The Maturational Processes and the Facilitating Environment* (New York: International Universities Press, 1965), pp. 145–46.

12. See Winnicott, ibid., pp. 148–49. The conception of the "true self," first articulated by Winnicott, includes spontaneous gesture, tissue liveness, continuity, creativity. In our true self, we feel real, distinctly our own person, and know ourselves in relation to others in the world.

13. See Ann Belford Ulanov, *The Feminine in Jungian Psychology and in Christian Theology* (Evanston, Ill.: Northwestern University Press, 1971), chap. 9.

14. See David Holbrook, *Masks of Hate* (London: Pergamon, 1972), Part II.

15. See David Holbrook, *Human Hope and the Death Instinct* (London: Pergamon, 1971), pp. 165–67.

16. See David Holbrook, *Education, Nihilism and Survival* (London: Darton, Longman & Todd, 1977), pp. 21–25.

17. Holbrook, *Human Hope*, pp. 196, 226.

18. The master of this lightning-rod ritual in painting in René Magritte. We go everywhere that fantasy, dream, a calculated consciousness or uncalculated unconscious can take us. See, for example, *"La reproduction interdite"* (Not to be reproduced), in which reality and unreality meet as a young man looks at a mirror and sees not his face, but the back of his head, with all that that might suggest about unfinished or unfulfilled self-encounters. The point is seconded by the book shown on the fireplace mantle at the man's left, Edgar Allan Poe's *The Narrative of Arthur Gordon Pym*, a tale of fantasized great adventure. Magritte's sense of reality in this area, which is perhaps "surreal" in the worlds held up to sorrowful inspection by Holbrook, is conveyed by these words: "The work of most artists is conceived under the illusion that it needs to be done—that the world would be somehow endangered if it weren't, and that it is therefore necessary to the world. (Unless of course it is just done to make money.) It would be all the same to me if my paintings were destroyed. Life continues." See David Sylvester, *René Magritte* (New York: Praeger, 1969), p. 9. The painting discussed here is reproduced on p. 118.

19. See Holbrook, *Human Hope*, p. 236, and C. G. Jung, *Mysterium Coniunctionis, Collected Works*, Vol. 14 (New York: Pantheon, 1954), par. 511.

20. See *C. G. Jung Speaking*, eds. William McGuire and R. F. C. Hull (Princeton: Princeton University Press, 1977), p. 419.

Cupid and Psyche: Understanding the Workings of the Female Mind

Pamela Taylor

Fictional encounter.

The doors which opened into the empty room swung apart with furious energy and a woman stepped confidently into the empty space. She seemed blazingly, violently angry despite the sense of self-possession which masked the rawest edges of the emotion. A tall woman followed immediately after her, a woman whose face, sensitive and delicate, wore an expression of distress.
"*I think you are too indignant.*"
The first woman stopped, turned, smiled ironically. Her voice was deep and rich.
"*Jumping to conclusions? He insinuates that I am some kind of maniac, he accuses me of being a witch, a sorceress, a destroyer . . .*"
"*He has suggested nothing about you that he has not also suggested about me.*"
"*And that is supposed to help me? I just accept it?*"
"*We have little choice. Consider our position.*"
The scorn on the first speaker's face was evident.
The rapidity of her angry movement brought her several steps away from the door and towards the french windows that looked over the unkempt garden. Impatiently she pushed the handle and the door swung out. As the cooler air began to fill the room a pale figure appeared outside the doors and stared coldly at the two women inside.
"*Esther Greenwood,*" *she said.*
The other two women glanced at each other.
"*Esther Greenwood,*" *repeated the newcomer, more hesitantly.*
The other two women drew closer to each other, slightly turning so that they excluded the third figure from their muttered conversation.
"*Who is she?*"
"*How should I know? I came to hear this talk at your instigation. I have no idea who else will be here.*"

They swung back to face the third woman.

"Why have you come?" asked Ursula gently.

"I want to get free, clear things up, start again. I'm sick of the stigma. I've been mentally ill, broke down. It's no crime but I am never allowed to forget it."

There was silence.

"It's no crime," repeated the stranger insistently.

"My name is Gudrun. My sister and I also feel indignant that we've been called schizoid, superior, contemptuous of the world. It is inaccurate."

"I am not sure," began Ursula and then paused and asked, "What caused your breakdown?"

"Life in general; being female in particular," whispered Esther. "I got so tired of misuse, abuse, lack of meaning in what I was doing, the inability to have a relationship based on someone knowing me rather than screwing me."

Ursula and Gudrun moved closer.

"Don't we know it; don't we just know it. Yet this man sees us in terms which will never acknowledge the wholeness of our character."

Gudrun's pale face did not change colour but the vehemence of her speech made her shake.

Ursula looked pale, tense.

"He might have a point. We are none of us free from the control of those who gave us life. And each of us was engendered by someone with difficulties, sickness of some kind.

We grew from disturbed minds and must carry the seeds of that within us. We must acknowledge our inner self."

"What are you talking about? Your self? The self the author wished you to have? Children always leave home, you know. Characters can escape their creator. Don't you know that each of us is read differently depending on who encounters us? It's what life is about, it is what fiction is about and it is certainly what being female is about. No one is only one thing. No one fits easily into the stereotypes and yet what happens? All of us are held up as examples of schizoid, damaged women who cannot cope with life. Just because this man has a pet theory gleaned from a reading of psychoanalysis, it has to be applied to every woman, every female character; we are all so different, so various and yet here we are in the same old straitjacket. It's the old story . . . label women, cause them to be taken less seriously."

"Oh, you aren't being fair. He wants to know about women . . . that is fairly rare. He's trying to discover what makes us tick; what motivates us and those who create us."

A new voice was suddenly heard from the hall into which the double doors led. The three women walked quietly into the hall and from there into a lecture room which led from the hallway. At the far end was a suspended gallery labelled Contributors. In this a number of eminent-looking people sat. At a wooden lectern in the centre of the stage a middle-aged woman in a navy blue dress was announcing the title of a talk. In front of her sat a handful of oddly and variously dressed women. Gudrun, Ursula and Esther moved quietly to find their seats and the voice began. . . .

Starting Points

The critical writings of David Holbrook bring together fascination with literature, an interest in psychoanalysis and a near obsessional attempt to understand what it is to be female. This dynamic urge to understand women is not all that Holbrook's criticism is about but it is a major concern. This concern is both engrossing and unsettling. Holbrook's insistence on the differentness of women is both alienating and fascinating. Whilst he strives to close the gap between male and female experience he nevertheless widens it, placing woman as "the other," forever moving in a foreign state of being. There is much of fairy tale in this—woman as entowered Rapunzel, Sleeping Beauty, glass-coffined Snow White or alternatively as witch, wicked stepmother or calculating sorceress. In *The Quest For Love* (1964) Holbrook declared an intention to

> make connections between the recent findings of psychoanalysis about love and our dealings with reality, and the poet's preoccupation with these.

He argued that in psychoanalysis was to be found

> an attempt to make a rational approach to the nature of being, a use of reason and intelligence in exploring the spirit.

He argued too that new writing of any significant creativity would only emerge if artists searched for

> insight into such profound truths as have to do with love and our dealings with reality, such as are being revealed by our increased insight into the mind.[1]

A highly personal interest is declared which is illuminating and startling in its honest acknowledgement of emotional commitment to an area of exploration:

> My interest in psychoanalytical themes has been impelled by the experience of being presented with the inescapable truth of at least some of psychoanalytical theory and practice, first hand enough in terms of actual living since I have been in love with and married to the subject of treatment.[2]

It is this honesty which gives Holbrook's critical work its intensity and passion. It also gives perhaps some insight into his own deep interest in the working of the female mind.

Essentially *The Quest for Love* is an attempt to revalue the creative, pro-life values represented by the fulfilled love of male and female; this relationship is seen as central to balance human experience. In attempting to illuminate how psychoanalysis and literature can combine to reveal the self and the nature of reality, Holbrook also seeks to show how humans can be enabled to love, to engage in creative emotion. Woman, he argues, can be both the enabler and the destroyer and as a result takes on a role of central importance in literary texts. The influence of psychoanalysts such as Guntripp, Winnicott and Klein on Holbrook's view of woman is undeniable. The argument is succinctly distilled in *Where D. H. Lawrence was Wrong about Woman (1992):*

> Woman stands for, symbolizes, is the focus for our awareness that we need to be in touch with being, and able to find a meaning in life in a world that is menaced by the lack of meaning and the elimination of being.[3]

Included in this is Winnicott's claim that the fear of woman is natural because in infancy the mother is crucial to healthy development. Fear is a natural acknowledgement of both this debt and of the absolute domination which would also be made possible by this dependence. In order to avoid such subjugation, man may attempt to dominate woman and to overcome her role as sorceress. This is a recurrent theme in Holbrook's work.

The Problem of Woman

Holbrook recounts the story of how when he was working on *Images of Women in Literature* a colleague heard that he had entitled the book *Literature and the Problem of Woman* and responded that it should be called "the problem of man" since it addressed the problem that men had with women. This designation of woman as problematic informs Holbrook's critical approach and arouses both interest and indignation. Maggie Humm (1986), in a discussion of the ideology of male criticism, examines the place of psychoanalysis in critical approaches and asserts that:

> the pioneers of feminist literary criticism established that one of the features of patriarchal literature was its ability to use language to naturalize stereotypes of women.[4]

This assertion may be as true of male criticism as male literature since it could be argued that male critics are shaped by patriarchal literature, are inevitably part of the male perspective on the world and are working within a male-dominated academic culture. Add to this Deborah Tannen's thesis (1991)[5] that men and women use language in distinctively different ways and the question of whether or not male critics can find any reality in the delineation of women in male authors or appreciate fully the impulse behind female writing emerges in all its impossibility and complexity despite the simplistic nature of such polarization.

The fact that a phrase such as "the problem of woman" is acceptable to Holbrook may be indicative of a belief in the polarity of male/female experience in his approach. In one sense this polarity cannot be denied but it may not prove a useful way of understanding the diversity of human experience or of approaching the nature of reality. This is not to deny difference, simply to argue the need for a less oppositional view. Polarity is not confined to male critics. Simone de Beauvoir claimed that male writers only wrote about women to learn more fully what they were themselves and Humm states that:

> de Beauvoir's legacy to feminist criticism . . . is her implicit assumption that women can never be adequately portrayed by male authors, determined as they are by their own male myths.[6]

Yet uniting all human beings are questions about life and the nature of reality which transcend difference and unite us in a search for understanding. These major points of contact are often neglected. The search for insight, understanding of self, authenticity in becoming oneself is a common search with different paths and goals for all humans.

Finding a Scapegoat

Both literary critics and psychoanalysts become expert in reading between the lines, at interpreting the telling gaps. Both may also rewrite the text and conjecture may replace probability. In this section I intend briefly to consider Holbrook's interpretation of the presentation of women characters in two male novelists. He offers us an interpretation of both the Lawrentian and the Dickensian woman. There are profound differences of attitude, characterization, depiction, and understanding, influenced not a little by the historical context both between and within the novelists. In *Where D. H. Lawrence was Wrong about Woman* (1992) Holbrook has a powerful chapter on *Women in Love*. The discussion of this moving and exasperating novel offers us a window into both the novelist's and the critic's view of woman. The chapter on *Women in Love* is subtitled *and the Man from the Infinite*. This encapsulates Lawrence's treatment of the ostensible focus of the book. It is not the women in love which concern him, it is the men. Interestingly this is true of Holbrook too although Lawrence's depiction of the two sisters is fascinating if only for its inability to penetrate the real issues of the relationships on which they embark. Holbrook opens his discussion with the fatal boating party and a claim that the love which Birkin feels for Ursula is "full of death." The focus of *Where D. H. Lawrence was Wrong about Woman* is Lawrence himself. The novels are used as documentary evidence in the psychoanalysis of Lawrence and they reveal, it is argued, a tormented and disturbed man at the root of whose disturbance lies "the problem of woman." Lawrence's dominating mother, his inadequate wife and his rapacious female friends are psychic ghosts who permeate the novel and who reveal themselves in the characters devised for them by the novelist as dangerous, unstable, and untrustworthy. The lucid and persuasive analysis of this novel illuminates both the literary and the psychological games played by the novelist. Holbrook's critique focuses most intensely on the failure of Lawrence to understand the nature of passionate love and on his flawed, pseudo-religious presentation of male strength. But these great Lawrentian flaws are explained through reference to his unhappy experiences with male/female relationships of every kind. In this adherence to a specific and idiosyncratic view of the role of woman in influencing and controlling Lawrence's view of life, Holbrook does women no favors. It is not that he gives Lawrence unqualified approval—far from it: Holbrook pinpoints in Lawrence an inability to cope with the reality of life and a pseudo-religious instinct to "escape his mortality as a tubercular and schizoid individual. . . ." *Women in Love*, argues Holbrook:

assails courageously ... the problem of the meaning of existence, but the novel was written out of a tormented condition of persisting grief for the mother whose funereal presence persisted in his consciousness.[7]

Yet one of Holbrook's central arguments, that woman is a source of creative life and a means of making sense of existence, is not fully explored in relation to this novel and it would have been a valuable counterbalance to the picture which is offered of the novel as an arid and cynical attack on women.

Holbrook pinpoints a lack of authenticity in *Women in Love*. He acknowledges that it is perhaps "Lawrence's most important novel" and claims that:

> It is about the relationship between man and woman in relation to questions of being, our fundamental needs, the meaning of existence, and the nature of the cosmos. The best art in this novel comes where he shows the man and woman being forced to accept their deepest needs in surrender to the love that is growing between them.[8]

Yet, like Lawrence, he avoids too direct a confrontation with why the treatment of woman in *Women in Love* is so halfhearted. There is a detailed analysis of the chapter "Excurse" which argues that here Lawrence manages to convey a sense of the "real woman."

> For once Lawrence happily embraces a woman's needs, her reality and her "separate, separate existence."

This section of the novel concerns the quarrel of Ursula and Birkin over his continued relationship with Hermione. The quarrel itself is described by Holbrook as realistic and powerful; in this passionate encounter, this assertion of Ursula's wishes, this attack on Birkin as "a foul, deathly thing, obscene ... obscene and perverse" Holbrook sees Ursula claiming womanhood and becoming real.

Yet the language Lawrence gives to Ursula is stilted, rhetorical, self-righteous and accusatory. There is nothing of the free flowing linguistic creativity of genuine anger. The contrived repetition and emphasis of

> Then go to her, that's all I say, go to her, go. Ha, she spiritual, spiritual she! A dirty materialist as she is. She spiritual? What does she care for? What is her spirituality? What is it? ... I tell you it's dirt, dirt and nothing but dirt.[9]

has a ranting violence which sounds more like a hellfire preacher than a passionate woman claiming her true self. As a piece of rhetoric it has all the characteristics of an artificial performance—a mechanically satisfying balance, a juggling with words and phrases which heightens emotion and yet which lacks reality.

When the writer is most struggling to convey the truth of the relationship he seems to be most artificial, over-inflated and false. Lawrence's language (which Holbrook argues reveals the writer's inadequacies and obsessions) is most deeply eloquent when he conveys the fact that deep emotions lie beyond the power of words. The following passage gets much closer, I believe, to the reality of self-expression in emotional situations:

> There was silence for some moments.
> "No," he said, "It isn't that. Only—if we are going to know each other, we must pledge ourselves for ever. If we are going to make a relationship, even of friendship, there must be something final and irrevocable about it."
> There was a clang of mistrust and almost anger in his voice. She did not answer. Her heart was too much contracted. She could not have spoken.
> Seeing she was not going to reply, he continued, almost bitterly, giving himself away:
> "I can't say it is love I have to offer—and it isn't love I want. It is something much more impersonal and harder—and rarer."
> There was a silence, out of which she said:
> "You mean you don't love me?"[10]

This language and these silences seem much more realistic, less forced, and more authentic than many other more violently emotional scenes. There is perception here about the struggle of the inner life. Yet it is not specifically female inner life but rather a way of conveying the universal pain and inarticulacy which so often accompanies emotions which lie beyond words. The incident of the wild cat in the section called *Mino* offers the reader a chance to see the Lawrentian interpretation of the male/female conflict. Here there seems to be an attempt on the part of the novelist to come close to offering both perspectives on sexual attraction. Nevertheless there is a continuing emphasis on male dominance and male cruelty. The argument which Ursula advances is never allowed to have any weight. For Birkin, advancing the male argument, females are "a fluffy sporadic bit of chaos." For Ursula, this is a giveaway of the true male attitude—"you want a satellite, Mars and his satellite." This leads to a description of her as "quick, so lambent, like discernible fire, and so vindictive, and so rich in her dangerous, flamy sensitiveness." Holbrook's thesis of the female as mother and witch could, it is true, be discerned here too. But there is an admiration in these adjectives and an acknowledgement of woman's creative and positive qualities. It is true, as Holbrook asserts, that Lawrence has an obsessive, unhealthy fascination with man as a godlike figure subduing and possessing women. There are violent and sadistic images in the descriptions of Gerald which have sinister overtones.

Repeatedly Lawrence expresses Gerald's sexuality in near-rape fantasies which emphasize pain and terror. When the character fails to overcome the woman, he chooses to die, yet the sense of blame being laid firmly upon the woman is disturbing in both the novel and Holbrook's analysis. The women of the novel carry the characteristics which render woman problematic for both writer and critic. Ursula and Gudrun are strong and determined. They have minds of their own which are concerned with love as a gentle and positive emotion as well as with love as a powerful passion. Love is a way for woman to explore herself and her partner and yet social mores have dictated that it is often the male who initiates the relationship. This leads to an imbalance of power which upsets the equilibrium of the relationship. Interestingly Lawrence does identify the need for balance but it is rhetoric without substance. Woman as an independent and whole human being does not emerge in the novel, nor is this identified as a positive possibility by Holbrook. Perhaps this is because it is not seen as a solution which would offer psychic wholeness. It is in the relationship with another that we find a reflection of our self.

Holbrook argues that the ability to make relationships through the reflection of self in the maternal eyes may be undermined and that this in turn impairs the ability to have a mature male/female relationship. But rather than blame the female influence for constraining the ability to discover one's self reflected in the other, it may be more helpful to discuss how women develop the intuitive ability to be sensitive to others both as mothers and as partners. It is in the development of this sensitivity that women become able to perceive their own true self reflected back to them through the sense of self which they give to others. Relationships may become the blank walls of a prison rather than the revelatory surface of a mirror, however. If relationships are rejected then woman becomes free to be individual and perhaps free to become problematic. For many women, the loss of psychic wholeness has been a result of the subservient role which they have had to play in a relationship. They have not been permitted to have a self because others' needs have always been given priority. Perhaps this can only be appreciated when it has been experienced. Edith Wharton, for instance, offers her reader deeper insights into how women can exist alone and yet be whole, as will be explored later.

Interval

With an explosive sound Gudrun leapt to her feet.
"Problematic! Why is it us who are problematic? We have wasted hours trying to communicate how we feel to two selfish men who are caught in an adolescent time warp ... One over intellectualizes and the other just wants to kick the stuffing out of everything. Why is it our fault? Why can't anyone see that we are the victims of male selfishness, wrongheadedness, inability to connect? The terrible male urge to compete, to win, to save face, to control all gets put down to our enveloping and faulty maternity. I can't stand it!"
Esther Greenwood turned to gaze up at Gudrun.
"Men are unreliable, insignificant, unhelpful, unsatisfying ..."
"You are right, Esther."
A pleasant-faced woman with a scarred complexion reached out her hand to the speaker. "If I may join your discussion? I can't help but feel that you are a little harsh. Men have cared for me all my life and I feel that they are always so ill-understood by our sex. I was born illegitimate, poor, a nuisance to my relatives and yet ..."
Gudrun glared fiercely at her. "I can do without this," she interjected.
"Sit down," hissed Ursula.

The presentation of women as problematic for the author is not confined to Holbrook's discussion of Lawrence. In *Charles Dickens and the Image of Woman* Holbrook argues that:

> Dickens associates woman with the dreadful possibility of being deprived of one's emotional inheritance and so of being blighted or falsified.[11]

Holbrook's analysis of *Bleak House* is richly persuasive and the above statement is, in some ways, the pivot of the argument. No one in *Bleak House* is free from the consequences of emotional deprivation. Again, woman is the reason for this deprivation and a focus for blame. It is the women who fail to mother; Lady Dedlock, Esther's godmother, Ada, Mrs. Jellyby, Mrs. Pardiggle. Only Charlie, who becomes Esther's maid, is capable of mothering and even she is a substitute for the real thing since her own mother has died. There is apparently no denying Holbrook's thesis here.

And yet it is possible to turn it on its head too. There is no responsible fathering either—Harold Skimpole, Richard, even Jarndyce himself, all either avoid responsibility or are so prodigal of it that they do the recipient no favors. It is the women in the novel who sacrifice their health, their happiness and their sanity to cope with the male world in which they find themselves and it is the women who perceive consequences, including even Miss Flite who sees that death brings freedom to those enmeshed in the courts of Chancery and so releases her caged birds. This metaphor moves beyond the obvious for Richard's death also spells freedom for Ada and for the others involved in the Jarndyce case.

The chapter which discusses this novel, *Bleak House: The Dead Baby and the Psychic Inheritance* is unremitting in its pursuit of the theme of the blame laid upon women in both the novel and the novelist's life. Dickens, it is alleged, was destroyed by women— his uncaring mother, his unacceptable wife, and his threatening mistress. There is an unconsidered alternative argument which might concentrate on Dickens's feckless father, Dickens's own cruel treatment of a wife who bore him so many children and the inadequacy of Dickens's moral and emotional life. This surely also raises questions about the nature of personal responsibility. The lack of focus on the role of the father/male may seem to be beyond the remit of Holbrook's argument. He is, after all, declaring an interest in understanding the "problem of woman." But it is unrealistic to divorce the two. In exploring the role of the father in the upbringing of women we may, *pace* Freud, begin to understand more fully the roots of later female sexuality or of emotional growth.

This is particularly true of Dickens where the character of Estella or of Nell, of Charlie or of Esther, might be explored in relation to the lack of a father and where a character such as Little Dorrit or Bella may be profitably analyzed in terms of that central relationship with their father. Holbrook's concentration on the "problem of woman" may close our eyes to "the problem of man"! Inevitably the recurrence of such a dominant theme overshadows more valuable points and the phrase "the problem of woman" may irritate some readers of this critical consideration of the work of Dickens into hurrying past more sensitive and important insights such as:

> The real clue to solutions of the problem of relationships between men and women is that of freedom; the need for mutual regard and

respect—the capacity to let one another go in terms of the life solutions of each.[12]

This wise statement is a helpful way into the consideration of Dickens's characters, both male and female, and it offers particular insight into the ending of *Great Expectations* where it is in the letting go that the hero finally comes close to understanding both his own needs and the needs of Estella. This novel opens up the area of child abuse to new insights and in examining the damage done to children by adults who are themselves damaged it has a particular message for today's society. It is in illuminating the relevance of Dickens's work for understanding society in the post-industrial era that Holbrook's latest book has great power.

In discussing the unnatural and repressive life expected of Victorian woman, Holbrook touches on a theme which has relevance for modern woman at a time when there is a backlash against the "strident" feminism of the early eighties and a call for women to reconsider the role of the mother. To seek balance is healthy but we need to be on our guard against the return of repression, particularly in a time of recession. For Dickens, woman was a source of danger and threat. As Holbrook points out, it was Dickens's fixation with the death of Nancy that led to his own death. Victorian woman was either the angel or the whore, there were no in-between stages. Interestingly this is more complex in the case of Esther Summerson. She loses her image by losing her looks and then has to retrieve her sense of identity. Only when she has lost her power as an attractive female is she regarded as having expiated her mother's crime. Her own sexual attractiveness has to be lost before she can be a real woman and marry. Yet the injustice of this passes without comment; it is her saintly acceptance of her fate which wins her the author's approval. The unfairness of the hand dealt to Esther by fate never calls forth the anger which she might be expected to feel—only regret.

As Holbrook points out, Dickens could only cope with woman as angel;

> The woman as angel cannot be reconciled with the real world, its mixedness, its ambivalence in the subjective realm.[13]

So Little Nell becomes a churchyard angel: "as far as you can get from the libidinal woman".

This failure to achieve identify leads to death for Dickens's women. For many of them, it is only by becoming identified with others, sometimes by subsuming themselves in their husband's wishes, that they survive. Little Dorrit steps into the role of daughter with her husband as easily as she did with her father. This theme of loss of identity appeared in an earlier work by Holbrook on the work of Sylvia Plath:

> identification becomes a process not of being reflected by others so much as desiring to become them, in a desperate search for a sense of identity . . . In our society . . . it is difficult enough . . . for human beings to feel whole and able to exert their freedom and autonomy. The schizoid individual especially is tormented by these problems of being a person.[14]

Interpreting the Evidence

"Ah well! Now you're closer to it." Esther Greenwood leaned over Esther Summerson's shoulder. Surprisingly the second Esther leapt to her feet and shouted: "No one ever wanted to know what I thought. He's right! This man Holbrook is right. Abandoned by my mother, hated by my godmother, looking after a bunch of half-witted men and then being married to a man who couldn't even save my looks for me. I'm a possession, someone to own, I'm expected to mother all of them. Me, who never knew my own mother. It is a miracle I haven't broken down."

"Look," said Esther Greenwood. "At least you are sane. My character is a complete wreck and I ended up half-dead and tied to an E.C.T. machine. I get analyzed both as myself and as the product of my creator's twisted psyche. And what do you mean he is right? Has he really understood your point of view? Are you not seen as an example of his theory?"

Is Holbrook's interpretation of "the problem of woman" different in the work of women writers?

Two of his most interesting studies, *Sylvia Plath: Poetry and Existence* (1976) and *Edith Wharton and the Unsatisfactory Man (1991)* endeavor to explore the female mind in two dimensions, fictional and in the life of the writer. It is in the works which bring these themes together that we see the power of Holbrook's thesis in illuminating the literary themes through a personal interpretation of both the text and the hidden life of the writer. Holbrook rehearses a belief that Sylvia Plath was a schizoid personality whose view of male-female relationships was "distorted and false." He claims elsewhere in the book that her work is dangerous for the young because of the damage it may do to the undeveloped mind in offering ideas which are obsessed with death. This perhaps underestimates the ability of readers to disentangle reality and fiction or reality and poetry. Holbrook argues that the world in Plath's view is schizoid and meaningless yet goes on to claim that she was searching for meaning. He quotes Daly in support:

> The ideationally schizoid individual quests for the truth in the language of ideas. He is always in the process of searching for, engaging in or disengaging from a doctrine, a concept, a set of terms or a final life giving and occasionally life taking principle. His transitions occur between being and nothingness.[15]

Through the character of Esther Greenwood in *The Bell Jar*, Holbrook suggests that because Sylvia Plath's mother was unable to help the young Sylvia mourn her father's death and to offer her a reflective model, this led to a loss of sense of identity for Plath. Like Esther Greenwood, she can only find herself "in the life rhythms and symbols of madness."[16]

Holbrook argues that *The Bell Jar* demonstrates:

> the desperate need of the schizoid individual to love and be loved, to be understood and to begin to be, rather than be "done to."[17]

This is one of many recurring themes in the work of David Holbrook and it prompts the question: What is it that the critical writing of Holbrook adds to our reading of those authors whose work he discusses?

There are several key themes. The theory that it is in the earliest relationship with the mother that the child develops her ability to make healthy relationships and through these, to make sense of the world is predominant. In his readings of Lawrence, Dickens, and Plath, Holbrooks traces the effects of failed mother/child relationships upon the authors and demonstrates how the characters express this theme. It is through the relationship between men and women that human beings give meaning to the world. This central relationship, it is argued, provides stability and a sense of the future through the birth of children. Yet it is also emphasized that this is not to deny individuality. If lovers identify too strongly with each other then there is the danger that they may not be capable of individual existence. The themes of psychic health and the wholeness found in fulfilled love inform Holbrook's writing and give readers signposts to an investigation of the inner life of both author and character. The themes are argued with passionate belief and the attractive vitality of the writing carries one along. But the question which arises concerns the interpretation of woman as problematic, as threatening, and as blameworthy. This strikes me as a one-sided and therefore unbalanced account of the part played by the women characters even when the writer in question has a curious view of women.

Both Lawrence and Dickens offer a curiously unfinished view of woman and it is the male characters who seem to have greater life. Yet this is an incomplete reading for there are other interpretations possible and that which the reader brings to the interpretation of Ursula Brangwen's situation may be very different from the Lawrentian view. Ursula shows a kind of despair in her love for Birkin which, I would argue, grows out of an awareness of Birkin's limitations in male/female relationships. It is also alleged that it is in woman's failure to fulfill her role as mother or as lover that psychic decay begins. This is a terrible responsibility for woman. It denies both the male role in nurturing the child and also the importance of fulfilled relationships other than the male/female lover relationship. It sets up polarities of existence between male and female that seem extreme.

The readings which Holbrook offers of these texts give us an interesting but dangerous perspective on the authors. Psychoanalysis is an interesting approach to literature but it may, ultimately, narrow our appreciation of the text. Texts are more than an account of their author and more than an analysis of human characteristics through the medium of fictional characters. Psychoanalysis gives insight into the workings of the mind but may not reach the deeper narrative structures which convey issues of more general concern. It may also lead to an unhealthy concentration on character or on biographical detail. Similarly the focus on woman as problematic may narrow our appreciation of both text and author by an over concentration on woman as metaphor or as sign of the authorial psyche rather than as the fictional presentation of female dynamic. This may cause a lack of perception about the implications of the fictional creation for an understanding of the reality of the parallel human situation. This is, I think, particularly true in relation to Holbrook's reading of Edith Wharton. In *Edith Wharton and the Unsatisfactory Man,* Holbrook concentrates fiercely on the power of love:

> What each human being needs is a love relationship in which he or she can find his uniqueness and so find a confirmation of his being; this is perhaps as near as we can get to anything that we can call meaning.[18]

He points out that Wharton herself had unsatisfactory relationships with men and claims that it is likely that her father abused her sexually, a claim he sustains by analysis of a short passage of pornography written by Wharton. It is also claimed that there is:

> a certain inclination on Edith Wharton's part to deny in women the capacities for sexuality and the forfeiture of innocence that such awareness must bring.[19]

Wharton, it is argued, was strong in her ability to show how females were damaged by male inauthenticity and Holbrook feels that "her acute judgment of women is not matched by an equal ability to present and judge men."[20]

He argues that her dread of sexuality leads to a distortion of relationships and men are presented as unsatisfactory because her own perception was damaged by her father and not repaired by her relationships with lovers. This seems to ignore Wharton's sharply critical yet very positive perceptions about men in, for example, *The Age of Innocence*. Holbrook's thesis illuminates a particular aspect of the literature which he discusses with startling and sometimes shocking clarity. He raises vital questions about our ability to cope with life. But there are important elements of life which are missed. An understanding of humor is perhaps one of these elements. Edith Wharton's dry, precise humor allows her to delineate the character of Newland Archer, "hero" of *The Age of Innocence*, without overt criticism:

> He did not in the least wish the future Mrs. Newland Archer to be a simpleton. He meant her (thanks to his enlightening companionship) to develop a social tact and readiness of wit enabling her to hold her own with the most popular married women of the "younger set," in which it was the custom to attract masculine homage whilst playfully discouraging it. If he had probed to the bottom of his vanity (which he sometimes nearly did) he would have found there the wish that his wife should be as worldly wise and as eager to please as the married lady whose charms had held his fancy through two mildly agitated years; without, of course, any hint of the frailty which had so nearly marred that unhappy being's life, and had disarranged his own plans for a whole winter.[21]

In this short passage Wharton manages to indicate a social structure in which women are used and abused, in which men are encouraged to believe that this is permissible (a view in which the women collude, it has to be said), in which hypocrisy and cruelty are rife and in which fidelity is devalued. She conveys the lightness of Archer's character as well as indicating that there are other possibilities within him—he nearly manages reflection. She indicates vanity and innocence in this man and all this is done with a deft, light, and devastating irony. And it is because of her ability to handle the lightness of tone which belies the seriousness of the scene that Edith Wharton is then all the more powerful when she writes of the moment at which Archer realizes that the woman who would fulfill his real needs so much better than the woman he has married has to remain beyond his reach:

> She leant forward and seemed about to speak, but he had already called out the order to drive on and the carriage rolled away while he stood on the corner. The snow was over, and a tingling wind had sprung up, that lashed his face as he stood gazing. Suddenly he felt something stiff and cold on his lashes, and perceived that he had been crying, and that the wind had frozen his tears. He thrust his hands into his pockets and walked at a sharp pace down Fifth Avenue to his own house.[22]

This is simply but powerfully expressed and the astonishment he feels at his own tears is a symbol for his gradual self-realization. This insight into male thinking seems to me perceptive and it is matched by the subtle portrait of Archer's wife May winning back her husband through the only weapon she has, which is her body. Absorbed by the portrait of the affair we hardly register that his wife knows until Wharton begins to drop clues such as the fact that May is wearing her wedding outfit or putting on a little weight. When she finally traps Archer by declaring her pregnancy, her "eyes wet with victory," we are shocked to find the net drawn so tightly about Archer. The exquisite detail of Wharton's writing brings the psychological reality of the marriage sharply to mind. She triumphs in her understatement:

> Something he knew he had missed: the flower of life.

This also underlines the fact that the life lived by every woman in this novel is constrained by social expectation and all the women are victims of circumstance as are all the male characters also. The balance and understanding of Wharton's work serves to decry the social system whilst demonstrating deep compassion for the human beings involved in it. It is this compassion that sets her work apart from the sentimentality of Dickens and the rhetorical religiosity of Lawrence and which gives it a less disturbing quality than the work of Plath.

The ability to convey a moral stance without proselytizing is something which Dickens and Lawrence might have envied Wharton. Her ironic and humorous vision of the world gives us a wholeness of view which the self-generated "gods and the daughters of men" of Lawrence or the caricatures of Dickens do not provide. It would, I think, have been illuminating if Holbrook could have discussed the refinement of Wharton's sensibilities by the process of her own sentimental and sexual education, rather than concentrating on the extreme conjecture into which his theories have led him.

It has to be said, however, that without the brave and illuminating light shed by Holbrook on the "problem of woman" the question of how writers portray women at the subconscious level might not even be considered. It is valuable, too, to have such consideration offered by a critic of Holbrook's reputation. The sincerity of his writing is never in doubt even if some of his theories may seem to narrow the approach to literature. The questions he raises are about how we approach some of the most fundamental questions of life. I would argue that these questions need to be seen in the context of the mutuality of human experience rather than as part of the polarity of experience but this is *my* hobby horse and I appreciate that it may be as unpalatable as Holbrook's will be to some readers. Nevertheless I feel disconcerted by the lack of balance which sometimes emerges in the argument. Being female is different from being male in biological, social, and emotional ways. Yet all humans face questions about the meaning of life, the difficulties of moral choice or the need to find a philosophical base to guide our choices in life. It is the parallel dilemmas within competing or opposed or varied contexts which create the tensions exploited and explored so positively in fiction. Holbrook does not always address the area of overlap. Yet our readings of these texts are challenged and therefore enriched even by our indignant reactions. What does not come through often enough is the sense of woman as a source of creativity. The writings of both Plath and Wharton offer real opportunities to celebrate the creativity of woman as writer and as character, but the nature of the analysis tends to focus on what is seen as an unbalanced and threatening manifestation of female psychic energy.

Searching for Divinest Sense

"Indignant reactions is right!" hissed Esther Greenwood to Gudrun. Gudrun sat up thoughtfully.

"So where does that leave us?" she asked.

"I think," said Ursula, calmly "that it should leave us feeling that attention has been drawn to our place in the novels and so we should be prepared for reaction to this."

"But I want to react on my own behalf!" said Gudrun indignantly. "I feel as though I have been made to fit a theory. I'm a woman for goodness sake. We're more complex than that."

"Critics all make us fit a theory, dear. It's all a matter of whether you agree with the theory. Life is too complex to be categorized but if we didn't keep on trying we'd go crazy with the senselessness of it all. That woman on the platform is trying to make sense of Holbrook; that lot in the gallery have all got to have their say now and make sense of it in their way. It doesn't really matter which theory you float—someone will always disagree and in that disagreement find their own theory."

"I'll tell you something," said Esther Greenwood. "It takes a woman to make sense of the nonsense of life and the craziness of the world we live in."

She pulled a book from her pocket and began to read:

Much Madness is divinest Sense—
To a discerning Eye—
Much Sense—the starkest Madness—
'Tis the Majority
In this, as All, prevail—
Assent—and you are sane—Demur—you're straightway
   dangerous—
And handled with a Chain—[23]

Together the women rose and slowly left the room.

Notes

1. David Holbrook, *The Quest for Love* (London: Methuen, 1964), p. 24.
2. Ibid., p. 15.

3. David Holbrook, *Where D. H. Lawrence Was Wrong About Woman* (Lewisburg, Pa.: Bucknell University Press: Associated University Presses, 1992), p. 35.
4. Maggie Humm, *Feminist Criticism* (Brighton: Harvester Press, 1986), p. 24.
5. Deborah Tannen, *You Just Don't Understand* (London: Virago, 1991).
6. Humm, *Feminist Criticism*, p. 28.
7. Holbrook, *Where D. H. Lawrence Was Wrong*, p. 233.
8. Ibid., p. 184.
9. D. H. Lawrence, *Women in Love* (Harmondsworth: Penguin, 1969), p. 345.
10. Ibid., p. 161.
11. David Holbrook, *Charles Dickens and the Image of Woman* (London: Vision Press, 1993), p. 29.
12. Ibid., p. 176.
13. Ibid., p. 182.
14. David Holbrook, *Sylvia Plath: Poetry and Existence* (London: Athlone Press, 1976), p. 109.
15. Ibid., p. 124.
16. Ibid., p. 107.
17. Ibid., p. 125.
18. David Holbrook, *Edith Wharton and the Unsatisfactory Man* (London: Vision Press, 1991), p. 8.
19. Ibid., p. 14.
20. Ibid.
21. Edith Wharton, *The Age of Innocence* (London: Vitago, 1988), p. 26.
22. Ibid., p. 248.
23. Emily Dickinson, *The Complete Poems of Emily Dickinson*, ed. Thomas H. Johnson (London: Faber, 1970), p. 209.

England's only Existentialist Philosopher

ROGER POOLE

An Alternative Existentialism

David Holbrook is England's only native Existentialist philosopher. Jean-Paul Sartre and atheistic Existentialism he early rejected. But, substituting a positive value for every negative value in Sartre's system, he has developed, over a lifetime, a system of thought which is consistently Existentialist. If he has had difficulty in getting his doctrines across, it is only because Existentialism as such is completely foreign to British philosophic orthodoxy, unintelligible where it is not simply wrong. For this reason, a lifetime's consistent philosophical effort has gone unrecognized and unrewarded.

In a very illuminating autobiographical account of the books he has read over a lifetime, David Holbrook describes, with typical frankness, to what an extent a youthful encounter with Sartre alienated him:

> One of the most disturbing experiences I had as a boy of seventeen was seeing a play by Sartre, *Huis Clos,* put on with Beatrix Lehmann, and enthusiastically supported by the leftwing "People's Convention" of those days (1940). I was appalled by the work, because of its hatred of human beings, and its nihilistic picture of the inevitable frustration of inter-human relationship and love. I have loathed Sartre ever since.[1]

This early recoil from Sartre in 1940 marked out a necessary philosophical career. It was necessary to oppose Sartre term for term. This decision was reinforced by a second "experience of mass human hate" which was the War. The shock of a young man exposed to the dangers of the Normandy invasion is brilliantly captured in *Flesh Wounds,* a novel only published in 1966.

At this early stage of Holbrook's development, the relationship to Sartre is still ambiguous. It is an ironic tribute to such a novel as *La Nausée,* which came out in 1938, that *Flesh Wounds* should offer an experience so uncannily like Sartre's hero Roquentin, the world almost unbearably "present," sight, sound, smell, and light all existentially experienced to the degree that Sartre called "superfluous" and "absurd." During three endless and terrifying minutes of a mortar shelling, for instance, Paul Grimmer, Holbrook's hero

> suddenly saw that the early morning grass was full of rich beetles ... The insects crawled untroubled through the thick stems beneath his face, as the smoke and dust flew in the air. There were black beetles with rainbow colours in their backs, their shells engraved with ribs finer than the grooves on gramaphone records, and beetles with moth-like patterns on them, wood-colours. There was one large green creature, shaped like a shield, jewelled like a brooch, catching gleams from the morning sun. With long delicate twig-like legs, it made its awkward way from small clod to small clod. Paul felt a great wave of empathy with the beetle, and pressed his face down to it. He saw it retract a step once as the ground shook with a heavy stinging blast from a mortar bomb. But, Paul wagered, if he gets to that clod six inches away, I shall survive this. If not, he, the green jewelled one, and I, will perish together.[2]

Just as Sartre's Roquentin stares with horror at the sheer existence of the black tree-root, and deduces only the fact of "contingency," so Holbrook's Paul Grimmer stares at the beetle and feels "a great wave of empathy with it." A lifetime's work is implied in that one reversal.

Sartre's "nihilism" then, and "the experience of mass human hatred" which was gained through the War, provide the antetexts (and the antitexts, for every writer writes *against* a preceding text) for a lifetime's philosophical writing. All that Holbrook writes will be in opposition to nihilism and to hate. All that he writes will be a search for that "necessary opposite": for the affirmation of life.

It was then inevitable that Holbrook should identify an alternative tradition of existentialist writing and thinking. He does so in that self-same essay on his reading, just after the passage on Sartre:

> The whole strand of positive existentialism, delineated in Rollo May's introductory chapters in *Existence-A New Dimension in Psychiatry,* is virtually unknown to most people. Yet it is a substantial movement, beginning with Husserl, Brentano, Binswanger, and others associated with the work of Martin Buber, Tillich, Marcel and Merleau-Ponty. Paul Foulquié's *Existentialism* is perhaps the best introduction to this new

existentialism. In psychotherapy some of the best writers are Viktor Frankl, as in *The Doctor and the Soul;* E. K. Ledermann in *Existential Neurosis;* Rollo May's *Love and Will;* Leslie Farber's *The Ways of the Will,* and Peter Lomas, *True and False Experience.*[3]

But if "high" French existentialism itself, in the form of Sartre, de Beauvoir and Camus, has never been more in the English-speaking philosophical world than an agreeable if irritating literary oddity, how much less will Holbrook's "alternative" tradition of existentialism be received, understood or welcomed, engaging frontally as it does not only with official "objective" behavioural psychology but also with the massed phalanxes of self-interested psychiatry! And when Holbrook, grasping the full import of Edmund Husserl's *The Crisis of European Sciences* and the importance of such thinkers as Michael Polanyi and Marjorie Grene, begins to promote the cause of phenomenology and "philosophical anthropology," the immensity of his intellectual undertaking in a world still dominated by Oxford positivism will be grasped, and, in the same moment, the utter impossibility of its success.

Philosophy and the History of Ideas

It is because the intellectual climate in England, at least since A. J. Ayer's *Language, Truth and Logic* in 1936, has been deeply hostile to "European" ideas; and because David Holbrook's writing is allied at every point with European or expatriate-European existential attitudes, that his work has never been accorded the dignity of a properly philosophical critique. Oxford distinguishes between "philosophy" and "the history of ideas." What Oxford does is "philosophy." What the rest of the world does is "history of ideas." David Holbrook's writing then, is seen as a restatement of certain decadent subcategories of European "history of ideas" and hence of possessing no intrinsic philosophical interest. The result is that, so far as I know, there has never been a single serious philosophical engagement with Holbrook's work in England. To deny debate to a position is to kill it, slowly and effectively and without public fuss. Thus it is that David Holbrook has been ignored by the official philosophical establishment for thirty years. Thus because his work has never been engaged with seriously, the benefits it could have offered, at many points of intellectual life, have been unavailable. In a world of self-satisfied Cartesians, this Vico of the mind has never been allowed to speak.

Holbrook's work has been deliberately and consistently ignored. Faced with the suggestion that there might be something in "European" or "Continental" thinking of some intrinsic philosophical validity, the British philosopher is inclined to strike that attitude of pained and baffled incomprehension which indicates that, here, we stand in the presence of a mere oxymoron. There is an elegant illustration of this on the cover of a book issued as late as 1990 from the Cambridge University Press. The book, Frederick Newhouser's *Fichte's Theory of Subjectivity*, appears in a series called "Modern European Philosophy." But in order to drive home the merely oxymoronic nature of this title, the cover is embellished by an elegant logo, which expresses in stark black and white a recognizable though geometrized map of Europe. The map stretches from Czechoslovakia to Spain, and from Greece to Finland. But, pointedly, the British Isles are omitted. There is a kind of epistemological "absence" just off the coast of France. "Modern European Philosophy" means exactly what it says, and British philosophy is not part of it.

The provocation offered by the wretched Fichte, who died in 1814 and might thus be considered to qualify, on basely historical grounds, for inclusion in the purview of "philosophy," is, however, as nothing compared to the provocation offered to the philosophical establishment by the honorary doctorate conferred upon Jacques Derrida in June 1992. Convinced that they have been conned into conferring their highest mark of academic recognition upon a mere sophist who has sold the philosophical world a bottle of pink water which claims to be a cure *(pharmakon)* but is in fact nothing more than a poison *(pharmakon)*, certain Cambridge philosophers, in a special issue of *The Cambridge Review* for October 1992, reach heights of invective and contempt against Derrida which are little short of hysterical. The plain (and quite unphilosophical) message of this publication is that, when philosophy has decided not to discuss European ideas, it is a scandal when such an unimportant and merely formal organism as a degree committee manages to subvert its long-continued embargo of silence by a single and inadvertent administrational *faux pas*.

Unfortunately, no degree committee has hit upon the idea of naming David Holbrook for an honorary doctorate, and thus the long stranglehold of silence on his work has never been relaxed, even by a clerical accident. The war of silence against Holbrook, over so many years, has been completely successful. That is one of the reasons for issuing a celebratory *Festschrift* of this kind, to honor his seventieth birthday. It puts on record, permanently, and in bound, volume form, the history of a willful and continued injustice against him.

Education, Dehumanization, Culture

I cannot attempt here a biographical account of how and why Holbrook's thematic preoccupations developed in the order that they did. It seems to me, though, that his writing falls into three phases, each one a logical development of the preoccupations of the last, and that all three are fundamentally existential in preoccupation and concern. The phases allow of course, of movements forwards and backwards across the divisions, but I see him as involving himself, firstly in the theory and practice of education as such, the period of the sixties; secondly, in a frontal assault on all forms of dehumanization, brutality, hate, and cultural decadence, in his writings of the seventies; and thirdly, falling back from both of these in the eighties, to a meditation on the philosophical underpinnings and presuppositions necessary to the formulation of a culture which would be in some degree responsible to its cultural mission, and to some degree aware of its philosophical, anthropological and scientific duties in front of a world much more complex than official philosophy and science allowed of.

The first period then, the period specifically devoted to the problems of education as such, would run from the famous *English for Maturity* (1961) and *English for the Rejected* (1964) up to *English in Australia Now* (1972). The second period, the period of cultural critique as such, opens with an angry burst of philippics in the early 1970s: *Human Hope and the Death Instinct* (1971), *Sex and Dehumanisation* (1972), *The Masks of Hate* (1972), *The Pseudo-Revolution* (1972), *The Case Against Pornography* (1972). This period would include and carry within it the highly pointed critique of nihilism and narcissism in the studies of *Dylan Thomas* (1972) and of *Sylvia Plath* (1976) as well as the richly orchestrated encomium to Gustav Mahler for precisely his ability to overcome hatred, despair and nihilism in *Gustav Mahler and the Courage to Be* (1975). His coordinates now stated for the second time, this period would end with *Lost Bearings in English Poetry* (1977), which substitutes "lost" for F. R. Leavis's "new" in Leavis's significantly titled *New Bearings in English Poetry* (1932), a book which established the criteria for significance in English poetry for thirty years—the point being that there *were* criteria for significance in 1932. With its gloomy inspection of the present scene—"Poetry has lost confidence in itself"; "Criticism has lost confidence in itself"; "The lack of a creative theme"; "From Vitalism to a Dead Crow: Ted Hughes's Failure of Confidence"; "Modern Poetry and the Death of Sympathy" are some of the chapter headings—*Lost Bearings in English Poetry* really does come to the conclusion that we are sitting fishing in the dull canal on a winter evening round behind the gashouse and shoring fragments against our ruins. This is confidence Degree Zero. This phase of Holbrooks' meditation can go no further. His own "subject"—English—has three times failed him: as poem, as criticism, as grounds for hope. (It is this constant desire for hope which marks him off so significantly from Sartre, who thought that it would be mere "bad faith" even to hope for hope). In all this ever-increasing gloom, the book on Mahler shines out like a good deed in a naughty world, a book which affirms that, even in spite of all Mahler *knew* about the world, he still had the courage to *transcend* it. It is the failure of courage which so dispirits Holbrook, a failure which is particularly of our time. Hence the bravely worded title *Gustav Mahler and the Courage to Be*. Citing as it does Paul Tillich's *The Courage to Be* (1952), Holbrook's title reaffirms the possibility of a positive existentialism, the one that would defeat Sartre at his own game. Tillich is invoked as a covering cherub against Sartre's malign influence.

The massive assault on pornography is accompanied by a series of texts in existential psychoanalysis and "object relations" theory. The fact that Holbrook chooses an existential form of psychoanalysis and post-Freudian psychotherapy is to be expected, but that most of the implied positives are "essences" underlines once again the ambivalence of his philosophical position. The study of Dylan Thomas, for instance, is conducted under the aegis of Harry Guntrip's "object relations theory" and there is free use of the theories of Melanie Klein, D. W. Winnicott and W. R. D. Fairbairn. Dylan Thomas is presented in terms of a "schizoid diagnosis." His ontological insecurity, his desperate effort to recreate a mother he never had, his effort to "develop and sustain a human identity and sense of meaning in life"[4] is part of a wider description of "existence" in the Sartrian manner, except that, once again, Holbrook is concerned to demonstrate the possibility of a struggle *for* meaning, rather than its impossibility. "As Viktor Frankl has pointed out, the capacity to question the nature and point of our existence is that which makes us man. To suffer from existential frustration and despair is not to be 'sick', but to be human."[5] (Both the use of "man" here, and of "human," explain much of what is implied in the purview and indeed the titles of much later books.)

The same concern to understand the search for a "missing" mother is evident throughout the book on Sylvia Plath (1976) as well. She too is analyzed in terms of Harry Guntrip's "schizoid diagnosis" and the same authorities are cited, as well as Robert Daly, Aaron Esterson, Marion Milner and Rollo May. R. D. Laing's *The Divided Self* plays an important role. "It is immediately clear that Sylvia Plath had a "dividual self." Throughout her work there are images of selves which are petrified, cracked, automaton, patched up, and divided against themselves." But once again, the aim of an existential psychoanalysis is to examine an entire society through an individual case: "There is a schizoid condition in her: but this cannot be discussed without reference to the problem which the schizoid individual is singularly equipped to recognise—the problem today of living in a schizoid society, in a world which seems to have lost its meaning."[6] As with Dylan Thomas, so with Sylvia Plath, the individual singularly deprived of a meaning-source in his or her life throws a kind of indirect light on the nature of the quest for meaning in an environing society. Existential psychoanalysis allows us to reconstitute the childhood origins of the schizoid personality, while phenomenological analysis allows us to enter into the lived world of the poet and to make connections of a subjective kind across the poems which traditional literary criticism would not allow of.

The same type of existential-phenomenological analysis of a writer whose fantasies comment directly upon the need to create meaning in a threatening and meaningless world, is evidenced as late as the book on C. S. Lewis of 1991. *The Skeleton in the Wardrobe: C. S. Lewis's Fantasies: A Phenomenological Study* carries out a quite unexpected analysis of the *Narnia* stories in terms of the mother whom Lewis lost as a child of just under ten years of age and to whose loss he never adapted.

To have this massively masculine intellect reconstructed in terms of a lifelong search for a missing mother might appear unlikely of success, but Holbrook's analysis is in fact convincing and adept. The mother is 'missing' and the Narnia imagery constantly reevokes her. But, when and if found, she might also turn out to be the "rejecting mother," and the fear of being rejected a second time leads to a considerable unconscious evasion in the writer. The effort to bring meaning into being is accompanied by a consistent desire to deflect one possible set of results. In an attempt to avoid a rejection that he could not survive, Lewis carries out "an ultimate surrender to a dominating authority," and this authority has of course to be male: "There is a profound distrust of the world, of the body, and the self: all are rejected, including the imagination. Everything is surrendered, in favour of an absolute, ideal, ineffable and intangible essence, whose authority is harsh and total. I suppose this is Christianity in one of its modes; but it seems to me to mark a failure, in terms of the problem of life."[7] The use of "life" there carries full existential force, and forms an exact parallel to another remarkable modern "failure" in dealing with "the problem of life."

Where D. H. Lawrence was Wrong about Woman (1992) again locates the problem of the writer in an unsatisfactory relationship to his mother. With Lawrence, of course, this is easier to do than with Lewis. Lawrence felt himself to be an object of greater emotional significance in his mother's life than he could bear, and the solution in the fiction is to exercise a repressive control over women. In scene after scene in his work women are badly treated, tortured, and put to death (as in *The Woman who Rode Away*); "sodomized in contemptuous anger" (as in *Lady Chatterly's Lover*); or submitted to "the fascistic domination of two murderers who are running a new religious-political campaign, while forfeiting even [the] capacity for orgasm" (as in *The Plumed Serpent*). This domination of woman Holbrook sees as a "denial of woman" (hence the point of the title). Instead of considering, as F. R. Leavis in his time did, Lawrence's fiction as "normative" and "celebratory," Holbrook finds Lawrence's work to be "full of hate and death."

What is significant about this series of case studies in "schizoid" personality is that it seems to David Holbrook to "speak to our condition." The implied premiss throughout is that only through "schizoid" poets can we experience the full complexity and horror of a "schizoid" world. Holbrook, like Sartre, is a moralist. Just as Sartre had offered the moral authenticity of existential stoicism to a world besotted with "inauthenticity" and "bad faith," so Holbrook offers implied positives ("love" instead of "hate," normality and "hope" against pornography and despair). But in his affirmations Holbrook seems often to be kicking against the pricks. Life may or may not be as Sartre says it is, but it is very rarely what David Holbrook wants it to be.

Sartre mocked the idea of "perfect moments" in *La Nausée*, just as he simply replaced "essence" by "existence" in his famous lecture of 1946. But Holbrook seems to be working always with the sense of a Fall, the sense that things were once much better than they are now. In Viconian terms, he sees us as having degenerated from the age of gods, through the age of heroes, to the age of men, and indeed to be on the extreme outer reaches of that, awaiting the crash of thunder that will signify collapse and the *ricorso*.

In his treatment of sexuality and the "schizoid," in his war on pornography and in the psychoanalytic studies, Holbrook thus becomes what one might call a transcendental existentialist, if that is not, as it is not meant to be, a mere contradiction in terms. He wants all the old "essences" back—love, wholeness, completeness, being, mutuality, "perfect moments" and all. He may have "loathed Sartre" ever since his experience of *Huis Clos* in 1940, but this may be because Sartre "tells it like it is." It may be that Sartre was right about the twentieth century, and that nihilism, indifference and egoism in sex *is* the twentieth century "truth."

Nevertheless, Holbrook's rejection both of Sartre's doctrines and of twentieth century sexual decadence and inversion is itself an existentialist move, because he is himself insisting upon the necessity of authenticity, responsibility towards the other, and subjection to some kind of unstated moral law. In this, of course, Holbrook appears rather to belong to a brand of existentialism which descends from Kierkegaard through Jaspers, Marcel and Maritain and includes his own favorites Buber and Tillich. It is a "religious" existentialism, which may or may not have God explicitly at its center.

If Sartre was an atheistic and nihilistic existentialist then, Holbrook turns out to be a humanistic and idealistic existentialist. Neither Sartre nor Holbrook believes in God, which is why whole tracts of experience about love in the world, the reality of love in action, *agape* rather than *eros*, are unsuspected by both of them. This great abeyance skews their analyses towards negative conditions which are conceived of as *a priori* (there is no God, no disinterested love, no possibility of sainthood, etc.). Perhaps, indeed, Holbrook at seventeen reacted so strongly to *Huis Clos* because he realized that that play does indeed express the eternal and perpetual condition of men and women who live in a post-theological space.

Elective Affinities

If I am right in my reconstitution of the three phases of Holbrook's work, and if in fact the second phase goes through the curve I have described and for the reasons I have suggested, then the whole odyssey of consciousness had come to an end in the late seventies. Education had failed. Poetry had failed. Criticism had failed. That only left philosophy. Philosophy—as a ground for hope? But during the seventies, Holbrook had been falling anew under the influence of F. R. Leavis, Leavis Mark II we might call him, because the later Leavis began to consider philosophical questions quite seriously, after a lifetime's denial that they could be relevant to "English." In such works as *Nor Shall My Sword* (1972) and *The Living Principle: "English" as a Discipline of Thought* (1975) Leavis began to consider such thinkers as Michael Polanyi and Marjorie Grene as being of direct relevance to English studies. The fact that Leavis's mantle had fallen directly on Holbrook, and that he was now Director of Studies in English at Leavis's own college in Cambridge, Downing College, could only have had the force of an "election" upon him, a kind of reestablishment of an "elective affinity" that went right back to the days when Holbrook had been an undergraduate student of Leavis. Now that Leavis had been one way round the circuit, and come to recognize the necessity of philosophy to the critical enterprise, and Holbrook had been the other way round the circuit, and come to recognize the necessity of philosophy to the cultural enterprise, then Holbrook could suddenly see a quite new relevance in Leavis's thinking for his *own* project: provided that "philosophy" were defined, not as "English" philosophy (Oxford and Cambridge positivism) but as philosophy as the rest of the world understood it, the philosophy of France and Germany and America.

Although Holbrook was fully engaged in the battle against pornography and the development of a specifically existentialist psychoanalytical literary criticism in the 1970s, something caught his attention in 1972, and that was Husserl's *Crisis of European Sciences*. I think it would be true to say that Holbrook first came across this masterwork of existential responsibility through a reading of my book *Towards Deep Subjectivity* in 1972. In the fourth chapter, "Subjective objections to Objectivity", I present Husserl's ideas about the imminent decease of the European "Lifeworld" in some detail. I myself had only recently become aware of the full importance of this marvellous work of Husserl's late maturity (he composed it between 1934–37), although I had possessed a paperback translation of part of it, translated by Quentin Lauer, in the Harper Torchbook edition since 1965. It was only when the full translation by David Carr came out in 1970[8] that I understood the extent of Husserl's genius, and my enthusiasm spilled directly over into the writing of *Towards Deep Subjectivity,* which was composed at Paunat, in the Dordogne, during the summer of 1970.

The exposition of Husserl obviously connected with something that Holbrook was searching for himself. In September 1972 I got my first letter from him. It was completely unexpected. We did not know each other at all, but typically, it introduced subjects of common interest at once, and without preamble. This letter was followed by several others, mostly written from Newton Abbot, but some written on trains as he travelled around the country. All these letters were written on the spur of the moment to explore some point of contact between Husserl and what he was reading himself: Erwin Straus's *The Primary World of the Senses,* Marjorie Grene's *Approaches to a Philosophical Biology,* E. K. Ledermann's *Existential Neurosis,* R. W. K. Paterson's *The Nihilistic Egoist: Max Stirner* and a host of others. Just as he was most deeply engaged with his antipornography drive, David Holbrook had seen the significance of the Husserlian thought-world, and it began to form a framework in terms of which he could think through those specific forms of Western decadence with which he was at that time most deeply involved.

Husserl's contention in *Crisis*—that, since the Renaissance, philosophical and scientific reason had lost their "telos," and hence that civilization itself was at risk—became a common obsession. In July 1973, David Holbrook and I organized a "Subjective Disciplines" seminar at Downing College, to see whether people working in other germane disciplines were as aware as we had become of the extent of the danger from "objective" philosophy and psychology. In July 1974, we both delivered papers on related topics at an In-Service Training Workshop at the International Schools Association in Geneva. (The excitement of the conversations at that period is recalled in a poem, *Picnic in the Jura,* in David Holbrook's collection, *Chance of a Lifetime.*)

Another work of my own which may have fitted into the new Husserlian phase of Holbrook's thought in the early seventies, was a long essay on the concept of "life" in the later criticism of F. R. Leavis.[9] This use of the word "life" may have connected up with Husserl's concept of the "Lifeworld." David Holbrook's "existential psychoanalysis" gradually transmuted into a "philosophical anthropology" which began to scrutinize modern post-Darwinian thought for its nihilistic implications. A third essay of mine which may have led David Holbrook's thought in ways it wanted to develop was a long review of Maurice Merleau-Ponty's *The Prose of the World*, which appeared in 1974.[10]

Subjectivity in a World of Meaning

Thus it is that *Education and Philosophical Anthropology* (1987), *Evolution and the Humanities* (1987) and *Further Studies in Philosophical Anthropology* (1988) form a full-scale frontal attack upon behavioral-positivist-reductive theories of human life, and a restatement of alternative modes of assessing creativity and creation, derived from existentialist and phenomenological thought. I have set out elsewhere[11] what I take to be the main thrust of the argument.

These three books are like the struggle between Sherlock Holmes and Professor Moriarty on the edge of the abyss. Holbrook has by now fixed his major adversary, abstraction, as the proper object of sustained existential critique. In the "Conclusions" to *Education and Philosophical Anthropology* he generously acknowledges my own *Towards Deep Subjectivity* for insisting upon the importance of subjectivity and intentionality for bringing into being a series of choices in a world retrieved for meaning. In his exposition of Husserl's *Crisis,* in his third chapter in *Further Studies in Philosophical Anthropology*, he refers to my book again in his attempt to reanalyze those elements in the Husserlian argument which most obsess him. These elements all have to do with finding our way back from abstraction to reality, to choice, to meaning, in a lived world. There is a motivation, unacknowledged because unperceived, in contemporary science which repeats the naïveté by which Galileo simply substituted an *Ideenkleid* or web of abstractions, for the world of nature in his own time. As against that abstracting movement, Holbrook wants to insist that the movement towards the acting subject ought to be primary. If the *Lebenswelt* is anything, it has to be a lived world in the sense that it has to be brought into being by the conscious decisions of freely acting subjects. And hcw can that be achieved, when science is constantly pretending, like an anxious virgin, that such decisions are sub- "scientific"?

The fourth chapter of *Further Studies in Philosophical Anthropology*, on Maurice Merleau-Ponty, continues the argument at the level of the body. How is intentionality visible in the world, and what are the rules of communication? Once again David Holbrook very generously acknowledges my contribution to this line of thought by citing the review of Merleau-Ponty's *Prose of the World* in which I contend that "there may be moments in the history of philosophy where a traditional conundrum is solved, not by an act of intellection, but by an act of moral sympathy, and I believe that this is one of them."[12]

The whole of the latter part of *Further Studies* is an exploration of how to carry this "act of moral sympathy" further. Erwin Straus, Ludwig Binswanger, Rollo May, F. J. J. Buytendijk, Helmuth Plessner and Michael Polanyi all represent ways of approaching intersubjective meaning in the world. The passages from Buytendijk on "encounter" and "meeting" are particularly fascinating, linking back to Merleau-Ponty, but also forward to the idea of "reciprocity" in encounter which completely transcends "objectivist" measurements.[13] "We cannot study encounter as the objectivist does ... As a mode of being-in-the-world it can only be understood if we share it, if we ourselves live encounters with others and so approach our subject by participation as well as by observation ... encounter demands a certain reciprocity. There is a parallel between encounter and perception."[14]

Positive Values

It is at this point of the book that Holbrook's "new" existentialism is officially launched as a positive existentialism which is explicitly and as such a rejection of negative existentialism. "This is where Buytendijk introduces 'loving encounter' of person with person, *liebende Wirheit*. It is possible to find the other ... This marks the fundamentally different attitude in the "new" existentialism and phenomenology ... these philosophical scientists cannot accept as realistic the philosophies of isolation, alienation and despair, of Sartre and Heidegger. They do not find with Heidegger that *Mitsein* is an aspect of inauthentic existence or with Sartre that each *pour-soi* is for ever alienated from every other."[15]

This "new" existentialism is now becoming quite explicit as to what its differentiations are with "classical" existentialism. There is one final volume which needs to be noted, and this is a kind of Coda to the trilogy entitled *What is it to be human? New Perspectives in Philosophy* (1990). This volume contains the proceedings of a conference held at Downing College in 1987. It shows, though, that the "widening out" of existentialist criteria in the very broad and all-inclusive manner of the trilogy, is not without its cost. The terminology used by the participants may overlap at many points, but there is a severe loss of precision, because of the generosity of the enterprise itself. The term "man" itself is now today, after relativistic anthropology, radical political (including feminist) philosophy, and deconstructive literary theory, rendered pretty well useless. "Human" has suffered the same fate. Holbrookian existentialism is itself seen as isolated from quite another kind of philosophical debate than the one it takes itself to have a quarrel with. There has been a war of attrition, for instance, from Lacan and the Lacanians against the very concept of anything that could be called an individual "self," and feminist Lacanians would have a particular quarrel with the refusal of gender distinctions implied by the generic term "man." Deconstruction has thrown into question whether philosophical positions are anything more than rhetorical strategies for persuasion—a position that one could imagine Holbrook finding particularly irritating, in view of his commitment to a philosophical position which he obviously conceives of as urgent and important. Neo-Historicists and Foucaultians have queried whether it is even possible to have any knowledge about "man" or "being human" or indeed about anything at all, which is not quite simply a function of the "archive" of knowledge (or *episteme*) which is available in any particular epoch, and which can never in fact be "transcended" in some transhistorical flight of "consciousness."

Yet, in his introduction and closing chapter to the volume, Holbrook makes it clear that the point of the discussions at the conference was to focus on and investigate the problem of *values* from several different angles, and in making this move he shows himself to be indifferent to the three kinds of contemporary philosophizing to which I have just referred. They *will* not speak about "values" in Holbrook's sense, and Holbrook is determined *to* discuss them, whatever philosophical objections to his project may be made. In this, once again, he shows his Viconian side: the Cartesians may cavil in any new-fangled terms they wish, but meaning and value are existential concerns, and remain so even if the referents of these terms are questioned or denied. If anything, Holbrook's "positive" existentialism is reinforced by having three new sorts of negative philosophising to contend against. For if we are to go on living in any sort of *Lebenswelt* at all, we must generate and project values, and be responsible for them. That means to say that the concept of meaning itself becomes the unique subject of existential philosophising.

If one reads David Holbrook's own essay at the end of *What Is It to Be Human?* attentively, one becomes aware that his central contention is that the universe is itself inherently meaningful, and that therefore, without needing necessarily to invoke the concept of God as such, we can and indeed must see the universe as being in some sense theologically significant. This passage is typical of many:

> But it is also true to say that philosophical anthropology is a stream of thought by which the universe is redeemed, because it becomes no longer a universe of matter-in-motion merely, operating by chance and necessity, but a universe in which living things "strive," whatever that may mean, and in which consciousness has a place. Science itself is matter become conscious of itself, and capable of knowing—a development in evolution which places an enormous burden upon us, and moral responsibilities (as "objective" science often fails to do).[16]

Almost exactly the *Pari* of Pascal against the mathematics of Descartes! Chapter 1 of *Les Pensées*, "Man's place in Nature: The two infinites"[17] rehearses the same arguments against the overweening Cartesians as David Holbrook rehearses against the modern evolutionists and necessetarians. Does not *Fragment* 194 say it all?:

> I cannot forgive Descartes. He would gladly have left God out of his whole philosophy, But he could not help making Him give one flip to set the world in motion. After that he had no more use for God.

and, even more to the point, *Fragment* 195:

Descartes, useless and questionable.

David Holbrook's argument, then, through the three volumes of 1987 and 1988, as well as in the Coda of 1990, is not quite a restatement of the Argument from Design (except perhaps in some modern mode in the manner of Teilhard de Chardin) but an insistence upon the inherent meaningfulness of matter, of evolution, and of consciousness. In this sense, it is a Pascalian *wager*, a wager on the possibility of there *being* meaning in a world which "science" regards as an inanimate lump of rock rotating in space and obeying only mathematical, physical, chemical, and biological laws. From that position, the scientific one, it is but a short step to what Pascal calls Pyrrhonism, or radical sceptical doubt. But, says Holbrook, very much in the manner of Pascal, what explains the inherent meaningfulness of evolution itself? What explains the meaningfulness of human emotion, thought, and behavior?

The detailed, patient, exploratory, investigatory essays gathered together in *Evolution and the Humanities* show again and again, and in explicitly technical terms, that science which operates without allowing for the concept of meaning and purpose in the materials it studies, is just missing the point. Chapter 7, for example, a detailed exposition of the theory of DNAs inherent purposiveness based upon the work of Michael Polanyi, raises a philosophical problem at the heart of what appears to be scientific fact. There is "intentionality" within what appears to be a purely mechanistic system. The longest chapter in the book, and the origin of the book itself, Chapter 9, "The Selfish Gene: dangerous extrapolation from microbiology," thirty pages of detailed technical argument against Richard Dawkins's book *The Selfish Gene*, is a masterpiece of patient and willing exposition, full of goodwill and showing every desire for intelligent debate. There has not, to my knowledge, been any such forthcoming. Alone, as usual, David Holbrook has to carry on the debate for himself, by writing a succeeding chapter on Michael Denton's *Evolution: A Theory in Crisis*, every bit as technical as chapter 9, in which he submits Richard Dawkins's case to rigorous critique. The technical grasp that David Holbrook shows in *Evolution and the Humanities* is quite as astonishing as the technical grasp he shows of musical theory and orchestration in the book on Gustav Mahler, and, were his critics to be in any way conscious of their own limitations, would put them to shame.

In the end of all then, David Holbrook is not a Sartrian existentialist, nor an atheist existentialist, but a Pascalian existentialist. And to have been that, to have set out the necessity for hope and purpose and meaning so consistently for thirty years in the face of almost total neglect (and, yes, often outright derision), is a very great achievement indeed. Those who have failed to listen to what he has to say for so long, and those who scoff, exhibit merely the limited scope of their own intellectual sympathies.

Notes

1. David Holbrook, "Reading and Discrimination" in *Bookmarks*, ed. Frederic Raphael (London: Quartet Books, 1975), p. 84.
2. David Holbrook, *Flesh Wounds* (London: Methuen, 1966), p. 137.
3. Holbrook, "Reading and Discrimination," pp. 84–5.
4. David Holbrook, *Dylan Thomas: The Code of Night* (London: Athlone Press, 1972), p. 4.
5. Ibid., p. 2.

6. David Holbrook, *Sylvia Plath: Poetry and Existence* (London: Athlone Press, 1976), p. 7.

7. David Holbrook, *The Skeleton in the Wardrobe: C. S. Lewis's Fantasies: A Phenomenological Study* (Lewisburg, Pa.: Bucknell University Press; London: Associated Universities Presses, 1991), p. 117.

8. Edmund Husserl, *The Crisis of European Sciences and Transcendental Phenomenology*, trans. David Carr (Evanston, Ill.: Northwestern University Press, 1970).

9. Roger Poole, "Life *versus* death in the later criticism of F. R. Leavis," *Renaissance and Modern Studies* 16 (1972), pp. 112–41.

10. Roger Poole, "The bond of human embodiment," *Universities Quarterly* 28:4 (Autumn 1974), pp. 488–500.

11. Roger Poole, "Education and Philosophical Anthropology; Evolution and the Humanities; Further Studies in Philosophical Anthropology," *The Heythrop Journal* 32:1 (January 1991), pp. 111–3.

12. Quoted by David Holbrook, *Further Studies in Philosophical Anthropology* (Aldershot: Avebury, 1988), p. 122.

13. Ibid., see pp. 183–7.

14. Ibid., pp. 183–4.

15. Ibid., p. 185.

16. David Holbrook, *What is it to be Human? New Perspectives in Philosophy* (Aldershot: Avebury, 1990), p. 121.

17. Blaise Pascal, *The Pensées*, trans. J. M. Cohen (Harmondsworth: Penguin Books, 1961), p. 51 ff., and p. 82.

Part IV
Poet and Novelist

Introduction

David Holbrook's poetry and novels, as Geoffrey Strickland points out, are not so well known generally as his works on literature and education. In part this may well accrue as a consequence of having acquired a reputation within those critical endeavors which have included, significantly, outspoken views upon various aspects of contemporary writings and cultural issues. The lack of notice, however, may have much more to do with the essential nature of the poems and novels which Holbrook composes. Just as Holbrook's literary criticism avoids the cultural fashions of deconstructionism, for example—simply because it does not serve the purpose of his intent—so do the novels and poems avoid the fashionably creative. His novels do not play with inventions of narrative technique, of dislocation, of alienation, of magic realism, of metafiction—those devices which call attention to the text as a self-enclosed reference system. Nor are his poems self-consciously experimental either in construction or language deployment. For Holbrook's poetry and novels are always directed (to use his own words from another context) to "that which is *beyond the words,* in life."

Holbrook's art rests, therefore, entirely outside contemporary modishness and its associated stratagems for achieving impersonality and disengagement, or for indulging in willful "play" or trickery, in the completed work. For his poems and novels are, with very few exceptions, both intensely personal and direct. His poetry, as he declared himself, is the essential means by which he "can maintain touch with . . . "the true self" . . . and maintain a sense of "what it is to be human," and cherish that, in oneself and others." The novels, in the main, are fictional only at a remove—and, in the case of the Paul Grimmer novels, a small remove at that (Grimmer being, as Boris Ford pointed out, the maiden name of Holbrook's mother). Holbrook's concerns, in his literary art as with his critical writings, are with the inner realities of being. The art springs from the determination to confront, reflect, and make realizeable, the realities of experience itself. Such is the authenticity of Holbrook's own writings.

Creative composition, in practice, operates largely through connecting sets of intuitive improvizations. Some measure of unconsciousness is subsumed in the activity itself of making the work. Alongside, or following, the making there may well issue a critical attitude both to one's own work and to the work of others: a matter posed in the Introduction through the example of D. H. Lawrence, and a process clearly exemplified in the writings of T. S. Eliot. John Ferns, in his contribution to this section, explores the relationship between Holbrook's critical method and his poetry and finds a similar anticipation, in the poems, of perceptions subsequently explored extensively in the criticism. The same themes feature in both forms of engagement. The "phenomenological" criticism widens and deepens responses to creativity, changes the meaning of poetic metaphor, and may well lead to further creativity.

Ian Robinson, who helped Holbrook to choose the pieces to be included in his *Selected Poems* (1980), here appraises the achievement of Holbrook's poetry. He acknowledges some of the criticisms which can be and have been made against the work, whilst affirming, within the whole output, a corpus of poems which have enduring distinctiveness. Indeed, the key to Holbrook's philosophical anthropology, he suggests, actually resides in certain of the poems—in that lived sense of reality with which they are invested and from which they issue. Robinson's appraisal concludes that: "At his best, if there is now a poet addressing the common reader in English, it is David Holbrook."

Geoffrey Strickland provides an introductory essay to Holbrook's novels. Read sequentially (though not in the order published) they "give every appearance of being close to autobiography." Unlike the retrospective self-justification of much autobiography, however, the traditional forms of the novel which Holbrook adopts enables him to explore the limitations and possibilities of experience. The process is one of illumination, through identification, in the search to discover the authentic being of persons. In this regard, Holbrook's novels are themselves creative embodiments of the central issues which he has been concerned to identify and delineate in his critical works. Yet they have their own autonomy. And as works of art in their own right it is absurd, as Strickland concludes, "that writing as powerful and intelligent" as Holbrook's novels "is not better known."

"The Petals of the Man": The Relationship of David Holbrook's Criticism to His Poetry

JOHN FERNS

A Critical Connection

In recent years as David Holbrook has been writing and publishing novels he has also written and published books about novels and novelists: Charles Dickens (1993), *Wuthering Heights* (1990), Edith Wharton (1991), D. H. Lawrence (1992), T. F. Powys, C. S. Lewis (1991), and *The Novel and Authenticity* (1987). It would appear that the two enterprises are connected. Writing novels, he reads and reflects on novels and novelists as he ponders the novelist's art. Earlier, as he was publishing poetry during the 1960s and 1970s, Holbrook was also publishing books about poets and poetry: three books about Dylan Thomas (1962, 1964, and 1972), a book about Sylvia Plath (1976), *The Quest for Love* (1964), and *Lost Bearings in English Poetry* (1977). As he attempted to diagnose critically what was wrong with English poetry, Holbrook was also writing poems that embodied his critical ideals. Indeed, Holbrook's poetry-criticism and poetry may be even more intimately connected than this later fiction and criticism of the novel. It is the relationship between his literary criticism and poetry which I wish particularly to explore here.

The period I will consider (1960–80) is also the period in which an important development in Holbrook's critical thinking took place. This development is clearly evident if we compare *Llareggub Revisited* (1962) to the later book on Dylan Thomas, *The Code of Night* (1972). What happened in the interim was that Holbrook embraced what he calls "philosophical anthropology," more particularly the psychoanalytical theories of Fairbairn, Guntrip, and Winnicott, even entitling his poetry volume of 1967, *Object Relations*. In his response to contemporary culture and the situation of poetry, Holbrook's criticism and poetry of the 1960s and 1970s involved a response to Thomas Hardy's injunction, "if way to the Better there be, it exacts a full look at the Worst."[1]

If we can describe *Llareggub Revisited* as a *Scrutiny*-inspired book, the turning point in Holbrook's thinking appears to have come in *The Quest for Love* (1964). In *Llareggub Revisited* Holbrook wrote:

> the strangest feature of Dylan Thomas's notoriety—not that he is bogus, but that attitudes to poetry attached themselves to him which not only threaten the prestige, effectiveness and accessibility of English poetry, but also destroyed his true voice and, at last, him. The lesson should be taken as a stern one for English letters.
>
> One does not have to look far to find confirmation of my diagnosis in the poems themselves. (I don't, by the way, put it forward as a psychoanalytical theory since this is something I know nothing about . . .).[2]

Two years later, in his Preface to *The Quest for Love,* he wrote of "psychoanalytical philosophy and practice": "We can no longer ignore these fresh lights. Indeed, if we can understand them, we may perhaps find in them the basis for better criticism of works of literature, for fresh creation, better methods of education, and a new (and more real) morality."[3] All of Holbrook's interests in criticism, in creativity, in education and in morality are present here, but we should note in particular the collocation of "better criticism of works of literature" and "fresh creation." For Holbrook literary criticism and the "fresh creation" of poetry go together. So it is hardly surprising that the literary-critical works of the 1960s and 1970s and the volumes of poetry of the same period culminating in *Selected Poems* (1980) should be interwoven.

From Practice to Theory

But how are the literary criticism and the poetry related? Surely the relation lies in the fact that the same mind, the same thinking, the same feeling inform both. I think it was T. S. Eliot who argued that any new development in poetry required an attendant ground-breaking effort in criticism. This is certainly true of Eliot himself, earlier it was true of Wordsworth, and it is true of Holbrook.

Concerns with love, art and "moral issues in life" that are continuously tackled in Holbrook's criticism are also engaged in his poetry. As he puts it in *The Quest for Love:*

In each personal life the growth of love is the root of our personal stability and is interwoven with the growth of our capacity to deal with reality. Since society is composed of individuals the growth of love is thus the basis of the stability and effective vitality of all human societies. Love is, indeed, the basis of human evolution and civilization: in this sense it is truly love that makes the world go round.[4]

His poetry would seem to have anticipated such perceptions as we see in the presentation of family life in relation to art in *Reflections on a Book of Reproductions* from *Imaginings* (1961):

> Then we all gather round for the tea,
> All laying claim to her, or informing me,
> Under the candles, about how they bought
> A pair of shoes, and how the bus they caught
> Struck the branches of trees, and what
> The old man in the seat behind
> Said to his wife, while they sneezed and grinned.
> Yet this is the family food of the aspiration
> To celebrate order: Bach's elation
> Was nourished on soup and hearth,
> And worked among insolent men; . . .
> . . . .
> So we are not demeaned by simplicity, or banality,
> By our cars, electric kettles, or lamps; the finality
> Of our death, even, in the mass-produced chest:
> Burial may ennoble us, that we watch our best
> From time to time put in the ground. From such roots
> We may draw from the soaring elms, the yellow
> Pillars of poplar, as each great red ball sinks below
> Our pathetic horizon, some share of the significance
> The great painters saw, between the small hours and the
>   natural world's magnificence.[5]

The same argument of the prose of 1964 is present in the poem of three years earlier. Holbrook sees how great art, like Bach's, grows out of the love present in everyday family living. So in the books on Dylan Thomas and Sylvia Plath he seeks to expose the hate-filled false solutions of schizoid poetry, while in *Lost Bearings in English Poetry* he shares the pessimism of Leavis's *Retrospect 1950* to his *New Bearings in English Poetry* (1932) that the new realism of modernism has failed since Eliot and Yeats to bear new fruit. For his part, Holbrook, both in his literary criticism and in his creative practice, sought to return poetry from the sensationalism of false solutions to celebrating the loving essences of meaning and being present in ordinary human life.

Just as Holbrook's poem of 1961 anticipates his critical perception of 1964, in *The Quest for Love* he notes that great writers like Shakespeare and Dickens had anticipated psychoanalytic theory in their understanding that life at its best involved more than a mere struggle to survive:

> The truth as seen by later psychoanalytical theory is rather more as it was seen by writers such as Shakespeare and Dickens who valued human ideals, creativity, and 'good' feelings in sincere relationship, by intuition, as our greatest reality.[6]

Indeed, Holbrook's Preface to *The Quest for Love* directly links critical to creative practice. He is quite explicit:

> My purpose in writing this book is to urge that we are unlikely to have new writing of any consequence, minority or popular, unless the writer-as-artist makes his own positive quest for insight into such profound human truths as have to do with love and our dealings with reality, such as are being revealed by our increased insight into the mind, through recent psychoanalytical philosophy and practice.[7]

Trying to reach beyond the violence and despair so present in "the new poetry" anthologized by Alfred Alvarez in the early 'sixties, Holbrook continues in a vein that stresses the interconnectedness of criticism, poetry and life:

> The question is not only one of writing: it has to do with our attitudes to life at large, our acceptance of possibilities of new growths in living power, based on hopefulness about the future, a belief in the continuity of life, creative attitudes, and positive values. There can be aims and values in our living, even in the absence of religious faith, if we listen to our deepest inward needs. The writer, teacher and critic who has to do with fiction, drama and poetry inevitably has to do with such aims and values, and such visions and concepts as we develop to help us to come at them. The writer is inevitably concerned with promoting (or obscuring) insight and understanding. There is no way of escaping this responsibility—one's literary work inevitably touches life thus.[8]

Intuition and the Reasonings of Psychoanalysis

The period 1961–65 spent as a Fellow of King's College seems to have been decisive in Holbrook's "conversion" to psychoanalysis. This period is partly dramatized in his autobiographical novel

Nothing Larger Than Life (1987). If *The Quest for Love* marks a decisive shift away from the critical method of *Llareggub Revisited* in its incorporation of psychoanalytical methods into literary analysis, the volume of poems *Object Relations* (1967) appears to be the one in which Holbrook attempts to incorporate particularly Harry Guntrip's psychoanalytical thought into his poetry. On the Contents page of *Object Relations,* we are told that "The poems are arranged roughly in groups dealing with Love and Hate; Time, Death and Mutability; various places; and Birth. Within the groups they are arranged in more or less chronological order." These permanently important subjects are Holbrook's continuous concern both in his literary criticisms and his poetry.

The volume begins in depression:

> Nothing responds: even the reeds are bruised with frost,
> Bent in the stream. At each corner comes regret:
> Homing I watch the pebbled surface pass beneath my feet.[9]

Swifts which follows the just-quoted poem *Depression,* lifts us out of that state even as it reaches through animal vitality to human renewal:

> Round and round whirl the swifts, in the oncoming rain.
> You love them too, I see:
> You smile and wave at me!
> They soar between us, charming close the fissures of our
>   pain![10]

The final clause, "charming close the fissures of our pain!" has a psychological resonance yet is a convincing and responsible use (to invoke Holbrook's criteria in *Llareggub Revisited*) of poetic metaphor. We do not feel any strain on Holbrook's part to write specifically psychoanalytical poetry. Even if the volume's title *Object Relations* has a clinically psychoanalytic timbre, Holbrook meets the challenge of making the term work poetically. This is best illustrated in the poem *Beggar-beads* in which a single bead reminds the poet that the string of beads from which it comes was a love-gift. After a quarrel, the bead helps to lead the poet back to his beloved:

> I've lost it now—but still am dazed with how
> This self-formed crustacean could speak of you
> And your identity, and how it broke from your soft neck,
> And lay in its curled shape of love, waiting to bring me
>   back.[11]

The psychoanalytical idea of "object relations" is realized in a poetically convincing way here.

Nowhere in the volume is there a sense of inhibition by the psychoanalytical reference in the volume's title. In *Italian Moments,* Holbrook's response to Botticelli reveals completely what Holbrook himself seeks to achieve in his art:

> At last I find Botticelli—and vindication.
> Everything else falls away, and I stand numb and chastened.
> The hair and draperies float, the moment of birth, dance or
>   cloaking,
> Forever hanging in air, about to happen; the Spring, or
>   Woman,
> Caught just about to bloom, and transfixed for ever
> On the windswept delectable brink of ebullient ripeness.[12]

Life, for Holbrook, is active and sympathetic living. So in the poem *Maternity Gown,* he discovers "the need to be, and make, even where annihilation threatens,"[13] and in *Shared Shore* he finds again, "the shoal of joys that once our marriage meant."[14] Marital problems confronted and resolved that are dramatized in the autobiographical novel *Nothing Larger Than Life* (1987) also find their resolution here. One feels that Holbrook's whole critical-creative enterprise is rooted in the reality of a complete marital and family life, one that also incorporates the natural world. Thus, in the poem *The Rewards,* Holbrook's response to nature is modified by his response to human life so that he sees natural objects "in the brightness of your eyes, / And all is changed;"[15] or in *Sanaigmore,* in which we see the interrelationship of the natural and the human dramatized in the image, "This sea eats at the beaches of my brain."[16] Finally, in *The Master,* human life is celebrated as Holbrook affirms the life of his infant son:

> We can't get away from him.
> Who wants to anyway?—He's our love-lord,
> Greater than canvas legacies or ten libraries of verse![17]

Holbrook reveals his clear grasp of the importance of life in relation to art. As Gerard Manley Hopkins once remarked, "if we care for fine verses how much more for a noble life."

The relationship between Holbrook's literary criticism and his poetic practice seems clear enough; the two activities are dynamically and organically related. They are also mutually illuminating. But a question remains: if poetry anticipates the perceptions of psychoanalysis, why is it necessary to engage in detail with psychoanalytical theories and incorporate them so completely into one's criticism and poetry? The answer may be that the perceptions of poetry are intuitively, perhaps even unconsciously, grasped, whereas the reasonings of psychoanalytical theory bring the unconscious or intuitive to full consciousness.

Second Thoughts: A Revaluation

In conclusion, I would like to consider why David Holbrook chose to write a second book on Dylan Thomas. Doing so involved a significant development in method that embraced psychoanalysis. Also, I would like to consider what further implications, if any, this critical development had for his practice as a poet.

In *The Quest for Love* Holbrook makes the reason for his 'conversion' to psychoanalysis crystal clear:

> my interest in psychoanalytical theories has been impelled by the experience of being presented with the inescapable truth of at least some of psychoanalytical theory and practice, first-hand enough in terms of actual living, since I have been in love with and married to the subject of treatment.[18]

Seeing, at first hand, the help that psychoanalysis provides in personal living, Holbrook naturally drew it into his creative and critical thought. In *Dylan Thomas: The Code of Night* (1972) he canvasses some of the problems that his development in critical method might have raised:

> A hostile reader may say that for me my critical role has become merely a mock therapeutic one, in which I can play at being a psychoanalyst. To this I could only retort that in discussing Dylan Thomas again I only began with the utmost reluctance, since I recognized that my point of view had completely changed since *Llareggub Revisited* and to face up to this would be awkward and embarrassing. But I was driven to write this second book because I wished to find good grounds for discriminating against the prevalent ethos of our fashionable literary world, and its concern to endorse schizoid false solutions, while neglecting the underlying problems of existence which the schizoid writer forces us to consider. I hoped to become able to "hear" Dylan Thomas as he had not yet been "heard."
>
> I have discussed the same problem in connection with Sylvia Plath, and in trying to "hear" in this way (when the avant-garde hear some-

thing quite different) I believe I am trying to apply the kind of insights to literary criticism which D. W. Winnicott emphasizes for psychotherapy.[19]

Holbrook could hardly be clearer than he is here. What his engagement with psychoanalysis has brought him is a deepened sympathy for human suffering. Increased sympathy deepens our own human being:

> In literary criticism, of course, often, as with Sylvia Plath and Dylan Thomas, the "patients"—the subjects—are dead. But to try to hear or see them as they are in their works is also a way to try to find "a way to exist as oneself" and to share this quest with others. As Farber says, what we are here forced to concern ourselves with is the nature of humanness: and this can be both exhausting and satisfying.
> The first problem, then, is to recognise that Dylan Thomas was sensitive, intelligent, and painstaking. The present writer acknowledges that it is very little credit to his former study that he tried to deny this.[20]

It would be hard to think of many modern critics prepared, as Holbrook is here, to admit in print that they were wrong. One might even think that Holbrook carries his apology too far when he writes:

> Since reading Thomas's letters and his life I have come to accept his integrity as a writer, and I believe he was sincere in these comments on his work. He was aware of all the faults with which I charged him in *Llareggub Revisited:* he was not mocking us by deliberate irrationality.[21]

It seems to me unlikely that Thomas *could* have been aware of "all the faults" with which Holbrook charged him in *Llareggub Revisited.* However, Holbrook's principal concern is to identify confusion in our response to life. Of Thomas he notes that, "Like Sylvia Plath, he confuses the grave with the womb . . ."[22] In discussing the poetry of Dylan Thomas (1962, 1972), Sylvia Plath (1976) and the work of other contemporary poets such as Robert Lowell and Ted Hughes in *Lost Bearings in English Poetry* (1977), Holbrook is discussing what he calls in *The Code of Night* a "whole false posture," "because the mode is now more fashionable than the modes of true creativity. Sylvia Plath's psychotic *Daddy* and Ted Hughes's cynical and nihilistic *Crow* poems are among the most popular poems of our time. The implications are serious, not only for our attitudes to life, but because of the effect of such fashions on creativity itself."[23]

This was basically Holbrook's position in *Llareggub Revisited.* What has changed is his increased sympathy for Dylan Thomas and, in *Poetry and Existence* (1976), for Sylvia Plath. At the close of *The Code of Night* Holbrook writes:

> Exploration of the meaning of poetic symbolism "phenomenologically," as a manifestation of consciousness in the here and now can, I believe, deepen and extend our response to creativity. In this we are no mere "outsiders," but draw gladly on the "psychosynthesis" offered by the poetry itself. In this we can find gratitude in ourselves for the immense efforts a poet has made, not least in the face of desperate life-problems. Such an approach recognises that his efforts have contributed to our capacity to find our own deeper potentialities, and our own sense of meaning, by the symbolic energy he has managed to exert and develop between separation and union, in the sharing between man and man that we call culture.[24]

For Holbrook, then, the psychoanalytical method of literary analysis affords a deeper and more sympathetic understanding of poetic metaphor and of the poet himself.

Being and Meaning

In Holbrook's view of life without religion, our principal problem is to discover being and meaning in the face of death. In *The Code of Night* and in some nearly contemporary poems in his fourth volume *Old World, New World* (1969) David Holbrook deals with the problem of the death of near relations both in Dylan Thomas's poems and in his own. I believe that we can see here how Holbrook, whether consciously or not, responds to poems that he finds unsatisfactory or only partially satisfactory with more life-affirming poems of his own. As well, we can see how his preoccupation with "philosophical anthropology" has deepened his sympathy and understanding not only of the work of others but also has enriched his own.

In the case of Dylan Thomas's poem *After the Funeral,* Holbrook presents evidence from Thomas's letters that indicate Thomas's inability to "feel" his aunt's death. As Holbrook notes, "this failure to become able to mourn was at one with the failure to be able to find reality, because of the failure to find substance in inner reality." This is what leads to the poem's egocentric rhetoric. As Holbrook comments, "the poem for Ann is therefore in the light of this something of a fake, an attempt to feel feelings of which he was incapable."[25] In contrast, Holbrook's poem *Step* from *Old World, New World* that recounts his mother's death is a deeply moving poem because it is fully felt. In part it recalls the emotion of Lawrence's *Piano*. Perhaps it would be stretching things to say that the engagement with psychoanalysis has helped Holbrook to express his feelings more fully, yet the poem seems to me the most deeply felt poem thus far encountered when we read Holbrook's poems chronologically:

> But then I'm lost, and for a moment stand inert
> In the old way, as when, dying and dead, she took my heart
> Down to the subsoil where the stumbling priest, that autumn
>   day,
> Recited to our tears and she was lowered far away—
>
> She on whose breast I sobbed, she whose piano melody
> Thrilled on my child's nerves in that long Eden holiday
> Between birth and the gradual separation till the grave
>   ropes creak
> And bitter apprehension of implacable truths come break
> In great sobs as the shovels heave the earth back on the
>   box.[26]

Although David Holbrook (rightly I think) finds *Fern Hill*, "the most successful and beautiful of all Dylan Thomas's poems", he argues that "in *Do not go gentle* death seems more real than anywhere else in Dylan Thomas."[27] Yet I would ask the critical reader if death is not "more real" and more fully dealt with in David Holbrook's remarkable poem *My Father's Gay Funeral* from *Old World, New World*. Though one could not say directly that Holbrook's "conversion" to psychoanalysis informs the poem, it does seem to me that the poem is a fully convincing and striking enactment of the critical ideals expressed in such preceding works as *The Quest for Love*. Though death is engaged in the poem, the overriding impression that emerges from it is of life. Ian Robinson is right that Holbrook's "strength is as an artist even more than as a critic and philosopher, important as some of his critical writings are." The "philosophical anthropology", as Robinson has argued, has been "necessary" for the poetry.[28]

Reading from *My Father's Gay Funeral* seems to me an appropriate way to celebrate and honor David Holbrook's contribution over seventy years. The critic and the poet finally are one. Certainly David Holbrook the poet deserves the last word:

> Weep as we could, his coffin sailed vivid and gay
> Through the September noon, lurched through the archway
> Where he stood ten years ago to be photographed
> After his second wedding: wreath-roses flipped the stone,
> The air filled with torn blossom because we were late,
> The air tearing garlands form his roof:
> How he would have laughed:
>
> Veiled, his widow,
> After the Blessing snaps a rose from the cross,
> Her hand on the ridge of the long box:
> Then we go out, crying bitterly, among the sun-warm flowers.
>
> But through our tears the massed petals under the walnut trees
> Dance and are sparkling gay. So we comfort one another.

Despite the pain of death, Holbrook's final memory is of his father's life. In the case of Holbrook himself, we feel the full force of his courageous creativity, the sense of what an impressive poet he is. There is no essential difference between the man and his work:

> But uppermost in the memory, in the mind's eye of him,
> Is the man as a spoiled flower, all there filled
> By the past bloom of him, the blossom dust we gathered,
> As I saw gather bees from the plump grapes on a market stall,
> On that same vivid day, when everything I saw
> Spoke stubbornly not of trouble, but of the petals of the man.[29]

Notes

1. Thomas Hardy, "In Tenebris," II, in *The Collected Poems of Thomas Hardy* (London: Macmillan, 1965), p. 154.
2. David Holbrook, *Llareggub Revisited* (London: Methuen, 1962), p. 129.
3. David Holbrook, *The Quest for Love* (London: Methuen, 1964), p. 11.
4. Ibid., p. 13.
5. David Holbrook, *Imaginings* (London: Putnam, 1961), pp. 19–20.
6. Holbrook, *The Quest for Love*, p. 13.
7. Ibid., p. 14.
8. Ibid.
9. David Holbrook, *Object Relations* (London: Methuen, 1964), p. 3.
10. Ibid., p. 4.
11. Ibid., p. 5.

12. Ibid., p. 44
13. Ibid., p. 13.
14. Ibid., p. 6
15. Ibid., p. 25.
16. Ibid., p. 34.
17. Ibid., p. 51.
18. Holbrook, *The Quest for Love*, p. 15.
19. David Holbrook, *Dylan Thomas: The Code of Night* (London: The Athlone Press, 1972), pp. 65–6.
20. Ibid., p. 66.
21. Ibid., p. 140.
22. Ibid., p. 164.
23. Ibid., p. 220.
24. Ibid., p. 261.
25. Ibid., p. 194–6.
26. David Holbrook, *Old World, New World* (London: Rapp & Whiting, 1969), p. 5.
27. Holbrook, *Dylan Thomas: The Code of Night*, p. 207, p. 197.
28. Ian Robinson, "Philosophical Anthropology," *The Human World*, no. 11 (May 1973), p. 81.
29. Holbrook, *Old World, New World*, p. 46–7.

The Probes That Are Creation

Ian Robinson

A Criticism of David Holbrook's Poetry[1]

This is not meant as a survey of David Holbrook's verse, for two reasons. The first, no doubt less respectable, is that though I think I know most of it I would feel uncomfortable if I were taken to be covering the ground, that occupation critics share with nettles and brambles. There would probably be gaps. Anyone looking for a survey (and a judiciously critical one, not just covering the ground) should read John Ferns's essay "David Holbrook."[2] My second reason is that I think it will be more useful, and a more genuine tribute to Holbrook, if I try to work out a criticism of his poems that I have had half-formulated for a long time. He deserves criticism.

Holbrook has been publishing poetry for more than thirty years and continues to do so. The same could be said of his activity in most of the other traditional creative modes, as well as criticism and philosophy: Holbrook goes on producing quite voluminously. The present occasion being, I trust, very far from a collection of obituaries in which Johnson says that one is not on oath, one has to salute David Holbrook warts and all; any possibility of getting more and better attention for his work must proceed from the clear recognition that some common objections to it are not unjust. There is no denying that his work can appear irritatingly paradoxical. His concerns are above all those of the all-round man of letters, for value in language, for what is significant in writing, as well as in living; but when not at his best (which is, not surprisingly given his output, quite a lot of the time) he can be stylistically careless and seems not to worry too much about whether he has said exactly what he means; i.e., he sometimes writes as if language is not of the first importance.[3]

He is, also, surely (with the possible exception of Iris Murdoch) the most prolific contemporary author with any pretension to seriousness, an all-rounder in the Victorian mode, who publishes more volumes a year even than those who admire his work can keep up with, but who is still very willing and able to produce more criticism, fiction, "philosophical anthropology" (as he calls it) and verse than the market can bear; he makes public complaints about not getting published and, when they become (a good thing too!) too implausible, complains that nobody reviews him.

The latter has, however, much truth in it, and it is to be hoped that the present volume will go some way toward making amends. I think it is a mark of his original genius that the literary-academic establishment finds Holbrook so hard to "take on board," and that his attitude to the contemporary academic and metropolitan establishments has to be largely one of antagonism. But one can't help thinking that he would probably make more of an impact if he poured himself out rather less and reworked rather more.

Holbrook does produce literary work of all sorts, though, as the tree produces leaves in spring. And other work as well: his paintings are always well worth putting on the wall (they improved his handsome but rather formal room in Downing). It is natural to the man to be very prolific and in the end one couldn't wish it otherwise without wanting him to be another man.

As it happens, being as an undergraduate several years behind Holbrook at Downing, I first came across him as a practitioner of that minor but interesting *genre,* the letter to the press. In the late fifties and early sixties it often happened that *The Manchester Guardian* (as I think it still then was?) was momentarily enlivened by a Holbrook letter. Such a letter always stood out from the gray mass of the new enlightenment in its vividness of feeling, directness of humane comment, forcefulness of language. I think it goes on being true that these momentaneous little responses to some particular bit of the life of these times can be more interesting, better written, more *lively,* than some at least of the paragraphs in Holbrook's weightier philosophical books. Thereby hangs my argument, for the one word I would need for many of Holbrook's letters to the press is *poetic.* They are, of course, prose criticism, but criticism as it creates judgment out of feeling as well as ratiocination, comment coming from a whole human response, criticism as it belongs (as Arnold thought long since) with creativity.[4]

Holbrook as a critic is admirable and necessary, all the way from *Llareggub Revisited* to *Lost Bearings in English Poetry* and the recent book on C. S. Lewis, *The Skeleton in the Wardrobe;* and the philosophical anthropology is at least something that ought to be taken seriously—what an age we live in when the self-important self-contradictions of Deconstruction obsess the academy but nobody has any time for Holbrook's much more interesting acclimatization in England of such continental thinkers as Cassirer and Merleau-Ponty, any more than for his bringing into literary criticism the work of the more humane psychological writers! But often in the philosophical anthropology he seems to me to be writing in chains which drop off instantly when he writes fiction or verse. I can't remember any clumsily written passage in the novels; on the contrary he often rises to a poetic freshness and witty precision that remind one of the verse of the metaphysicals on which, at Downing, we were all brought up.

I don't think Holbrook is a novelist of the order of Lawrence or a poet of the order of Eliot or Yeats, but the first and smaller claim is to say that after long experience I have never failed to enjoy his fiction and his verse, that both are unfailingly easy, fresh, close to the author's own life (perhaps too much so in the case of the fiction) and thoroughly decent in feeling. If this seems faint praise, bear in mind that it is written at a time when the predominance of what one critic has called the "black beetle" school of fiction shows no sign of abating. I once had to stop reading a Holbrook novel on a railway train because it was reducing me to tears by the beauty of its presentment of human emotion.

I think this is a hint about understanding what is enigmatic about Holbrook's work, the really huge *oeuvre,* always worth attention, so decent, often so likable, which so often doesn't quite come off, but which in the moments when it does can remind one of D. H. Lawrence, or Blake, or Yeats.

The larger claim, that is, that I have to make for Holbrook's poetry is that the best of it is much more than the "engaging minor verse" (as Inglis called it) thrown off by a literary all-rounder, though often one has to agree that the phrase is just enough. At best it is the poetry that gives the figure in Holbrook's carpet.

This again, though, is not a straightforward matter, and I will confess that, as I shall explain, the dawning of this answer to what must appear a kind of conundrum came to me not because I can claim any great superiority of insight but because, two decades ago now, I happened to be in a situation in which I would hardly miss it.

But at first sight, in the *Selected Poems*[5] the verse may well appear to conform to the standard Holbrook pattern. It is always readable, often engaging, unfailingly sound and good in feeling: but it may seem rarely if ever to rise above that level, which would make the word *minor* appropriate.

There are some ominous symptoms. Holbrook is unobtrusively skilled in the use of the traditional modes of English verse, though not an innovator; but he is not always good at knowing where to stop. I don't know whether he adopts the D. H. Lawrence method of cutting off a text with a pair of scissors when he thinks it has gone on long enough, but it sometimes reads like that; or one turns a page and finds to one's surprise that a poem is continuing when it seemed to have ended (e.g., "A Child Said, 'I am Smoke . . .'," pp. 49–50). When I had the privilege of helping Holbrook choose the poems for the selection it wasn't easy, and I remember suggesting, without much success, that if some of them were pruned there would be room for more. Similarly, he often writes blank verse or an Eliotic four-beat freer line, but the lines tend to expand as the poem goes on, and it is quite common, and not I think a good thing, for the *verse libre* to expand in length, or the pentameter to expand into hexameter and even, on one occasion, into heptameter. *Song of the Seasons* (p. 36), expands from very pleasing four-foot verse into, in the last line of the penultimate stanza, not so pleasing pentameter; *A Moth in a Morning* expands from a rather free blank verse into free hexameters, while *Cardoness Castle* (pp. 45–6) goes all the way from blank verse into something rather like poulter's measure, and not, I think, to the advantage of the poem. Holbrook has not the kind of technical originality and tightness of control that allowed the septuagenarian Yeats, for instance, to develop a sort of tetrametrical blank verse, shorter than the usual blank verse line, for *Purgatory*.

It may seem, again, and on occasion truly, that the fault of the poems is the same as the fault of the novels, that they are too much slices of life. To be sure, to have anything to do with life, if a fault at all, is a good one, and the slices are usually fresh and vivid *(Lynx, Bowling for a Pig)*. But coming cold upon the *Selected Poems* I don't think anyone would call Holbrook a Yeatsian kind of poet. I mention Yeats again, however, because, like Holbrook, his poems are often moments of life; they are often also closely related to the poet's philosophic/systematic grapplings (and I will say that I much prefer Holbrook's philosophical anthropology to Yeats's absolutely unvisionary *Vision*). The obvious difference is that for Yeats the poem is, at the same time as a mode of genuine thought, also the Grecian Urn, the monument of unaging intellect, the struggle to a perfection cold and passionate as the dawn. Even when Holbrook's poems are free from his characteristic fault of expansiveness, as in the just-mentioned *Lynx,* they are not *often* Yeatsian in concentration or artistic inevitability; which is only to say again that Holbrook is not a poet of the order of Yeats. I nevertheless make the comparison seriously to suggest a real similarity of effort concentrated, made whole indeed, in particular in formal poetry. Yeats too was an important critic and essayist, but the prose work is that of a man whose poetry makes the *oeuvre* a whole.

What can be said *for* Holbrook the poet, beyond the claims already made befitting a minor poet, that the poems are pleasing and about life, is that at his best they achieve a memorableness and succinctness not characteristically found in the prose philosophy, and that they fuse Holbrook's predominant concerns and bond the rest of the work together.

He is one of the few poets since Yeats whose lines do stick in the mind. Reading again all the way through the *Selected Poems* for the first time since I helped select them, I was agreeably surprised to find how many I hardly need to read, particularly the early ones I have known for a long time, like the one about Leavis with his head like an old corm *(Living! Our supervisors Will do That for Us!)*[6] and the good and beautiful poem *Unholy Marriage* about the wise virgin found watching on a fatal pillion seat.

The poems I have most in mind, however, as sticking in the mind, are not in the *Selected Poems,* being composed too late for inclusion.

The best way I can find of making my point is by way of reminiscence. In the early 1970s I was running a magazine called *The Human World,* to which Holbrook sent contributions that reminded me of a good plum year in a rather ill-kept orchard. They were all enjoyable, though not all seemed to me to be the man at his best—and there were just too many of them. If I remember rightly there were occasions when his method of delivery was parcel post. (All this without a penny offered to an author then trying to live by the pen, and for the sake of helping a magazine Holbrook thought deserved encouragement, though he was far from sympathetic to its politics and could have had no expectation that it would do his reputation any good at all!) This was at the beginning of his philosophical anthropology phase, and simultaneously other parcels were arriving, of review copies of his recent philosophical anthropological work. The magazine had a series called "New Scrutinies," and Holbrook's work, as a whole, was an obvious subject if the editor could find anyone of sufficient appetite to tackle it. A. A. H. Inglis did, and contributed the critique already mentioned above, which I thought well argued and just, but rather severe in perhaps understating the virtues of the work. So I asked Peter Abbs to contribute a kind of counterbalance, which he duly did. Being still unsatisfied, I tried to write an editorial postscript, and I think it was while I was agonizing over that that yet another Holbrook envelope arrived, this time containing some verses.

Now any editor of a literary magazine knows all too well that in this world there are more magazines than readers, and more poets than magazines. We always tried to take seriously anything that came in, and we made a number of enemies by giving, instead of the usual slip, reasons for rejection. What is more, we had more borderline cases of verse than anything else. The ordinary fate of the verses that came through the letterbox, nevertheless, was to be rejected instantly as being obviously not poetry.

This batch of Holbrook's was one of the two I had during the four years' life of the magazine (the other being some of Christopher Morgan's) which had the other effect. Phrases like *the shock of reocognition* seem appropriate. I was sure at once that these were the real thing, the making in language that is at the same time the individual voice of the real man. You can find these poems in *Human World* no. 12, and then again in the collection *Chance of a Lifetime*. Small objections fell away and I was captivated.

I tried to say some of this to Holbrook and he, true Blakean, was annoyed that I preferred "little poems" (as I think he called them) to the philosophical work into which he had put so much serious effort. He was at least unique amongst our poet contributors in preferring to be thought something else.

But in the end my judgment was that these poems, in the act of being closer than anything else by the author to the making of something shapely and, who knows, eternal, in language, were also more deeply philosophical than the prose works.

A Kind of Consciousness is actually, and clearly, a poetic working-out of Holbrook's thinking about what humanity consists in, about how our consciousness resembles and how it differs from that of the animals, and about how these questionings link with his thoughts about poetry, culture, the state of the language. I think the poem needs to be quoted in full:

The Probes That Are Creation 251

A Kind of Consciousness

A wink of flame through the hedge:
The sun falls into Sharpitor.
At the other end of the fading sky
An orange mass pushes out of the horizon.
Darkness closes round my bonfire.
I drag at unseen branches while the moon
Climbs golden into her black epoch.

I hear a munching: a black shadow
Warm in the shadows, chewing holly.
Our neighbour's horse likes company,
Studies my fire over the gate, his presence
Clouding warm through the darkness,
A consciousness of me. Understanding,
I go to touch the hard ridge of his nose,
His downward silky, upward bristly pelt,
His white flash in the dark, over the bone.

A long dry grey bone, under the hedge,
Does not sense me: the horse does,
Tugs the tough spiny bunches yet more vigorously.
In the dark I spin my senses out like threads:
A child half way down the hill, you in the wood,
A lad asleep by the fire: a daughter
Far away, up in London. I come indoors
And hear her voice, over the telephone:
The moon is white now in a black crystal.

I shake the long life-line across a kingdom:
Tremors of consciousness. She responds,
Fills in her scene. Outside the horse is basalt,
Sleeping: the hills fall away,
The moon's a black ring of matter,
Not a face, not a bent man, until
Tom throws up his perceptual magic:
"Is that God in the Moon?"

The probes that are Creation, without which
All would be formless void.

The Edward Thomas-like precision of "His downward silky, upward bristly pelt" and the like, the evocation of the familiar experience of meeting a big harmless animal by night, may be what strike the reader first, or the stark contrast between the horse's sensation of the poet (and vice versa) with the long dry grey bone under the hedge which "does not sense me" though the dog does. Poetry or platitude? We all know that bones have no sensations. But one useful formula for poetry is Lawrence's phrase, "From this I learn, though I knew it before . . . ." I do think this is poetry, in the first place, because of the power with which it invests the commonplace. Is it not one of the functions of poetry in all ages to redeem what we all know from "the boredom that there is in life itself" and to reendow it with meaning?

What makes the poem classical for me, however, is the way the poet places the encounter in family life, and quite magically incorporates the child's question "Is that God in the moon?" with the purely poetic, purely philosophical conclusion,

> The probes that are creation, without which
> All would be formless void.

The thought here points to the prose elaboration and working-out, but it is the poetry itself that is creating an alternative to chaos, the act of creation that validates the argument.

It may sound rash, but I want to say that the key to the philosophical anthropology is in these lines, and in some others of the poems in the same group, and not the key to the poems in the philosophical anthropology.

The immediately succeeding *In the Face of Nihilism* places the same questioning, questing consciousness in the inevitable context of our literary world. This poem is a kind of anti-Wordsworthian mood, connected with a severe but just judgment of the life of our times.

For a nature poet the two terms are always necessary. I used to think that Wordsworth could have done it anywhere, that wherever he had happened to live he would have endowed with poetic wonder, and I still think there is a kind of truth in that. But that was before I knew the Lake District, and I now think the relationship was more symbiotic. "Half perceive, half create" is the appropriate Wordsworth phrase: nobody before him had seen what he saw, and the seeing is creative and then common, offered to others. All the same, what he saw really is there to be seen. What Wordsworth managed to see, a century and more after Milton, was the beauty of nature as unfathomably significant for the human spirit. But what then if the meaning drains out of nature, as it did for E. M. Forster? *In the Face of Nihilism* is the Holbrook equivalent of the terrible sonnets of Hopkins, and worthy of the comparison. What saves the poem from being *only* anguish that "I cannot throw a mangle of delight / Over the frail flowers" is the judgment, rather Juvenalian in its ferocity, of the state of the culture that has reduced the poet almost to despair. The perception of the beauty of creation in Wordsworth went with a Blakean cleansing of the gates of perception and a renewal of language. The nihilism in this Holbrook poem is a mark of the irredeemable impoverishment of language, "mad and intolerable," in which the poet has to live as in a gas chamber. But the poem is nevertheless not just a cry of rage and despair because of the sane judgment of the situation, culminating in that upsettingly haunting line

> As mean as England and as meaningless.

The anguish, that is (need one say?) proceeds from love not from hatred. The poetry is a redemptive movement within language, even here, very unlike the work of one of Holbrook's subjects, Sylvia Plath.

Another poem in the same group, *Time*, must just be mentioned, though I am not at all sure I have fathomed it. Here the evocation of "an uncanny dreadful sense of time" is again both philosophical and purely poetic and here too there is the paradox that what is almost despair becomes, in this expression in verse, something positive.

> Everything seems to be, as I gaze around,
> Mementos to myself, and, as they fade,
> So does my confidence in anything I've made.

Oddly enough the poet in his more confident mood is not so creative: creation is itself affirmation.

Most of the time, of course, Holbrook is far from being in despair and is an enjoyer of life at the level of Eliot's "or even a very good dinner" without the Eliotic note of deprecation in that "even." I like very much the sequence of poems *Italian Moments* (pp. 74–81), also the one about arriving in Dieppe (*A Day in France*, p. 139): in both the poems and the novels the appreciation of wine is noticeable: not Rabelaisian but a proper tribute to something that can be magical!

All the same, I think Holbrook is at his very best when he is in anguish or awe. There is a concentration forced upon him by agonizing which one does not find elsewhere. And it certainly has continued in his poetry after the group I mentioned. I have taken the liberty of mocking an author who complains about being unpublished when the critique of his work mentioned above was accompanied by a bibliography (kindly supplied by the author) of his then-recent work that stretched to a page of small print. And since then he has regathered momentum. But it is true that his poetry should have much more attention than it has ever had yet; it is also true that the work of the last decade remains uncollected and to a large extent unpublished.[7] I have been privileged to see new work from time to time, and I can say that in my view it at best continues the development I noticed in *Chance of a Lifetime*. In 1986, for instance, I saw a collection based on a sequence called *Ignis Fatuus,* from which Holbrook was wondering whether to delete some poems as not positive enough. (This is my memory of my suspicion, not anything he said or wrote.) I urged him not to, because in my view these poems were of his best, in a way similar to *In the Face of Nihilism:* they were agonizing, but making philosophy and even a kind of belief out of the agony. I remember in particular one called *Erithacus Rubecula* which began as a Clare-like poem of precise observation/evocation and suddenly turned into a kind of enactment of the proof from design. If there is such a proof of divinity in the universe it certainly must be like this, poetic, a moment of created uncertainty, not philosophical argumentation.[8]

I need not have worried about Holbrook deleting the best things from his collection as, to the best of my knowledge, it never saw even the grey dawn of publication. Which, I think, is a suitable point to conclude for the present, with a question that I believe others have asked before me, and by which I do concede a large element of justice in Holbrook's complaints about not being attended to: where are the publishers capable of recognizing the worthwhile when it is laid before them? where the reviewers? and where the readers when at last they get the chance?

At his best, if there is a poet now addressing the common reader in English, it is David Holbrook.

Notes

1. Page references are to David Holbrook, *Selected Poems 1961–1978* (London: Anvil Press, 1980), unless otherwise stated.
2. John Ferns, "David Holbrook," in *Dictionary of Literary Biography*, vol. 40 *Poets of Great Britain and Ireland since 1960,* ed. Vincent Sherry (Detroit: Gale Research Co., 1985), pp. 229–37.

3. Cf. A. A. H. Inglis, "Philosophical Anthropology," *The Human World*, 11 (1973), pp. 64–74.

4. Cf. P. J. M. Robertson, *Criticism and Creativity* (Gringley-on-the-Hill: The Brynmill Press, 1987).

5. Holbrook's *Selected Poems* (which is still available in hardback) remains one of the few contemporary books of verse to be taken to heart. It needs expanding, however, in a revised edition.

6. Perhaps the time is coming when an Annotated Holbrook will be necessary. "Living, our servants can do that for us!" was one of Leavis's favorite quotations in support of his thesis that the English art of the nineteenth century was free from what he took to be the Flaubertian standing-off from life. I wonder, too, how many present readers will spot "Christ in the Cupboard" as a reference to one of T. F. Powys's short stories.

7. This also applies to some of the fiction. There is for instance a most charming Huckleberry Finn-like tale of Norfolk adolescence called *Getting it Wrong with Uncle Tom* and a philosophico-scientific thriller called *The Flask of Bouillon* both of which I would heartily commend to any enterprising publisher.

8. The question how Holbrook is and is not a religious writer is a good one that I have raised elsewhere. His recent book on C. S. Lewis seems to me to be judging from far more reliably Christian standards than those of the professedly Christian commentators on Lewis, but I do not expect Holbrook ever to make anything like a formal profession of belief—any more than Leavis ever did. (I do remember Holbrook saying in a letter that he has always believed the world to be fundamentally benign, which as a professed Christian is far more than I could take upon myself to affirm!)

The Novels of David Holbrook

GEOFFREY STRICKLAND

The name of David Holbrook is well known among students of literature and education but few who have heard of him seem aware of the many kinds of contribution he has made to our common culture over the past thirty years or of the existence even of some of his best writing. I forget how often someone has told me he didn't even know that Holbrook was a novelist or how often, when arguing with colleagues, I have been made to realize that in England, and English universities in particular, an unconditional commitment to ideas can earn a helplessly honest man the dangerous reputation of a crank. A professor of sociology and expert on the "sociology of humour" likes to tell how he once impersonated a badly briefed editorial assistant at the request of a publisher, who, when David Holbrook arrived at his office, hid in a cupboard until he had gone away. This would be quite funny in a West End farce but not when some of his finest work has still to find its way into print, when it is rare for reviewers to notice what does come out and when sales of these are accordingly so poor. Holbrook is not unmarketable but he has not yet been marketed. Meanwhile, first editions of his books may prove to be valuable investments for those who would rather have the last laugh.

Holbrook's poetry and novels, like those of Lawrence, give every appearance of being close to autobiography. Read sequentially, though not in the order in which they appeared, they tell the story of the only child of devoted, hard-working parents in Norwich before the Second World War; of the author's introduction to ancient learning and civilized modern values at a local grammar school and in the Norwich Maddermarket Theatre; of the formative and shattering experience of military training and tank warfare after the D-Day landings; and of life as a schoolmaster, Cambridge don and paterfamilias in the 1960s and 1980s, struggling to preserve the tenderness and unity of a marriage beset by all too familiar but mysterious inner demons. What he brings to the story is a philosophical awareness of the all-importance of the familiar—Blake's "minute particulars"—and of what is merely but thereby truly personal. In his essays on *The Novel and Authenticity,* he reminds us of Winnicott's distinction between the "true self," which retains a "sense of its own reality and integrity" and the "false self" which merely "keeps things going." It is in the novel especially, he argues, that the former is able to be recognized for what it is. Thus stated, his conception of the novel is fairly traditional and one that owes much, obviously, to the teachings of F. R. Leavis. What gives the creation of this kind of novel "a new validity" at the present time, he argues, are developments in psychotherapy and philosophy, that influenced by Heidegger in particular, which tell us of the conceptual irreducibility of our "Dasein," our being where we are.[1]

This does not mean that Holbrook either is or writes as if he were a philosophical novelist, like Proust or Kundera. Nor, despite his having been an English don, is he like David Lodge who, even in what is by far his best novel, *How far can you go?*, a searching exploration of the personal experience of fellow Catholics of his generation, never ceases to demonstrate his sophisticated awareness of the possibilities and limitations of the genre. Holbrook has made some bracing and well-timed comments on the kind of academic satire for which David Lodge is best known, together with Malcolm Bradbury and Tom Sharpe, and which while preserving their authors from what might seem in England the *gaucherie* of taking literature too seriously, encourages the Philistine prejudice against higher education in general and the humanities in particular.[2] By contrast with other academic novelists, Holbrook writes in a way which may appear at first unself-consciously conventional and in such a way as to appeal to those who borrow books from public rather than university libraries and in order to escape into a world of fantasy. Yet, as D. W. Harding has pointed out, there is no fiction, not even the most sophisticated, which does not depend, if it is to be understood, on vicarious enjoyment of this kind.[3] Holbrook's artistry, moreover, lies in the way in which he induces the reader to build on what he has at first casually imagined, to see it as progressively more real as it appears in startling new perspectives and in doing so, to participate in what he has called, speaking of *Wuthering Heights,* a "creative dream."[4]

His first published novel, *Flesh Wounds*[5] (1966), is still probably his best known and the only novel to have been reprinted. *The Eastern Daily Press* reviewer at the time described it as "the best war writing I have ever read," which, if he meant it, was praise indeed, though almost as disconcerting as if he were paying the same compliment to *War and Peace*. Mr. Holbrook would be the first to acknowledge that he is no Tolstoy, but the comparison may lead us to ask not only how immediately we can relate to a great classic of the past which for most of us is inaccessible except through translation; but whether, in his own story of war and peace, he has not illuminated aspects of human nature and experience of which Tolstoy was, if not more imperfectly, more remotely aware. It is the story of Holbrook's fictional alter ego, Paul Grimmer, a student of English at Cambridge of left-wing views who, having campaigned for a Second Front to relieve the Soviet Union, now accepts that he is under a moral obligation to take part in it, if possible, himself. It describes—and with the attention to detail of the military historian—the training for action, the landings on the beaches and the fighting of the tank crews with an often invisible army in the orchards, fields, and woods north of Caen; and it conveys the vulnerability and oddity of unthinking civilian life, when seen through a soldier's eyes: "the friendly muddle of the little old town" of Amersham, as it appears to the soldier on leave; the sight of a Norman peasant digging in his garden on a June day as the tanks roar past seeking the enemy. The evocation of the outer scene is also, as in Tolstoy, the alienation from itself of the human psyche, as the outer world is transformed beyond recognition. Not far from the center of the novel is Paul Grimmer's wartime affair with a fellow student, who becomes an actress and their, at first, magical reunions during weekend leaves:

> Uncertain what to do, he took his beret off. Lucy recognized him and laughed, with astonishment and gladness. She had expected him; but not so changed.
> "It's *my* soldier. It's Paul. They've made him a solider. Oh, darling, *darling*, what have they done to you?"
> She ran and put her head on Paul's battledress blouse and hugged him. She wanted to be a little theatrical in front of her theatre friends. But it didn't turn out like that: she burst into real tears of joy . . . (pp. 71–72)

What they have "done to him" is what army life and the quasi-mystical experience of concussion on the battlefield have done to Tolstoy's Prince Andrei; though the consequent failure of the latter's marriage lacks the physical immediacy of Paul's failure with Lucy as the training of body and mind for combat drives them apart during their meetings on subsequent leaves:

He seemed to caress her resentfully, and merely out of habit. Her body seemed to him a weak and childish thing. When she turned to him questioningly in bed, puzzled by his abstraction, he rejected her. He was repelled by her mood of beseeching. Her body seemed to him to have an unwholesome pallor, while his was all warm, active and tense . . . (p. 78)

This is not contradicted by our being told of Paul's sense of dismay and almost terrified loss when Lucy decides to end the affair.

Holbrook's extraordinary ability to convey the real, i.e., unpredictable, feelings of men and women caught up by events over which they have only rarely the illusion of control, makes this more than just "war writing," in other words. He writes as the chronicler of ordinary lives; and not, as one sometimes suspects in the case of Tolstoy, out of the piety of the aristocrat towards the peasant, but because of the need of the protagonist, who is also novelist, to know who and where he is; which he finds possible only through the contemplation of wholly different participants in the life they all share. Holbrook has the advantage of a remarkable ear for dialogue and dialect. Paul Grimmer, as a boy, speaks, like his parents, broad Norfolk. There is nothing remotely condescending in his portrayal of the North Country tank crew, discussing, during a lull in hostilities, the possible infidelities of each other's wives at home; or of his unassumingly efficient N. C. O., Sergeant Whatmough, for whose death Paul will later weep in a shell-shocked state. Paul contemplates Whatmough's "crumpled shiny photographs, black and white":

> A hatless and slightly bald Tom Whatmough in mufti knelt down beside a trim plump woman of about thirty-five, her hair neatly drawn to a bun. She had a genial attractive face, plain, maternal and careworn. Tom had his arm round a fair child of six, standing with her belly thrust forward in a Sunday frock, all lace and pink sateen. The child was laughing and her hand was on Tom's ear. Then there was a boy, plain with glasses about ten, standing in knickers on the grass plot by a garden fence of railway sleepers—a backyard in Keighley . . . (p. 113)

The all too human precision of this—its *punctum,* to borrow the terminology of Roland Barthes in his study of photography, *La Chambre claire*—is all the more poignant, as distinct from sentimental, in that Paul is unable, as the ship approaches the battle zone, to feel any real interest in the family. "He felt cold-hearted and repelled by the surge of feeling. He looked back at the great grey dividing sea . . ."

I have quoted from the novel at some length because I can think of no better way in which to make it clear what I think Holbrook means when he talks as a critic of the revelation of the "true self" and when he uses the Heideggerean concept of "Dasein." *Flesh Wounds* also, like all of his subsequent fiction, is concerned with the ways in which the authentic being of individuals, who in themselves are very different, finds itself at moments of heightened awareness in the knowledge of a hitherto unsuspected purpose and identity. As the great armada of ships and landing craft approaches Normandy, messages are read out to the assembled N. C. O.s and officers, for many of whom Paul feels an antipathy which is more than merely political:

> Bumpo [Major Bumpton] stopped. Then he read a message from the Colonel which said God Bless You at the end. Everyone stared into the bilges, embarrassed. And then the major became solemn for his own part, obviously with a great effort, and spoke of his "splendid team." Paul had a shock, because the words transcended the public school platitudes which he loathed so much. The emotions of men like Bumpo were sparse, taboo and firmly suppressed under a surface politeness, and a kind of *Tatler* and Cavalry Club orthodoxy of cliché. Their efforts to be grave and serious in matters of feeling came as a shock if ever, as now, they transcended their limitations. At this moment they did: they achieved gravity (p. 117)

The limitations that are transcended are those of Paul as well. As in the instance of his failure to feel interested in or moved by the Whatmough photograph and yet with acute registration of its human significance, the point of view of the protagonist, however sympathetically portrayed, remains clearly distinct from that of the novelist. It is this that raises the novel to the level of achieved drama. (*"Il faut,"* Flaubert insisted to George Sand, *"par un effort d'esprit, se transporter dans ses personnages et non les attirer à soi . . ."*[6]). Yet it is at moments such as this, at which the tank crews prepare for possible victory and inescapable sacrifice, that the reader who feels moved by their momentary gravity may respond to that sense of common humanity, none the less, to which the "true self" belongs.

The identification of what unites us, in a shared sense of nationhood initially, with its few genuinely common traditions, but also in a wider community is a constant preoccupation of the other novels which Holbrook has published since 1966. It is a sense of community, we are constantly reminded, to which the political radical is at least as likely to feel allegiance as the unselfcritical patriot. All these, with the exception of *Worlds Apart* and *Jennifer,* in which the central figure is a young woman, tell the story of Paul Grimmer as a boy and a married man. They belong, like the novels of Lawrence, to the tradition of the *Bildungsroman;* and as such, depend for their success on a protagonist who, while not perfect, has the courage and vitality that enable him to grow as an authentic human being.[7] They depend too, no less than *Flesh Wounds,* on the presentation of a social world of which the protagonist's life is an active part and which can be no less seriously envisaged or realistically shown than life. Holbrook's novels are about Paul Grimmer's England no more nor less than about Paul Grimmer himself.

A Play of Passion[8] is both a comedy and a tribute to the creator of the Norwich Maddermarket Theatre, Nugent Monck, who appears under his own name. Paul's blundering adolescent love affairs and experiments with left-wing politics are conducted under the protective eyes of this spinsterly, self-professed but "harmless" and unselfish homosexual who becomes his mentor, one of the founders of the original repertory movement in the British provinces, whose practical and disinterested devotion to the theatre and to the enlightenment it represents in pretelevision England the novel both records and celebrates. Monck has known, we are reminded, Yeats and the founders of the Abbey theatre in Dublin. The novel is also both candid and telling on the subject of social class. Holbrook has written elsewhere of the "coarseness, selfishness" and "unfeeling brutality" of a working-class love affair in Sillitoe's *Saturday Night and Sunday Morning,* which are obviously true to life but "inauthentic," insofar as the novelist is unconcerned with the "meaning" and the "inward needs" from which such behavior may arise. "From such coarse farce," he writes, "we learn to despise ourselves."[9] There is no contempt in a *Play of Passion* in the presentation of Paul's parents or their semi-detached home in an ugly group of houses outside Norwich. The family bond, despite explosions of mindless adolescent revolt, is shown as strong and normal. But nor is Paul or his creator inclined to the inverted snobbery to which those of us who came from similar backgrounds were encouraged to indulge in the heady egalitarian 'sixties. ("My tragedy is that I'm not working class," the director of the film of Sillitoe's novel once confessed in a television interview.) The limitations of Paul's home, which are limitations of opportunity, are shown for what they are and thus bring out by contrast the benefits and benevolence of the middle-class culture of Nugent Moncke. Paul learns in the theatre not only how the mind can be awakened to what is delightful and, in a performance of the *Norwich Passion Play,* venerable. Like Pip in *Great Expectations,* he learns also conventional table manners and the pleasures of neatness and good china, of a respect, that is, for the life of all the senses. The contrast with the bohemian digs which he shares, in which the pretty girl he adores succumbs to the gropings of an unprepossessing advanced thinker and pacifist, are among the lessons of the *Bildungsroman*. So too is his discovery of the conflicting forces at work within the middle-class establishment: that represented by the local school governors who seek, because of his unpatriotic views and the company he keeps, to deprive him of his exhibition to Cambridge; as it is also by a very different source of authority, that of his forbidding and far from indulgent Cambridge tutor, a classicist, and by Nugent Monck, who vouches for his good name:

> To read the classics, thought Paul, didn't exactly disqualify a man from understanding modern villainy. This short-sighted academic, with a high forehead and a bird-like manner, was really rather magnificent. Paul could see it was all what Short and his Left-wing friends would call "bourgeois" and despise. But he could see it was based on a deep and ancient approach to human truth they could not comprehend, on which "Cambridge," "Maddermarket" and civilisation, as he dimly apprehended its nature, rested ... (p. 204)

This is the ethos of E. M. Forster at its most courageous and fine, though without that "pressure of nihilism" which Holbrook detects in his work, despite the "intellectual honesty" in which Forster believed "passionately."[10]

The respect for that ethos and the awareness—not nihilistic but melancholy—of its vulnerability in the brutally materialistic England of the 1960s unites husband and wife throughout the neurotic traumas of their marriage in *Nothing Larger than Life.*[11] They are the trusted tenants of an ancient house in a Hertfordshire village, which, like Forster's Howard's End, owes some of its serenity to its previous occupant and owner:

> Mrs Thrower wore thick rather dreary tweeds and a brown felt hat, solid shoes and lisle stockings ... Her eyes were heavily lidded set in a wrinkled puffiness: but if you looked into the eyes with their large brown irises, you found a deep sadness and also a desire for affection. Daphne had no children, and all she could hope for was to save some-

thing of her corner of England, for the future. Her whole life was devoted to the quality of life of a village of some 1,200 souls—"quality" in this matter being determined by her . . . (p. 62)

She is resented by her tenants in the village, who pay rents well below the market rate, as are the Grimmers when they campaign and use Civil Service connections to preserve the village's crowning glory, Verderers Cottages on the main street, which the local council is determined to render derelict and then obtain planning permission to "develop." The Grimmers win. Their victory coincides with the recovery of their almost irreparably broken marriage and their preparations to move away; though it is with a sense of the artificiality, in a large degree, of their endeavors to keep the best of the past alive and their dependence in the future on their own resources, whatever these may be. A hint of that is given in the sympathetic but caustic account of the solicitude of Mrs. Thrower herself for the quality of life in the village, in which the "quality" is "determined by her."

The near hopelessness of the struggle to maintain belief in anything of value at all and the mutually destructive rage of husband and wife in this novel are reassuring only in that we are shown that no defeat, any more than any victory, is final and that the spirit has resources we can not foresee. The mood of much of this novel can be conveyed by quoting from one of Holbrook's finest poems, *Drought*, from his collection *Against the Cruel Frost* (1963):

> So we're estranged again—how it goes on!
> Your who-you-are dissolved: my disappointed me
> Skulking in silence. Rain falls, then it is gone.
> The sun's bright on wet roofs, every washed tree
> Has June's hard highlights, while a rivulet
> Runs down the road that has been dry a month.
> And with it run the feelings that I let
> Flow as I contemplate our last dry month . . .

The sonnet ends with the thought of "some sudden shower again" to "break our thoughts."

> Both of us are, I know, in our sorrow,
> Watching the same rain from our each window.

Yet, as in the poem, the human conflict gains dignity from the unsparing honesty with which it is recorded and a certain beauty, experienced by the couple themselves, from the natural setting, though this is never glamorized and retains the sharpness of outline and openness to the sky of the southwestern edge of East Anglia.

If there is one major criticism to be made of this novel, it is of the failure in writing so concerned with truth and justice to maintain an equal inwardness in its presentation of both partners. We are merely told, for example, that Paul's wife Frances undergoes what is for her agonizing psychotherapy. It is a novel about Paul's marriage with Frances rather than about what it is like to be married to Paul. And yet Holbrook's gift for portraying women and writing from the woman's point of view is evident both in his other novel and here: in his portrayal, for example, of the young half-French Cambridge student with whom he falls helplessly and to his astonishment in love, a woman keenly intelligent and attractive, though with her own deep psychic wounds.

By contrast, psychic wholeness and intelligent purpose are represented by his country-bred schoolteacher heroine of *Worlds Apart*,[12] the daughter of an East Anglian architect, who relives a number of Holbrook's own experiences as a visiting lecturer in the newly radicalized Australia and as a passenger on one of the last P & O liners to Australia before the days of the jet. She is the daughter of happily married and wise parents, a woman whose instinctive sense of a symbolic order surprises her and moves her to tears when at a port of call she watches the pilot come on board:

> She wiped her eyes on the sleeve of her dressing-gown. Fortunately, there was no one else on deck . . . She went down with a great sense of elation, with the word 'Pilot' shining boldly somewhere in her mind . . . She recognised that in her respect for the Pilot she was paying tribute to a male capacity. Of course, women nowadays could be in charge of ships or aeroplanes: but to guide a great vessel into harbour like that seemed to her a version of paternal love . . . (p. 85)

What may seem like impenitent or deplorably dated sexism here is perfectly consistent with the novelist's account of how she has to fight off an attempt at rape by one of the P & O officers and sexual harassment from one of her Australian hosts. (These are the liberated 'sixties when "harassment" has another name.) *Worlds Apart* asks to be read as an idyll of a still not distant past, ending with the reconciliation of former childhood friends who are destined to find themselves again as husband and wife. The assertively masculine Peter, an experimental scientist, chastened by the collapse of his belief in his science, is now responsible to her feminine insight and sensibility and to what is correspondingly intuitive in himself. To call it an idyll is merely to point out the extent to which it gives full play to ideal possibilities and to acknowledge that, like the requisite happy ending, these are possibilities only, in contrast to the menacing actualities which in the end are made to seem ridiculous and ineffectual. *Nothing larger than Life* is in no way idyllic, despite its happy ending. Its actualities are all too menacing.

In *A Little Athens*,[13] we return to the Norwich schooldays of Paul Grimmer and the narrator is for the first time Paul Grimmer himself. The little Athens is the city of Norwich School, a state grammar school and like *A Play of Passion*, the novel pays homage to those who exemplify for the young " a deep and ancient approach to human truth" in the often hostile and uncomprehending provincial England of the 1930s and 40s. The title refers to the funeral oration of Thucydides, a sacred text for the school's gentle and—in the England and Norwich of the time—heroically enlightened headmaster. Both school and home provide the setting not for an idyllic childhood but one in which the adolescent grows into mental and physical awareness under watchful and mainly protective eyes. It is under those of the kindly French teacher, Miss Alexander (whom nobody "rags") during a cricket match that Paul experiences his first orgasm:

> We had invented a game called bollock-snatching. It was, I suppose, a kind of boy's homosexual puppyish lark. You had to try to grab your opponent's genitals, though what you did when you seized them was not laid down. As interest in the cricket match waned, some of us began to play this coarse game. After a few scrambles, someone became huffy.
> "Leave me alone!" he shouted.
> Miss Alexander awoke, stared at the scrum of little boys grabbing at each other's trousers and said,
> "Tell those little asses to stop it!"
> So, we sat up respectably, some of us a little anxious, in case Alex had seen what we were doing. In a sense, I believe, she did see, and unconsciously was a little fascinated. At any rate, we were soon squealing at it again, while she watched in a half-doze ...

After the unthinkable has occurred, Paul can only walk back in to school by hobbling:

> Miss Alexander barely noticed, and only murmured "Silly little pups—what a way to behave." And yet I couldn't help feeling, in some

strange way, she had known and had condoned it, because it was unconsciously a glimpse of a world she had never known and yearned for ... (pp. 50–51)

Meetings with girls take place at street corners:

around the safety of bicycles: the bicycle was an important instrument in this kind of contact. It was, in a way, a symbolic, protective chaperone. You kept hold of it, and your partner kept hold of hers: it gave both of you something to do with your hands, and it looked all the time as if either could escape, rapidly out of the situation. This implicitly denied any commitment: you were both just passing the time of day, on your bicycles, under the lime trees at the corner ... (p. 89)

The deep enchantment of Paul's first love affair, while on a holiday in Lowestoft with his parents, in the tiny illuminated pleasure gardens on the edge of the salt marshes and meadows, is recalled with the same humor and the same sense of a note being struck which will remain audible throughout life. Countless writers have recalled the world of adolescence, but few with Holbrook's gift for evoking its endlessly varied drama and constant fesh changes of scene. Paul is aware, by contrast, of his father's stifling routine in a glass-roofed warehouse of bicycle parts and his youthful energy in devising schemes, into which Paul eagerly joins, for improving their distribution; and one of the novel's minor dramas occurs when Paul, the future conservationist, true to the enlightened ethos of his school, publishes a prize essay in the local newspaper condemning the bicycle wholesalers' plans for extending their premises into Norwich's now abandoned eighteenth-century Assembly Rooms. His father's career suffers. The directors are shocked to find that the son of one of their managers has "gone public over a planning issue, on leaked information." The painful lesson in the ways of the world proves to be a stage in the emergence from adolescence of the responsible adult.

Jennifer focuses on the adult consciousness in the contemporary world and like *Worlds Apart,* is a study of early womanhood.[14] It is the story of the courtship and marriage of an educated, highly civilized couple. It is also the presentation of lives that, like those of *Worlds Apart,* appear normative and exemplary. It is no wonder therefore that the reviewers have ignored it. It is less obviously idyllic than *Worlds Apart,* even though it is set in the same vividly beautiful rural Hertfordhire; but one may be reminded when reading it of what Holbrook has written of those heroines in Dickens and James who, like Shakespeare's Marina, stand for "the capacity of the human spirit to be good—to remain uncorrupted."[15] That incorruptibility, however, as he points out, tends in Dickens and James to be seen as virginal and in *Little Dorrit*, is that of the "redeeming daughter";[16] whereas Jennifer, who is herself a victim of the neurotic violence of her father, which threatens her parents' marriage and which, we are told, is a legacy of the war, is destined to succeed where her parents have failed. The measure of her fortitude is her ability to survive trauma after the cot death of her first child. In the closing pages, the baby twins born after this tragedy are carried by their parents on an early summer day through the petals and blossom along the banks of a stream, where the dead child is "more with them than absent," while the tears that rise in her eyes are "shed themselves like shreds of blossom into the spring airs." This may sound embarrassing in a writer of Holbrook's sophistication; but the intensity of the lyricism is proportional to the author's awareness of all that threatens hope and joy: the proposed new bypass, the death of the baby in its cot. For "there are moments when the relationship between the self and the film of time is brutally torn . . . Suddenly, the gulf of death and nothingness, over which we always dance on thin ice is revealed . . ." (p. 169). Superficially, if musical analogies are appropriate, *Jennifer* has more in common with the *Domestic Symphony* of Richard Strauss than with the music of Mahler. Yet in the sense of emptiness it conveys in its bleaker moments and its reaction against nihilism, the unashamed exuberance of its celebration of the supreme moments of ordinary lives can remind us of what Holbrook has written of Mahler's "greatness," which "was to meet the possibility that death and nothingness could extinguish all meaning, but then to wrestle with this nihilistic menace . . . enacting meaning as he doggedly strove to find it."[17]

Meanwhile, the risks that he is prepared to take with sentimentality are apparent in the very title of *The Gold in Father's Heart*,[18] which takes us back to Paul Grimmer's Norwich childhood and the Norfolk dialect and present the father as a comic character more extravagant because more credible than H. E. Bates's appalling Pop Larkin. It is the father's exuberant boyishness that is brought to life, as he enjoys, for example, a wonderful conflagration in a timber yard by the river, drawn away by the terrified infant Paul who sees only the leaping flames of the Hell of his Sunday religion; or as he falls, all too innocently, in love with the French lady lodger, who has to be asked to leave. One is left with a sense, however, in this novel, as in *Even if they fail*,[19] of personal experience vigorously recreated in dramatic terms, which has been somehow left on the novelist's hands and which lacks the sense of space and expanding significance of his finest work. *Even if they fail,* the last of Holbrook's novels, as I write, to have appeared, lacks any but an episodic structure. It is the story of Paul Grimmer's experiences as Director of Studies in a thinly, and almost unnecessarily disguised Downing College during the 1980s. Drama is provided and a dénouement by Paul's involvement in a libel action brought by an assistant lecturer in English who has failed to receive permanent faculty tenure and which is so close to recent history that I had better not be too specific myself. (In a *Punch* cartoon at the time, a wife was asking her husband who was reading the newspaper, if they had "caught the Cambridge structuralist yet.") Paul's generous but rash outspokenness on behalf of the colleague who was actually sued (and for those who know him, a well-drawn likeness) puts at risk not only his own income and property but those of Frances his wife, which she has recently inherited from her mother. His failure to confide in her even until the threat of libel has been withdrawn keeps the story going, in so far as there is a connected story, but we are told that they have mellowed since the days of *Nothing Larger Than Life* and the high-minded betrayal is all too readily forgiven at the end. Despite the potentialities of its theme, it is not exactly Conradian drama.

It is the work of a distinguished novelist, nonetheless, as engrossing, even if unconnected, episodes constantly remind us: supervisions, sometimes indicative of the lack of any common culture, with the undergraduates of the 1980s, the brilliantly told unmasking of a young biologist on the make, passing off his girlfriend's work as his own and given away by the unforgiving laser printer. It is remarkable for its portraits too, including that of the again easily identifiable Master of "Pemning College," a wise and plain-dealing Squire Headlong, who turns the ideal of the academic community into a humane and practical reality. It is a portrait, however, that leads one to regret that Holbrook has not yet published his own unfictionalized autobiography. As a novel, *Even If They Fail* is inferior to at least one of these which can still only be read in typescript, *A Flask of Bouillon,* whose repeated rejection I find unaccountable and which was written in the late 1970s. It is the story not of Paul Grimmer but of a Cambridge biologist, whose inability to believe in the reductionism of those who inaugurated the era of molecular biology is symbolized in a near breakdown of both his sanity and his marriage. The resolution of the conflict coincides with a rediscovery of the venerable origins of his science. The flask of the title is the one which is carefully preserved in the museum at Arbois of Louis Pasteur.

"He has," Angus Wilson wrote some fourteen years ago in a review of *A Play of Passion*, "an extraordinary range of sympathy and evocation . . . He is a master writer waiting to be found." However, the publisher is still hiding in the cupboard. An introductory essay of this kind is therefore bound to read more like an enthusiastic recommendation than a judicious appraisal. Had Holbrook been recognized as one of our finest living novelists, it would have been more appropriate, for example, to say more of those occasions when his work falls short of its highest standards; and in particular of those passages which read uncomfortably like an imitation of the Lawrence whom he is among the few critics to write about with respect but without constraint and to have, in various ways, outgrown rather than rejected. In spite of which, there are occasions when reading of the married life of the Grimmers, that one may feel some sympathy with Bertrand Russell's "I'm glad they've come through. I don't see why I should look . . ."; when one may be reminded too of Henry James's feelings about the "sexual passion" in D'Annunzio, which from "the moment it depends on itself alone for its beauty . . . endangers extremely its distinction, so precarious at the best."[20]

A more judicious account would also, however, have more to say of the subtlety of Holbrook's dramatic gift; of that of the episode, for example, of the seminar on *The Ancient Mariner* held in a study of "Prince's College" overlooking Henry VIII's famous chapel. Paul Grimmer, the supervisor, is grieving for his mother and at the same time lusting helplessly after the girl who is his best student. In this context, the "sexual passion" is entirely convincing, in that it is in no way whatever dependent "on itself alone for its beauty." The context includes the adulterously-inclined Paul's awareness of the all too human complexities beneath the surface of the institutionalized "English" and "Cambridge":

> The great cliffs of the Chapel, speckled with light in the afternoon; inside, he remembered, the panels gay with carved ribbons, H and A entwined in loveknots. Then, chunk!—the axe through the neck . . .

It is absurd that writing as powerful and intelligent as this is not better known.

Notes

1. David Holbrook, *The Novel and Authenticity* (London: Vision and Barnes & Noble, 1987), pp. 14–18.

2. Ibid., pp. 184–5.
3. D. W. Harding, "Psychological processes in the reading of fiction," in *The British Journal of Aesthetics*, II, 2 (1962), pp. 133–47.
4. *The Novel and Authenticity*, pp. 17–18.
5. David Holbrook, *Flesh Wounds* (London: Methuen, 1966; and London: Buchan & Enright, 1987). Page references here are to the Buchan & Enright edition.
6. Gustave Flaubert, *Correspondence*, 15–16 décembre, 1866. To be found in any complete edition of Flaubert's letters.
7. An exception to this is *Mr. Noon*, which Lawrence never tried to publish. The far from perfect Lawrence who emerges from the second half, which describes his early relations with Frieda, throws an interesting light on the more idealized protagonists of *Women in Love, Aaron's Road*, and *Kangaroo*. I confess that I welcome the revelations of *Mr. Noon*, part 2, and find it far less confused and perverse than Mr. Holbrook. (See David Holbrook, *Where D. H. Lawrence Was Wrong About Woman* (Lewisburg, Pa.: Bucknell University Press, 1992), pp. 241–69).
8. David Holbrook, *A Play of Passion* (London: W. H. Allen, 1978).
9. *The Novel and Authenticity*, p. 152.
10. Ibid., pp. 129–130.
11. David Holbrook, *Nothing Larger Than Life* (London: Robert Hale, 1987).
12. David Holbrook, *Worlds Apart* (London: Robert Hale, 1988).
13. David Holbrook, *A Little Athens* (London: Robert Hale, 1990).
14. David Holbrook, *Jennifer* (London: Robert Hale, 1991).
15. *The Novel and Authenticity*, p. 85.
16. Ibid.
17. *The Novel and Authenticity*, p. 113.
18. David Holbrook, *The Gold in Father's Heart* (London: Robert Hale, 1992).
19. David Holbrook, *Even if they Fail* (London: Robert Hale, 1994).
20. Henry James, "Gabriele D'Annunzio" in *Selected Literacy Criticism* (London: Heinemann, 1963), p. 295. Originally published in *Notes on Novelists* (1914).

Select Bibliography of Works by David Holbrook

I: Books

POETRY

Imaginings. London: Putnam, 1961.
Against the Cruel Frost. London: Putnam, 1963.
Object-Relations. London: Methuen, 1967.
Old World, New World. London: Rapp and Whiting, 1969.
Chance of a Lifetime. London: Anvil Press, 1978.
Moments in Italy: Poems and Sketches. Richmond, Surrey: Keepsake Press, 1978.
Selected Poems 1961–78. London: Anvil Press, 1980.

FICTION

Lights in the Sky Country: Mary Easter and Stories of East Anglia. London: Putnam, 1962.
Flesh Wounds. London: Methuen, 1966; London: Buchan and Enright, 1987.
"Youth's a Stuff Will (probably) Not Endure." In *New Stories I,* edited by Margaret Drabble and Charles Osborne. London: Arts Council of Great Britain, 1976.
"A Play of Passion." In *Writers of East Anglia,* selected and edited by Angus Wilson. London: Secker and Warburg, 1977.
A Play of Passion. London: W. H. Allen, 1978.
Nothing Larger Than Life. London: Robert Hale, 1987.
"Worse Than the Bombing." In *Words International, The Book,* 1987–88.
Worlds Apart. London: Robert Hale, 1988.
A Little Athens. London: Robert Hale, 1990.
Jennifer. London: Robert Hale, 1991.

The Gold in Father's Heart. London: Robert Hale, 1992.
Even If They Fail. London: Martin Breese International, 1994.

ON EDUCATION

English for Maturity: English in the Secondary School. Cambridge: Cambridge University Press, 1961; 2nd. edn., 1967.
The Secret Places: Essays on Imaginative Work in English Teaching and on the Culture of the Child. London: Methuen, 1964; University, Ala.: University of Alabama Press, 1965.
English for the Rejected: Training Literacy in the Lower Streams of the Secondary School. Cambridge: Cambridge University Press, 1964.
(with Raymond O'Malley and others) *English in the C. S. E.* Cambridge: Cambridge University Press, 1964.
The Exploring Word: Creative Disciplines in the Education of Teachers of English. Cambridge: Cambridge University Press, 1967.
Children's Writing: A Sampler for Student Teachers. Cambridge: Cambridge University Press, 1967.
English in Australia Now. Cambridge: Cambridge University Press, 1973.
Education, Nihilism and Survival. London: Darton, Longman and Todd, 1977.
English for Meaning. Windsor: National Foundation for Educational Research, 1980.
Education and Philosophical Anthropology: Toward a New View of Man for the Humanities and English. London: Associated University Presses, 1987.

LITERARY CRITICISM

Llareggub Revisited: Dylan Thomas and the State of Modern Poetry. London: Bowes and Bowes, 1962; abridged as *Dylan Thomas and Poetic Dissociation.* Carbondale: Southern Illinois University Press, 1964.
The Quest for Love. London: Methuen, 1964; University, Ala.: University of Alabama Press, 1965.
Dylan Thomas: The Code of Night. London: Athlone Press, 1972.
Sylvia Plath: Poetry and Existence. London: Athlone Press, 1976; Atlantic Highlands, N. J.: Humanities Press, 1976.
Lost Bearings in English Poetry. London: Vision Press, 1977; New York: Barnes and Noble, 1977.
The Novel and Authenticity. London: Vision and Barnes and Noble, 1987.
Images of Women in Literature. New York: New York University Press, 1990.
The Skeleton in the Wardrobe: C. S. Lewis's Fantasies: A Phenomenological

Study. Lewisburg, Pa.: Bucknell University Press; London: Associated University Presses, 1991.

Edith Wharton and the Unsatisfactory Man. London: Vision Press, 1991; New York: St. Martin's Press, 1991.

Where D. H. Lawrence Was Wrong About Woman. Lewisburg, Pa.: Bucknell University Press; London: Associated University Presses, 1992.

Charles Dickens and the Image of Woman. New York: New York University Press, 1993.

Creativity and Popular Culture. Madison, N.J.: Fairleigh Dickinson University Press; London: Associated University Presses, 1994.

MUSIC CRITICISM

Gustav Mahler and the Courage to Be. London: Vision Press, 1975; New York: Da Capo Press, 1982.

PSYCHO-SOCIAL AND PHILOSOPHICAL CRITICISM

Human Hope and the Death Instinct: An Exploration of Pyschoanalytical Theories of Human Nature and their Implications for Culture and Education. Oxford and New York: Pergamon Press, 1971.

Sex and Dehumanisation in Art, Thought and Life in Our Time. London: Pitman 1972.

The Masks of Hate: The Problem of False Solutions in the Culture of an Acquisitive Society. Oxford: Pergamon Press, 1972.

The Pseudo-Revolution: A Critical Study of Extremist 'Liberation' in Sex. London: Tom Stacey, 1972.

Changing Attitudes to the Nature of Man: A Working Bibliography. Hatfield, Hertfordshire: Hertis, 1973.

Evolution and the Humanities. Aldershot: Gower Publishing Company, 1987.

Further Studies in Philosophical Anthropology. Aldershot: Gower Publishing Company, 1988.

COMPILATIONS

Children's Games. Bedford: Gordon Fraser, 1957.

Iron, Honey, Gold: The Uses of Verse. 2 vols. Cambridge: Cambridge University Press, 1961; issued in 4 vols. 1965; 2nd edn., 1992.

People and Diamonds: An Anthology of Modern Short Stories for Use in Secondary Schools. 2 vols. Cambridge: Cambridge University Press, 1962.

Thieves and Angels: Dramatic Pieces for Use in Schools. Cambridge: Cambridge University Press, 1962.

Visions of Life (prose anthology). 4 vols. Cambridge: Cambridge University Press, 1964.

I've Got to Use Words (creative English texts for less able children). Cambridge: Cambridge University Press, 1966.

(with Elizabeth Poston) *The Cambridge Hymnal*. Cambridge: Cambridge University Press, 1968.

Plucking the Rushes: An Anthology of Chinese Poetry (translated by Arthur Waley). London: Heinemann, 1968.

(with Christine McKenzie) *The Honey of Man*. Melbourne: Nelson, 1973; London, Heinemann Educational, 1975.

The Case Against Pornography. London: Tom Stacey, 1972; New York: Library Press, 1973.

(with Elizabeth Poston) *The Apple Tree*. Cambridge: Cambridge University Press, 1976.

(with David Lamb and Wolfe Mays) *What is it to be Human?: New Perspectives in Philosophy*. Aldershot: Avebury, 1990.

II. Contributions to Books

"Nonne Preestes Tale." In *The Pelican Guide to English Literature*, Vol. 1, edited by Boris Ford. Harmondsworth: Penguin, 1961; 1983.

"Two Welsh Writers." In *The Pelican Guide to English Literature*, Vol. 7, edited by Boris Ford. Harmondsworth: Penguin, 1961.

"Magazines." In *Discrimination and Popular Culture*, edited by Denys Thompson. Harmondsworth: Penguin, 1965; revised edn., 1973.

"Poetry and the Inward Life." In *Teaching Poetry*, edited by Thomas Blackburn. London: Methuen, 1966.

Introduction to *Mr Weston's Good Wine*, by T. F. Powys. London: Heinemann 1967.

"Creativity in the English Programme." In *Creativity in English*, edited by Geoffrey Summerfield. Champaign, Illinois: NCTE, 1968.

"Psychoanalysis and the Teacher." In *The Impact of Psychology on Social Work and Teaching*. Shrewsbury: Shotton Hall, 1972.

"Pornography Educates," and "Historical Perspective." In *Pornography: The Longford Report*. London: Coronet Books, 1972.

"Sylvia Plath, Pathological Morality and the Avant Garde." In *The Pelican Guide to English Literature*, Vol. 7, edited by Boris Ford. Harmondsworth: Penguin, 1973.

"Ted Hughes's *Crow* and the Longing for Non-Being." In *The Black Rainbow*, edited by Peter Abbs. London: Heinemann, 1975.

"Reading and Discrimination." In *Bookmarks*, edited by Frederick Raphael. London: Quartet Books, 1975.

"The Problem of C. S. Lewis." In *Writers, Critics and Children*, edited by Geoff Fox and others. New York: Agathon Press, 1976; London, Heinemann Educational, 1976.

"The Need for Meaning." In *Human Needs and Politics*, edited by Ross Fitzgerald. Sydney: Pergamon Press, 1977.

"What it Means to be Human." In *What it Means to be Human*, edited by Ross Fitzgerald. Sydney: Pergamon Press, 1978.

"Hope for the Triumph of Truth About 'Life'." In *The Sources of Hope*, edited by Ross Fitzgerald. Sydney: Pergamon Press, 1979.

Introduction to *The Old Wives' Tale*, by Arnold Bennett. London: Everyman, Dent, 1982.

Introduction to *Phantastes*, by George MacDonald. London: Everyman, Dent, 1983.

"The Lesson of Children's Writing." In *The Pelican Guide to English Literature*, Vol. 8, edited by Boris Ford. Harmondsworth: Penguin, 1983.

"F. R. Leavis and the Sources of Hope." In *The Leavises; Recollections and Impressions*, edited by Denys Thompson. Cambridge: Cambridge University Press, 1984.

"Lawrence's False Solutions." In *Transitional Objects and Potential Spaces: Literary Uses of D. W. Winnicott*, edited by Peter Rudnytsky. New York, N. Y.: Columbia University Press, 1993.

III: Papers and Essays in Journals (excluding reviews)

"The Poetic Mind of Edgell Rickword." *Essays in Criticism* XII.3 (1962).

"Society and our 'Instincts'." *Universities Quarterly* 20 (1966).

"Creativity and Education." *Universities Quarterly* 21 (1967).

"R. D. Laing and the Death Circuit." *Encounter* (August 1968); reprinted in *Psychiatry and Social Science Review* 3.4 (1969).

"The Wizard and the Critical Flame." *Journal of Moral Education* 1.1 (1969).

"Sylvia Plath and the Problem of Violence in Art." *Cambridge Review* 90 (1969).

"The English Teacher, the Avant-Garde and the Revolution in Philosophical Anthropology." *English in Education* 4.1 (1970).

"The Politics of Pornography." *Political Quarterly* 48.1 (1971).

"The Dangers of Dogmatic Enlightenment." *The Critical Quarterly* 13.1 (1971).

"Out of the Ash: Sylvia Plath." *Human World* (May 1971).

"Out of the Ash: Sylvia Plath and the Death Camps." *Human World* (November 1971).

"The Misuse of Symbolism." *New Humanist* (July 1972).

"Pornography and Death." *The Critical Quarterly* 14.2 (1972).
"Pornography—the Ultimate Absurdity." *Tract* 2 (Winter 1972).
"The Corruption of Symbolism." *Tract* 10 and 11 (Spring 1974).
"F. R. Leavis and Creativity." *Universities Quarterly* 29 (1975).
"The Touch of Nihilism in E. M. Forster." *New Universities Quarterly* 32 (1978).
"Are We Losing the Next Generation?" *Journal of Moral Education* 10.2 (1978).
"Creative Disciplines in School English." *The Critical Quarterly* 20.3 (1978).
"Are we only DNA's way of making more DNA?" *New Universities Quarterly* 32 (1978).
"An Existentialist Approach to the Poetry of Thomas Hardy." *Tract* 16 and 17 (n.d.).
"Am I an Accident of Chemistry?" *Collaborations* (York University) 1.1 (Summer 1980).
"The Search for Meaning." *New Humanist* (September/October 1980).
"Dr. John Bowlby: No Need to Nod to Positivist Dogma." *New Universities Quarterly* 36 (1982).
"Edgell Rickword, 1898–1982." *Cambridge Review* 103 (1982).
"The Creative Approach to English Teaching." *Teachers' College Record* 84.3 (1983).
"Against a Curriculum in English Studies." *Cambridge Review* 104 (1983).
"The Humanities, Hate and Suffering." *Universities Quarterly* 37 (1983).
"The Real Discipline." *The Use of English* 35.2 (1984).
"Truth, Campaigns and Freedom: Reflections on a Prospectus." *Encounter* LXV.5 (December 1985)
"English Up Against It." *The Use of English* 42.1 (1990).
"Holy Vows: The Extraordinary Menage of John Chapman with George Eliot." *London Magazine* 30.7 and 8 (October/November 1990).
"Searching for Intelligence in Space." *New Scientist* 134.1822 (23 May 1992).
"Disciples and Enemies: on F. R. Leavis." *London Magazine* 32.3 and 4 (June/July 1992).
"In the Beginning Was the Word: Literature and Language Studies." *Meridian* (School of Education, La Trobe University, Victoria State, Australia). Special issue (Autumn 1992).
"Exorcist on an Unholy Crusade; on *Lady Chatterley's Lover*." *The Times Higher Educational Supplement* (9 July 1993).
"Natural Feeding and Sexuality in Literature." *London Magazine* 33.5 and 6 (August/September 1993).

Notes on Contributors

PETER ABBS is Reader in Education, University of Sussex, where he directs the M. A. course in Language, the Arts and Education. Author of a number of books on education and culture, and editor of the Falmer Press Library on Aesthetic Education, he has also published three volumes of poetry: *For Man and Islands* (1978), *Songs of a New Taliesin* (1981), and *Icons of Time* (1991).

ANDREW BRINK is Professor and Coordinator, Humanities and Psychoanalytic Thought Programme, Trinity College, University of Toronto. He has published an edition of the (1714) *Life of The Rev. Mr. George Trosse* (1974), and is co-editor of vols. I and XII of *The Collected Papers of Bertrand Russell* (1983, 1985). His major studies are: *Loss and Symbolic Repair: A Study of Some English Poets* (1977), *Creativity as Repair: Bipolarity and its Closure* (1982), and *Bertand Russell: A Psychobiography of a Moralist* (1989). He is currently preparing *Obsession and Culture: A Study of Sexual Obsessions in Modern Fiction*.

MICHAEL CHARLES began his teaching career in 1963. He taught first in a boys' secondary school, before moving on to a secondary co-educational school. At the start of his career his subject was History, but after several years he transferred to the teaching of English, subsequently becoming the Head of an English department.

JOHN FERNS is Professor of English at McMaster University, Ontario, Canada. He has published *A. J. M. Smith* (1979) and *Lytton Strachey* (1988), and has co-edited George Whalley's *Studies in Literature and the Humanities* (1985) and *The Poetry of Lucy Maud Montgomery* (1987). Author of the entry on David Holbrook's poetry in *The Dictionary of Literary Biography*, he has published five volumes of his own poetry.

BORIS FORD was Editor, then Director, of the Bureau of Current affairs; a member of the Secretariat of the United Nations; and the first Head of Schools Broadcasting with Independent Television. He has been Professor of Education at the universities of Sheffield, Bristol, and Sussex. A former editor of the *Journal of Education* and of *Universities Quarterly*, he is General Editor of: *The New Pelican Guide to English Literature* (11 vols.), *The Cambridge Cultural History of Britain* (9 vols.), and a forthcoming series of 9 volumes on the arts and civilization of the Western world.

ROGER KNIGHT is a Senior Lecturer in Education in the University of Leicester, and editor of the journal *The Use of English*. He is the author of *Edwin Muir: An Introduction to his Work* (1980); co-editor (with Ian Robinson) of *My Native English* (1988), and editor of *English in Practice: Literature at 'A' Level* (1989).

JOHN PAYNTER is a composer who has taught in primary and secondary schools and is now Head of the Department of Music at the University of York. His books on music education have been translated into several languages and he has travelled extensively, organizing courses for teachers in many parts of the world. His compositions include orchestral and choral works, two string quartets, a large-scale piano sonata, and the music-drama *The Voyage of Saint Brendan*, a community music project involving young performers with adult professionals. John Paynter was appointed OBE in 1985.

ROGER POOLE is Reader in Literary Theory in the University of Nottingham, and the author of *Towards Deep Subjectivity* (1972); *The Unknown Virginia Woolf* (1978, 1982, 1990); and (with Henrik Strangerup) of *Dansemesteren* (1975), in translation as *A Kierkegaard Reader* (London, 1989) and as *'The Laughter is on my Side': an Imaginative Introduction to Kierkegaard* (1989). A major study, *Deconstructing Kierkegaard*, has recently been published (1994). Roger Poole is also the author of a play about Kierkegaard, *All Women and Quite a Few Men are Right*, which was performed at the Edinburgh Festival in 1986.

GORDON PRADL completed his doctoral dissertation (on the work of David Holbrook) at Harvard and began teaching at New York University, where he is currently Professor of English Education and Director of Staff Development in the Expository Writing Program. He is co-author of *Learning to Write/Writing to Learn*, has edited *Prospect and Retrospect: Selected Essays of James Britton*, and is completing a book entitled *Literature for Democracy*. He also serves as co-editor of the journal *English Education,* published by the National Council of Teachers of English.

IAN ROBINSON studied at Downing College, Cambridge, under F. R. Leavis and has lectured in English at University College Swansea since 1963. His principal published works are on Chaucer, Chomsky's linguistics, modern liturgical language and, in *The Survival of English,* cultural criticism. He is currently working on a defense of classical English criticism, and on the tragic English novel.

GEOFFREY STRICKLAND was born in 1931 in Aldershot and educated at the local grammar school and at Downing College, Cambridge, where he read English and Modern Languages. He is Reader in French in the University of Reading and the author of *Stendhal: the Education of a Novelist* and *Structuralism or Criticism?; Thoughts on How We Read.*

PAMELA TAYLOR read English at Durham University and subsequently studied for a higher degree in Victorian Studies at the University of Edinburgh. She taught English in Finland before becoming a primary school teacher with a special interest in language development. She then undertook research in Education and moved into teacher education where she now teaches English once again. Her particular literary interest is in creative responses to text.

ANN BELFORD ULANOV is Christiane Brooks Johnson Professor of Psychiatry and Religion at Union Theological Seminary, New York; a psychoanalyst in private practice; a supervising analyst and faculty member of the C. G. Jung Institute, New York City. She is the author *The Feminine in Christian Theology and in Jungian Psychology, Receiving Woman: Studies in the Psychology and Theology of the Feminine, Picturing God,* and *The Wisdom of the Psyche.* Together with her husband, Barry Ulanov, she has produced several other works, including: *Religion and the Unconscious, the Witch and the Clown: Archetypes of Human Sexuality,* and *Anima and Animus: Archetypes of Transformation.*

BARRY ULANOV is McIntosh Professor of English Emeritus, Barnard College, Columbia University. Among his many books are: *A History of Jazz in America, The Literary Traditions of Christian Humanism, The Two Worlds of American Art: The Private and the Popular,*

Makers of the Modern Theater, and *Jung and the Outside world.* He has written for radio and television and lectured extensively in the United States, Canada, Europe, South America and India.

EDWIN WEBB has taught in secondary schools, a technical college, and a college of education. He is currently a Senior Lecturer in English within the University of Greenwich, London. His publications include a collection of poetry, *Notes on Spontaneous Cases,* and his latest book is *Literature in Education: Encounter and Experience* (1992).

MARGARET WELDHEN was educated at St Hilda's College, Oxford, where she read History. After teaching in secondary schools for some years, she took a degree in sociology at London University, followed by a doctorate in social philosophy. She was a lecturer at Goldsmiths' College, University of London, and a tutor in social studies, University of Bath. Her articles have appeared in journals such as *Universities Quarterly* and *The Use of English.*

Index

Works of David Holbrook are gathered separately within the following entries: Critical writings; Educational writings; Novels; Poetry; Psycho-social writings. In addition to the entry under Poetry, individual poems are indexed separately by title and identified as (D.H.).

Abbs, Peter, 250
Abrams, Mark, 38
Age of Innocence, The (Edith Wharton), 206–8
Ainsworth, Mary, 167
Alvarez, A., 162, 236
Animal symbolicum, 13, 68, 76. *See also* Symbolism; Symbolization
Archetypes, 119
Army Bureau for Current Affairs (ABCA), 29
Arnold, Matthew, 64–65, 68, 93–96, 97, 112, 115, 116, 246
Art: as cognition, 120–23; as metaphor, 73, 118, 153–55; as ordering of experience, 74–76, 84, 101–2, 186, 193
Arts, the creative, 18, 87, 103, 108–9, 116, 119, 171, 184–85, 186, 188; and art-making, 69–76, 81–82, 126–27; art-making and psychoanalysis, 72–74, 183; teaching of, 112–24, 127
Assessment of English, 60, 78–79, 85, 89
Attachment and Loss (John Bowlby), 166–67
Attachment theory, 167–68
Augustine, Saint, 180
Autobiography (John Stuart Mill), 115
Ayer, A. J., 213

Bach, Johann Sebastian, 179, 235
Bakhtin, Mikhail, 110 n.26
Barnes, William, 156
Barrie, J. M., 167
Barthes, Roland, 259

Bartók, Béla, 137–38
Bates, H. E., 267
Baudelaire, Charles, 98
Bawer, Bruce, 168
Beauvoir, Simone de, 195, 213
Beethoven, Ludwig van, 137
"Beggar-beads" (D.H.), 237
Bell Jar, The (Sylvia Plath), 163
Berlin, Isaiah, 126
Berryman, John, 168
Binswanger, Ludwig, 212, 223
Blake, William, 112, 247, 257
Bleak House (Charles Dickens), 200–202
Blunden, Edmund, 82
Bonham-Carter, Victor, 38
Boswell, James, 37
Botticelli, Sandro, 238
Bowlby, John, 166–68, 169
"Bowling for a Pig" (D.H.), 248
Bradbury, Malcolm, 257
Brentano, Lugo, 212
Brewer, Derek, 48
Bronowski, Jacob, 38
Buber, Martin, 104, 212, 219
Bullock Committee Report (1975), *A Language for Life*, 80, 86–88, 89, 90, 148–49, 151
Butterfield, Sir John (later Lord), 48
Buytendijk, F. J. J., 43, 117, 223

Cambridge Review, The, 214
Camus, Albert, 213
"Cardoness Castle" (D.H.), 248
Carline, Richard, 37
Cassirer, Ernst, 148, 159, 247

Chambre Claire, La (Roland Barthes), 259
Charlotte's Web (E. B. White), 106–7
Chaucer, Geoffrey, 115, 145
"Child Said, 'I am Smoke,' A (D.H.), 32–33, 248
Clayton, John J., 168
Cognition, 65, 67–68, 86, 120, 154–55. *See also* Intellection, in symbolic forms
Coleridge, Samuel Taylor, 71, 112, 118, 148, 156, 269; on language and thought, 67, 86
Comfort, Alex, 165
Cook, H. Caldwell, 69–70, 75, 77 n.12
Conrad, Joseph, 168
Couperin, François, 137
Cox Report (1989), *National Curriculum Proposals for English for Ages 5 to 16*, 57, 90, 91
Creativity: in children, 101, 103–8, 117, 119–20, 182; in culture and tradition, 122–24, 240–41, 246; in English teaching, 62, 69–76, 102–3, 122–23; in music teaching, 129–41
Crisis of the European Sciences, The (Edmund Husserl), 175–76, 213, 220–21, 222
Critical writings of David Holbrook: *Charles Dickens and the Image of Woman*, 200–203, 233; *Dylan Thomas: The Code of Night*, 162, 215, 233, 239–41; *Edith Wharton and the Unsatisfactory Man*, 49, 164, 203, 205–8, 233; *Gustav Mahler and the Courage to Be*, 37, 164, 167, 215, 226; *Images of Women in Literature*, 194, 233; *Llareggub Revisited*, 233–34, 237, 239–41, 246; *Lost Bearings in English Poetry*, 36, 37, 215–16, 233, 240, 246; *The Novel and Authenticity*, 44, 233, 257; *The Quest for Love*, 15, 193–94, 233, 234–35, 236, 237, 239, 242; *The Skeleton in the Wardrobe: C. S. Lewis's Fantasies*, 163–64, 166–67, 217, 233, 246; *Sylvia Plath: Poetry and Experience*, 11, 162, 203–4, 215, 217, 233, 241; *Where D. H. Lawrence was Wrong about Woman*, 49, 164, 167, 194, 196–99, 218, 233
Culture and creativity, 16, 73, 119–20, 122–24; and F. R. Leavis, 96–99; and language development, 80–83; and Matthew Arnold, 65, 93–96, 117; and tradition, 81–82, 84–87; child's personal, 17, 103–4, 120; origins of, 117, 119; popular, 59–60, 97, 100–101, 114–15; pre-industrial, 59, 89, 90–91, 97, 100–101, 115; social, 170–71, 184–85; verbal, 58
Culture and Anarchy (Matthew Arnold), 64–65, 93, 115
Culture and Environment (F. R. Leavis and Denys Thompson), 99, 114

Daly, Robert, 204, 217
Dance, 59
D'Annunzio, Gabriele, 269
Dante Alighieri, 98
Daquin, Louis Claude, 137
Dartington Hall School, 45–46
Dasein problem, the, 13–14, 17, 257, 260
da Vinci, Leonardo, 176–78, 179
Dawkins, Richard, 226
"Day in France, A" (D.H.), 253
Deconstructionism, 74, 119, 159, 169, 224, 247. *See also* Structuralism
da la Mare, Walter, 82
Delius, Frederick, 135, 137
Denton, Michael, 226
"Depression" (D.H.), 237
Derrida, Jacques, 170, 214
Descartes, René, 225
Dewey, John, 139
Dickens, Charles, 205, 208, 236, 266–67; David Holbrook on, 200–203, 204
Dickinson, Emily, 209
Dilthey, Wilhelm, 150
Divided Self, The (R. D. Laing), 217
"Drought" (D.H.), 263

Eastern Daily Press, The, 257–58
Education and the University (F. R. Leavis), 97–98
Education: conceptions of, 62–66, 68, 75, 78–79, 94, 112, 120; and English teaching, 55–61, 62–76, 78–91, 148–49, 168–71; and music teaching, 125–41
Educational writings of David Hol-

brook: "Against a Curriculum for English Studies" (essay), 150; *Childrens' Writing*, 127–28, 135; "Creativity and Education" (essay), 106; *Education and Philosophical Anthropology*, 44, 108, 222; *Education, Nihilism and Survival*, 11; *English for Maturity*, 39, 53, 55–56, 72, 79–82, 86, 108, 112–16, 122, 127, 152–55, 215; *English for Meaning*, 80, 81, 86, 88, 89, 112, 113, 148, 151–52, 155; *English for the Rejected*, 38–39, 53, 56, 107, 113, 117, 127, 215; *English in Australia Now*, 215; *Evolution and the Humanities*, 44, 222, 226; *The Exploring Word*, 113, 127, 155; *Iron, Honey, Gold* (anthology), 57; *The Secret Places*, 72, 74, 113; "The Wizard and the Critical Flame" (essay), 103
Education of the Poetic Spirit, The (Marjorie Hourd), 70–72
Education Through Art (Herbert Read), 71
Eliot, T. S., 235, 247, 253; on poetry, 155, 234; on tradition, 81–82
Ellis, Havelock, 163
Empson, William, 96
English: as communication, 80–81, 85, 119; as creative, 62, 67, 69–76; as moral force, 90, 93–109, 154–55; assessment of, 60, 78–79, 85, 89; mastery of, 58; models of, 86–91, 105; teaching of, 55–61, 62–76, 78–91, 148–49, 168–71. *See also* Language; Literature; Poetry: teaching of
English for the English (George Sampson), 63, 66
Enright, D. J., 96
Essences, 216, 218
Eroticism and sex, 165–66
Esterson, Aaron, 217
Evaluating with Validity (Ernest House), 149
Examinations, 139; in English, 60, 85, 89. *See also* English: assessment of
Existentialism, 75, 117, 170, 185, 211–26
Experience, shaping of through art-making, 70–76, 84, 101–2, 106, 116, 120–22, 148, 153, 156–57

Experiment in Criticism, An (C. S. Lewis), 153

Fairbairn, W. R. D., 17, 43, 117, 160, 166, 183, 216, 233
Fantasy, 69, 74, 104, 106, 164
Farber, Leslie, 213, 240
Faulkner, William, 168
Feeling and Form (Suzanne Langer), 121
Feelings, expression of, 60, 70, 104, 116, 121–22, 169, 170, 242
Feminine, the: female ways of looking, 180–83, 184, 185
Feminist Criticism (Maggie Humm), 195
"Fingers in the Door" (D.H.), 31
Flaubert, Gustave, 260
"Flies, The" (D.H.), 101–2
Folksong, 100
For Your Own Good: Hidden Cruelty in Child Rearing and the Roots of Violence (Alice Miller), 162

Gardner, Helen, 149–50, 155
Giedion, Sigfried, 126
Goethe, Johann Wolfgang von, 174, 177
Goldfinger (film), 185
Golding, William, 14–15, 16
Gorky, Arshile, 186
Great Expectations (Charles Dickens), 202–3, 262
Grene, Marjorie, 12, 117, 213, 220, 221; on knowing, 75; on origins of culture, 119
Grosskurth, Phyllis, 163
Guntrip, Harry, 14, 16, 43, 117, 160, 166, 183, 194, 216, 217, 233, 237

Harding, D. W., 257
Hard Times (Charles Dickens), 64, 80, 87–88, 115
Hardy, Thomas, 98, 156, 234
Hawkes, Jacquetta, 38
Heidegger, Martin, 13–14, 151, 223, 257, 260
Hellman, Lillian, 163
Hemingway, Ernest, 168
Hesse, Hermann, 168
History of Ideas and Philosophy, 213–14, 220–21. *See also* Existentialism; Philosophical Anthropology

Hoggart, Richard, 112, 115, 116
Holbrook, David: and character of writing, 10–11; novels discussed, 256–69; poetry discussed, 31–34, 101–2, 155–57, 233–43, 245–54; portrait of, 27–50. For entries to individual works, see Critical Writings of David Holbrook; Educational writings of David Holbrook; Novels of David Holbrook; Poetry of David Holbrook; Psycho-social writings of David Holbrook. See also poems indexed separately by title and identified as (D.H.)
Holland, Norman, 170
Holmes, Edmund, 69
Homer, 115
Hope, Christopher, 34
Hopkins, Gerard Manley, 238, 252–53
Hourd, Marjorie, 70–72, 75
House, Ernest, 149
How to Teach Reading (F. R. Leavis), 98–99
Hughes, Ted, 216, 240
Huis Clos (play, Jean-Paul Sartre), 211
Human World, The, 249–50
Humm, Maggie, 195
Husserl, Edmund, 12, 177, 212, 213, 222; and everyday experience, 151; and the "pregiven" or "Lifeworld," 174–76, 177, 189 n.1, 220–21, 222–23, 224
Huxley, Aldous, 38
Huxley, Thomas, 94

Idea of a University, The (John Henry Newman), 65
"Image Problems" (D.H.), 42
Imagination: and children, 117, 156–57; and fantasy, 104, 152; and knowledge, 149–51, 153, 154–55; Marjorie Hourd on, 70–71; and reality, 152; and subjectivity, 75. See also Creativity
In Defence of the Imagination (Helen Gardner), 149–50, 155
Individuation, 71
Intellection, in symbolic forms, 120–23
Intellectual Growth in Young Children (Susan Isaacs), 68–69
Intellectuals (Paul Johnson), 163

Intentionality, 222, 226
"In the Face of Nihilism" (D.H.), 252–53
"Italian Moments" (D.H.), 238

James, Henry, 168, 266–67, 269
Jarrell, Randall, 168
Jaspers, Karl, 219
Johnson, Dr. Samuel, 245
Johnson, Paul, 163
Jung, Carl Gustav, 71, 186, 189

Kant, Immanuel, 118, 119
Keats, John, 82, 86
Kierkegaard, Søren, 219
"Kind of Consciousness, A" (D.H.), 250–52
Kingman Report, The (1988), *Report of the Committee of Inquiry into the Teaching of English*, 87, 89, 90
Klein, Melanie, 17, 43, 117, 160, 163, 166, 169, 183, 194, 216; on fantasy, 104
Klingender, Francis, 37
Knowing: tacit, 75, 87; ways of, 120, 149–51, 225. See also Perception
Knowledge and imagination, 149–51
Kundera, Milan, 257

Lacan, Jacques, 169, 224
Laing, R. D., 217
Lady Chatterly's Lover (D. H. Lawrence), 218
Langer, Suzanne, 129; on feeling, 121–22; on music, 129; on objectivity, 12, 75; on symbolization, 104–5, 120
Language: and English culture, 80–85, 86, 112–13; and thought, 67–68, 86, 122, 154–55; as art, 75–76; as shaping of experience, 70–76; as symbolization, 68, 105, 148; mechanical models of, 78–79, 86–91, 148–49, 151–52
Language and Reality (W. M. Urban), 153–54
Language in the National Curriculum Project (LINC), 83
Language, Truth and Logic (A. J. Ayer), 213
Lao-Tze, 174

Index

Lawrence, D. H., 42, 115, 204, 205, 208, 242, 247; David Holbrook on, 164, 167, 168, 218, 269, 270 n.7; F. R. Leavis on, 97; on fullness of being, 81; on morality, 18; on poetry, 248, 252, 256; "pollyanalytics," 10; *Women in Love* discussed, 196–99
Leavis, F. R., 29, 36–37, 48, 112, 116, 117, 215, 220, 257; on culture, 97–99, 221; on literary values, 96–97, 113–14, 218, 235
Ledermann, E. K., 213, 221
Lee, Laurie, 58–59
Leibniz, Gottfried Wilhelm, 176
Lewis, C. S.: David Holbrook on, 163–64, 217–18; on literary experience and criticism, 153
"Lifeworld" of pre-given realities, 174–76, 177, 189 n.1, 220–21, 222–23, 224
Lindsay, Jack, 37
Literature and Dogma (Matthew Arnold), 64–65
Literature: and morality, 93–109; educative effects of, 65, 70, 74–76, 152–55. *See also* English: teaching of
Little Dorrit (Charles Dickens), 267
"Living? Our Supervisors Will Do That For Us" (D.H.), 37, 249
Living Principle, The (F. R. Leavis), 220
Locke, John, 166
Lodge, David, 257
Lomas, Peter, 213
Longford, Lord, 165
Lorenz, Konrad, 119
"Love and Let Die" (D.H.), 32
Lowell, Robert, 168, 240
"Lynx" (D.H.), 248, 249

Macdonald, George, 166
Macmillan, Margaret, 68
Maddermarket Theatre, Norwich, 256, 261, 262
Madge, John, 38
Madox Ford, Ford, 168
Magritte, René, 190 n.18
Mahler, Gustav, 167, 215, 216, 226; David Holbrook on, 37, 164, 267
Main, Mary, 167
Manchester Guardian, The, 246
Marcel, Gabriel, 212, 219
"March Evening" (D.H.), 34

Maritain, Jacques, 219
Marvell, Andrew, 165
Mass media, 98–99, 114–15
"Master, The" (D.H.), 238
"Maternity Gown" (D.H.), 238
Maude, Angus, 38
May, Rollo, 212, 213, 217, 223
McLachlan, Donald, 38
McLuhan, H. M., 96
Meaning: as act of interpretation, 12, 149–51; as existential, 13, 37, 75; in symbolic forms, 121–23; response to, 88. *See also* Metaphor: as making of meaning
Mellers, Wilfrid, 37, 126
Merleau-Ponty, Maurice, 212, 222–23, 247
Messiaen, Olivier, 137
Metaphor: as art, 74–76, 118; as extension of experience, 84, 121, 152, 155, 157, 241; as making of meaning, 152, 153–55, 156; as model of reality, 73
Midgley, Mary, 119
Mill, John Stuart, 84, 115, 159, 162, 166
Miller, Alice, 162
Milner, Marian, 43, 104, 180, 183, 217
Milton, John, 159, 162, 166, 252
Mitchell, Donald, 37
Monck, Nugent, 34–35, 261, 262
Morality: and value judgements, 159–61; in art and literature, 18–19, 93–109, 155
Morant, Sir Robert, 63–64, 69
Morgan, Christopher, 250
Morris, William, 38, 160, 162
"Moth in a Morning, A" (D.H.), 248
Mr. Noon (D. H. Lawrence), 270 n.7
Murdoch, Iris, 245
Music: as form, 128–29, 139, 140 n.9; education in, 125–41
"My Father's Gay Funeral" (D.H.), 242–43

Nabokov, Vladimir, 168
National Curriculum, The, 57, 59, 78–80, 88, 89, 90, 91, 121, 139
Nausée, La (Jean-Paul Sartre), 211
New Bearings in English Poetry (F. R. Leavis), 37, 215, 235

Newbolt Report (1921), *The Teaching of English in England*, 66, 86
Newhouser, Frederick, 214
Newman, John Henry (later Cardinal), 65
Nihilism, 13, 37, 162, 212, 240, 252–53, 267; of Jean-Paul Sartre, 163
Nor Shall My Sword (F. R. Leavis), 220
Norwich Passion Play, 35
Novels of David Holbrook: *Even if they Fail*, 267–68; *Flask of Bouillon, The* (unpublished), 255 n.7, 268–69; *Flesh Wounds*, 14, 28–29, 211–12, 257–61; *Getting it Wrong with Uncle Tom* (unpublished), 255 n.7; *Gold in Father's Heart, The*, 267–68; *Jennifer*, 42–43, 261, 266–67; *A Little Athens*, 265–66; *Nothing Larger than Life*, 15, 40–42, 47–48, 236–37, 238, 262–64, 265, 268; *A Play of Passion*, 35–36, 261–62, 266, 269
Nurturing of children, 17–18, 103–4, 160

Objectivity: as incomplete realization, 11–12, 75, 167, 174, 175–76, 220–21, 223; in relation to language, 87–88
Object-relations school of psychoanalytical theory, 216; and creativity, 104; and culture, 117; and development, 17, 160–61, 169, 216; and perception, 180, 188; and sources of love and hate, 165; and true self, 183
Oh! Calcutta (stage production), 165
O'Malley, Raymond, 40
Oral English, in the National Curriculum, 78–79, 80
Origins of Love and Hate (Ian D. Suttie), 14
Our Time (Marxist quarterly), 29

Pascal, Blaise, 225
Pasteur, Louis, 269
Perception: as a way of listening, 179–80; as a way of looking, 173–79, 180–81, 183–84; male and female looking, 180–83, 184, 185. *See also* Woman, male and female perception of
Perversion, the Erotic Form of Hatred (Robert Stoller), 165

Peterson, R. W. K., 221
Peerson, Martin, 135; *The Fall of the Leafe* (musical illustration), 136
Perse Play Books, The (H. Caldwell Cook), 69
Pestalozzi, Johann Heinrich, 68
Petrarch, 115
Phenomenology, 117, 213; and literary studies, 162–64, 241; and perception, 174–76; and understanding, 151
Philosophical anthropology, 75, 117, 118, 159, 213, 233, 241, 242, 246–47, 248, 252; and knowing, 120, 225; elements of, 44, 221; its character described, 11–13
Philosophy and the History of Ideas, 213–14, 220–21. *See also* Existentialism; Philosophical anthropology
"Picnic in the Jura" (D.H.), 221
Plath, Sylvia, 162, 208, 215, 235, 253; and schizoid solutions, 239–40; personality, 169, 203–4, 217; *The Bell Jar* (novel), 163
Play, as purposive and educational, 69–70
Play Way, The (H. Caldwell Cook), 69–70
Plessner, Helmuth, 223
Plumed Serpent, The (D. H. Lawrence), 218
Poems of David Holbrook: discussed, 31–34, 101–2, 155–57, 233–43, 245–54. *See also* individual titles indexed separately and marked (D.H.)
Poetic humanism, tradition of, 112–24
Poetic, nature of the, 83–85, 113–14, 148, 152–53, 156–57
Poetry: and experience, 151–53; and morality, 94–95, 96; teaching of, 59, 60, 70, 71, 75–76, 82–84, 86, 102, 122
Polanyi, Michael, 213, 220, 223, 226; and existential meaning, 75
Porn: Myths for the Twentieth Century (Robert Stoller), 165
Pornography, 43, 164–66, 215, 216
Postan, Elizabeth, 30
Powys, T. F., 38, 233, 255 n.6
Practical criticism, 16

Index

Pre-industrial culture, 59, 89, 90–91, 97, 100–101,115
Proust, Marcel, 257
Psychic weaning, 17–18
Psychoanalysis, 15–16, 71, 73–74, 116–18, 159–71, 193–94; and literary criticism, 159–64, 168–71, 205, 238–41. See also Object-relations school of psychanalytic theory
Psycho-social writings of David Holbrook: *Case Against Pornography, The* 43, 215; "Dr. John Bowlby: No Need to Nod to Positivist Dogma" (essay), 167; *Human Hope and the Death Instinct*, 16, 116–17, 161, 215; *Masks of Hate, The*, 215; *Pseudo-Revolution, The*, 165, 215; *Sex and Dehumanisation*, 43, 165, 215

Read, Sir Herbert, 71, 123, 129
"Reflections Upon a Book of Reproductions" (D.H.), 156, 235
Respighi, Ottorino, 137
"Rewards, The" (D.H.), 238
Richards, I. A., 96
Rickmann, H. P., 150
Rickword, Edgell, 29, 37
Robinson, Ian, 242
Rodin, Auguste, 165
Romanticism, 118
Rousseau, Jean-Jacques, 163
Russell, Bertrand, 166, 269

Sampson, George, 62–63, 65–66, 68, 75, 86, 112, 114
"Sanaiagmore" (D.H.), 238
Sartre, Jean-Paul, 163, 213, 216, 219, 223; and existential stoicism, 218; *Huis Clos* (play), 211; *La Nausée* (novel), 211–12
Savage God, The (A. Alvarez), 162
Schiller, J. C., 139
Science and meaning, 221, 225–26
Schizoid: personality, 160–61, 203–4, 216, 217, 218; solutions of, 17–18, 161–62, 182, 185–86, 219, 235, 239
Schoenberg, Arnold, 179
School Examinations and Assessment Council, 78–81, 83–84, 85, 88, 89
Schubert, Franz Peter, 32
Schwartz, Delmore, 168
Scrutiny, 29, 37, 48, 161, 234

Self-realization, 14, 18, 67–68, 69, 71, 85, 107–8, 113
Self: subjectivity of, 173–87; true and false sense of, 14, 17–18, 75–76, 161, 169, 189, 190 n.12, 257, 260
Sensibility, 65, 81–82, 83, 95, 98, 113
Shakespeare, William, 58, 84, 98, 112, 236, 266
"Shared Flame" (D.H.), 238
Sharpe, Tom, 257
Sillitoe, Alan, 261
Snow, C. P., 113
"Song of the Seasons" (D.H.), 248
Space, Time and Architecture (Siegfried Giedion), 126
Steiner, George, 80
"Step" (D.H.), 242
Stevens, Anthony, 119
Stoller, Robert, 165
Straus, Irwin, 43, 223
Strauss, Richard, 267
Stravinsky, Igor, 179
Structuralism, 154. See also Deconstructionism
Subjectivity, 74–75, 96–97, 173–87, 222. See also Self: true and false sense of
Sunday Times, The, 29
Suttie, Ian D., 14, 43
"Swifts" (D.H.), 237
Swingler, Randall, 29, 37
Symbolism, 116, 117–18, 241; as form and intellect, 121–22; as identity, 103, 105, 107–8; in culture, 99, 161, 185–87, 194. See also Symbolization
Symbolization: as realizations of consciousness, 13, 104–5, 148, 150–51, 188; within culture, 17, 18, 117, 120. See also Symbolism

Tannen, Deborah, 195
Teaching: of English, 55–61, 62–76, 78–91, 102, 122, 148–49, 168–71; of music, 125–41; of the arts, 112–24, 127
Teilhard de Chardin, Pierre, 225
Thomas, Dylan, 162, 215, 235; personality, 163, 216, 217, 234; and David Holbrook's approaches to his poetry, 239–42
Thomas, Edward, 82, 84, 118, 251

Thompson, Denys, 37, 40, 99, 112, 114
Thorpe, Geoffrey, 34, 35
Thucydides, 265
Tillich, Paul, 212, 216, 219
"Time" (D.H.), 253
Times Educational Supplement, The, 138
Tolstoy, Count Leo Nikolaievich, 258, 259
Tradition, 81–82, 115; of poetic humanism, 112–24. *See also* Culture
Trilling, Lionel, 96
True and false self, 14, 17–18, 75–76, 161, 169, 189, 190n.12, 257, 260
Tynan, Kenneth, 165

Understanding and the Human Studies (H. P. Rickmann), 150
"Unholy Marriage" (D.H.), 249
Updike, John, 168
Urban, W. M., 153–54
Use of English, The: founding of, 40

Virgil, 115

Weber, Max, 150
Weelkes, Thomas, 125
Wells, H. G., 168
Wharton, Edith, 164, 200, 203; novels discussed, 205–8
What Is and Might Be (Edmond Holmes), 69

White, E. B., 106
Whitehouse, Mary, 165
Wilde, Oscar, 169
Williams, Gertrude, 38
Williams, Raymond, 40, 112, 116
Williams, W. E., 38
Williams-Ellis, Clough, 38
Winnicott, D. W., 43, 117, 118, 160, 165, 166, 167, 194, 216, 233, 240; on creativity, 74, 103, 123; on moral growth, 103, 161; on mothering, 17, 182, 184; on psychic growth, 107; on teaching psychoanalysis, 169; on true and false self, 190n.12, 257
Witkin, Robert, 127
Woman: male and female perception of, 191–209
Woman Who Rode Away, The (D. H. Lawrence), 218
Women in Love (D. H. Lawrence), 196–99
Woolf, Leonard, 38
Woolf, Virginia, 115, 168
Wordsworth, William, 71, 84, 113, 115, 234, 252, 253
Worker's Educational Association, 38
Wright, David, 156
Wuthering Heights (Emily Brontë), 257

Yeats, W. B., 80, 81, 235, 247, 248, 249, 261